Politics and Scholarship

Politics and Scholarship

Feminist Academic Journals
and the Production of Knowledge

Patrice McDermott

University of Illinois Press   Urbana and Chicago

AUG 1995

Winner of the Illinois–National Women's Studies Association
Book Award

1 2 3 4 5 C P 5 4 3 2 1

This book is printed on acid-free paper.

Library of Congress Cataloging-in-Publication Data
McDermott, Patrice.
     Politics and scholarship : feminist academic journals and
the production of knowledge / Patrice McDermott
        p. cm.
     Includes bibliographical references and index.
     ISBN 0-252-02078-2 (alk. paper).—ISBN 0-252-06369-4
(pbk. alk. paper)
        1. Feminism—Political aspects.   2. Learning and scholarship—
Political aspects.   3. Authorship—Political aspects.
     4. Authorship—Sex differences.   5. Authors and publishers—
Political aspects.   6. Scholarly periodicals. I. Title.
HQ1236.M381994
305.42—dc20   93–31206
                                                               CIP

For my parents,

Jane Louise McDermott

and

John Francis McDermott

Contents

Acknowledgments

I would like to thank the many scholars at the University of Maryland College Park campus who encouraged me during the course of this study. I am especially indebted to the work and guidance of John L. Caughey. In addition, Evelyn Torton Beck, Claire G. Moses, and Carol Pearson from the Women's Studies Program, and the late Gene Wise of the American Studies Department, contributed enormously in formulating my analysis. I also appreciate the comments that Janice Radway and Patrocinio Schweickart made on earlier versions. At the University of Maryland Baltimore County, I am grateful for the encouragement of my teaching colleagues, Warren Belasco, Carole McCann, Ed Orser, and Leslie Prosterman. I wish to thank Carolyn Ferrigno for her organizational skills and endurance.

Throughout the research, writing, and revision of this book I have relied on the comments of my friend and colleague Kathy Scales Bryan. Of particular importance is Wendy Kozol, whose critical judgment, warm support, and model of scholarly commitment enabled me to complete my manuscript. Anne M. Collins and Sheila Sweeney know how personally essential they also were in the process.

Various phases of my research were supported by fellowships and travel grants provided by the University of Maryland, College Park Campus. The revision of the manuscript was supported by an Illinois–NWSA Book Award. I am deeply grateful for this assistance. In addition, I thank Carole Appel, Mary Giles, and Karen Hewitt at the University of Illinois Press.

Finally, I owe an enormous debt to the editors and staffs of *Feminist Studies, Frontiers,* and *Signs.* Despite overburdened schedules, they all gave freely of their time and expertise. My study was contingent upon their support and accessibility, and I am grateful for their continuous and patient cooperation.

introduction

A Cultural Approach to
Feminist Academic Journals

. . . the journal functions as a sign of contradictions
within academic institutions.

Signs, Autumn 1982

Since the 1970s, the feminist movement has formed an uneasy partnership with the patriarchal university in the production of new scholarship on women. The result has been an explosion of theoretically rich and complex information that spans the academy's disciplinary spectrum. Academic journals are the institutional entry point for private speculation to be transformed into publicly available, socially sanctioned knowledge. Feminist scholars are acutely conscious of the political importance of constructing an available and legitimated body of oppositional knowledge. As professional scholars, they are also motivated by the "publish or perish" dictum that has become a significant force in the economics of scholarship and in appointment, advancement, and the granting of tenure.[1]

During the 1970s, activists attempted to bridge the gap between the political interests of the grass-roots feminist movement and institutional demands of scholarly inquiry by creating feminist academic journals. These journals offer a rich area for research because they explicitly address the practices and processes of academic publishing while shaping the parameters of an available body of feminist research and contributing to the advancement of women's studies scholars. Consequently, the journals provide a model for understanding the mediation of feminist resistance and patriarchal authority in the production of cultural knowledge.

How is it possible for feminists to challenge, critique, and transform patriarchal institutions as they use such institutions as a resource? How do those dynamic, elusive standards of rigorous scholarship and effective politics converge in the production of feminist scholarship? How do political movements become institutionalized and legitimated in the wider social context? In what manner do the journals contribute to the construction, negotiation, and legitimation of feminist discourse in the academy, the contemporary women's movement, and the larger society? To answer such questions, I have relied on a diverse but integrated approach to the study of three major American, university-based journals: *Signs: A Journal of Women in Culture and Society* (University of Chicago Press), *Feminist Studies* (based at the University of Maryland), and *Frontiers: A Journal of Women's Studies* (housed at the University of Colorado at Boulder).

I have defined "feminist academic journals" as those fitting specific criteria. They are university based in terms of housing and financial support and operate under the acknowledged auspices of an accredited university. They state an intended feminist perspective in either their preface, editorial statement, or content. They use academics as editors and consultants. They adhere to conventional forms and styles of academic publishing as defined in such manuals as the Modern Language Association Style Sheet and the *Chicago Manual of Style*. They are bound and typeset in accordance with recognized journal appearance. They are abstracted, indexed, and microfilmed in such major academic reference services as the *Modern Language Association International Bibliography, Psychological Abstracts, Social Science Citation Abstracts,* and *Women's Studies Abstracts.* Finally, they are consistently published at regular intervals. These criteria define the parameters of this study but do not include many nonacademic feminist publications of serious intellectual inquiry, for example, *Trivia: A Journal of Ideas* (from Amherst, Massachusetts), *Hecate: A Women's Interdisciplinary Journal* (Madison, Wisconsin), and *Lesbian Contradiction: A Journal of Irreverent Feminism* (Seattle).

The selection of *Frontiers, Feminist Studies,* and *Signs* as the central focus of this study was determined by three important attributes of these particular journals. Each is interdisciplinary in its scope and attempts to address scholarly feminist discourse throughout the field of women's studies. Each was created early in the history of the field and directly addresses the concurrent development of feminist discourse in the academy. And, finally, each of these journals is positioned at a different location within the university. *Signs* is owned and operated by a prestigious university press; *Feminist Studies* has retained an independent ownership by a feminist collective but is housed and subsidized by a state university; and *Frontiers,* for most of its history, has been owned by a collective, operated through the personal resources of a nonacademic editor, and tenuously housed at a state university.

These selected attributes allow me to examine the institutional and discursive history of the field within the context of varying institutional affiliations. However, my use of these attributes is not meant to privilege the scholarly and political content of *Frontiers, Feminist Studies,* and *Signs* over other equally worthy feminist academic journals. For example, the *Psychology of Women Quarterly* (from Cambridge University Press) is one of oldest and most influential feminist academic journals in the field, but its disciplinary focus only allows for an in-depth analysis of feminist discourse in one arena. *NWSA Journal* (Ablex Publishing), the official journal of the National Women's Studies Association, is comprehensive and interdisciplinary but was not created until 1988. *Women's Studies* (Gordon and Breach Science Publishers) was first published in 1972. Although its institutional affiliation resembles that of *Signs,* unlike editors at *Signs,* Wendy Martin, who has been in charge of the journal since its beginning, rarely uses her editorial voice to intervene directly in the controversies and contentions of the field.

I have used the journals to examine the themes of politics and scholarship in the feminist production of knowledge. Although *politics, scholarship,* and the related terms *the university* and *the community* are familiar, their meanings both within the contemporary American culture and in feminist thought must be examined carefully. The discussion that follows generally characterizes traditional and feminist conceptions of politics and scholarship, even though these categories are, in reality, neither exclusive nor uncontested.[2]

The university is the powerful institution that produces, legitimates, and distributes scholarly knowledge. Knowledge can be produced in many cultural settings, but the university is differentiated from the wider community as a special site sanctioned for the purpose. Knowledge produced within the university can be used in the service of society, but the scholarship itself is supposed to remain free of nonacademic interests. Ideally, the university functions in relative isolation from the broader community, a boundary designed to protect the production of scholarship from the influence of outside interests. Commenting on the social responsibilities of the modern university, Harvard president Derek Bok cautioned scholars that:

> Certain people in society are thought to have an obligation to reveal the truth without regard to the consequences, save in the most exceptional cases. . . . a strong argument can be made that social scientists should recognize a similar obligation. If investigators began to censor their work in order to minimize the risk of abetting policies they consider wrong, the credibility of scholarship would very quickly deteriorate. . . . such moral inhibitions could distort the process of research itself. It is difficult enough to avoid personal bias in carrying out investigations of social problems. But such biases could become much more intense once investigators knew the price of arriving at certain findings. . . . scholars should remember that their primary obligation is to search for truth.[3]

The university is manifested as classrooms, libraries, research centers, and laboratories. However, it is equally a complex and diffuse system of institutions and relationships. The physical university provides an institutional framework, but the heart of the enterprise is comprised of scholars, their networks, conferences, associations, and publications.[4] The sociologist Philip Altbach calls this the "invisible college" and considers academic journals as its most visible form:

> Scholarly journals . . . provide a legitimation of knowledge by the decisions that are made on what to print. In this sense, the editors are key gatekeepers who in many ways control access to the field. Journals also permit relatively speedy communication of new knowledge to everyone involved in the network, and to those outside the structures as well. Invisible colleges have institutional forms that are important for knowledge creation and distribution and those who stand at the center of any of these communication or publication systems have considerable power. They are in a way the leaders of the invisible colleges.[5]

Scholarship is the specialized knowledge, constructed in accordance with Western philosophical traditions, which is produced and sanctioned by the university and its publication system.[6] The modern university considers political and emotional impartiality to be the hallmark of its rational discourse. This ideal of reasoned scholarly impartiality suggests a point of reference removed from any interests or desires—the impartial observer thus stands outside of, and above, the situation and is afforded a whole, rather than partial view. This Archimedean observer is then able to apply logic and empiricism to produce objective, value-free, and socially sanctioned scholarship.[7]

Feminists criticize the traditional view of scholarship as pervasively androcentric. They argue that scholars are not impartial observers, but socially located and gendered participants in the construction of knowledge. Many feminists contend that scholarship is socially produced, is based on important presuppositions, and is expressed in culturally and historically specific forms constructed from the perspective of race, class, and gender-specific groups. Traditional scholarship relies on a discursive inheritance that reflects the perspective of the white, male, Eurocentric institutions in which it was developed. Consequently, like all cultural productions, scholarship is inherently political.[8]

Feminist politics criticizes and reconceptualizes the particular role of gender in the distribution and functions of power. "Politics" refers to the distribution and functions of power as it is manifested in social institutions, codes, and relationships.[9] Critical, activist politics seeks to rebuild existing political orders in keeping with a new social vision. The task of activist intellectuals has been to use their scholarly skills to analyze existing relations of power and formulate conceptualizations of more just and humane social orders.[10] The heart of feminist political activism has been located primarily in what feminists call the "community" sector of the contemporary women's movement. Consequently, feminist scholars challenge the traditional dichotomizing of university-community relations by constantly attending to the political interests of the nonacademic feminist community.[11] The term *the community* has acquired a set of complex and shifting meanings, both essential and ambiguous, within the contemporary women's movement, as is evident from the following excerpts from feminist scholars:

> if our aim is to get closer to the truth and to develop a strategy for the future, then we have to have connections outside academia. If we work primarily within universities and colleges, then our scholarship will inevitably remain distorted and limited by the elitism and class bias of our environment. Only autonomous programs have any possibility of having significant involvement in the community and still survive.[12]

If a program is to reach out to the 'community,' what is it? Is it women in the women's movement, the neighborhood, or all women? Is the community to be defined politically, geographically, or sexually? . . . The question of what that relationship should be has been a barbed maze for persons interested in women's studies. Trying to resolve it has stirred up internal conflict and pain within various programs and among serious people. One part of the problem is that the question is a microcosm of a larger issue: the responsibility of education to society, the responsibility of society to education.[13]

For me, the community included working-class women who were never going to get inside the halls of the University of Colorado. It included women of color. It included feminist community organizations like NOW which was quite active in Colorado at that point, and it included folks like my mother and older women who had been feminists without being named so and had been working in isolation for some time.[14]

Thus, "the community" is variously, and at times simultaneously, constituted as a wider nonacademic, even nonfeminist, population; the nonacademic, generally feminist, although not necessarily activist population; and the nonacademic activist feminist population that includes reproductive rights workers, rape crises counselors, and feminist lawyers. But feminist editors' most specific use of the term denotes the cultural and activist remnants of the younger, more radical branch of the early contemporary feminist movement.[15] This group still produces most of the movement's radical and lesbian theoretical and literary publications.

The commonality in all of these conceptions of the community is that it exists outside the formal boundaries of the academy. It is a place where women, despite their proximity to the active "center" of the movement, are removed from the university. Even feminist institutions devoted to higher education, such as Sagaris, the Califia Community, Feminist Studio Workshop, and the Women's School of Planning and Architecture, were defined as "community" institutions by their nonuniversity location.[16] Similarly, when feminist academics work and write outside of the university, they categorize these projects as their community activities.[17] Thus, it is this generalized conception of the community as a variously engaged, nonacademic feminist population distinct from the university that predominates this study. However, from time to time,

I will use the term more specifically in keeping with my informants' usage. The feminist production of knowledge takes place from within a complex web of tensions created by these social constructions of the university and its scholarship and the community and its politics.

Feminist activists did not enter the university in search of protection, but, ironically, the ready-made infrastructure of university publishing has enabled feminists to sustain the development of critical theories that have done much to reorient traditional scholarship. Under the ambivalent sponsorship of the university, feminist academic journals have constructed and continue to maintain a domain of "cultural, social, and institutional space in which to go on doing things in feminism."[18] The feminist literary theorist Rita Felski calls this domain a "feminist public sphere: used for the development and preservation of serious oppositional research and debate." The rational republican public sphere developed in late-seventeenth- and early-eighteenth-century Europe was built on masculinist gender constructs that formally excluded women from public life.[19] Consequently, the feminist public sphere is not simply assimilated into the masculinist public domain, but operates as a "contestatory counterpublic."[20] Counterpublics use the legitimated authority of public sphere discourse "to critique cultural values from the standpoint of a marginalized group within society."[21]

The university has become an important site of counterpublic activity, and feminist academic journals constitute one of the many institutional locations of the feminist public sphere. The journals are a socially sanctioned channel of communications that disseminates the arguments of feminist discourse.[22] How have feminist activists used the interpretive authority conferred by their participation in a traditional institution to legitimate the politics of the contemporary women's movement? How has their location within the tension of scholarship and politics affected the production, legitimation, and distribution of feminist scholarship and affected their relationship to the community sector of the feminist movement?

The early 1970s witnessed an influx of feminists into the university, a growing reliance of the movement on the printed word, and the establishment of many and varied feminist presses. The alternative feminist press has changed and grown considerably since the early seventies, as periodicals, newsletters, and newspapers emerged to address specific feminist issues and constituencies. After growing at a prodigious rate throughout the decade, the initial wave of feminist presses and publications has begun to subside. Influential, formerly thriving feminist presses have closed, key feminist bookstores have gone out of business, and feminist classics have gone out of print; however, *Frontiers, Feminist Studies,* and *Signs* have been able to celebrate both growth and influence. It is within this context that I have chosen to study the experiences of the women who, from within a patriarchal setting, have created one of feminism's most successful institutions.

The character of this inquiry reflects my training in the anthropology of belief systems, the sociology of literature, feminist theory, and discourse analysis. I have drawn on methods from these diverse areas in an effort to develop an integrated approach that serves the scope of this study. I have several related goals. First, I provide a history of each journal's genesis and development within the context of the contemporary women's movement and university publishing. This account relies on a number of sources—organizing documents, journal records, published histories, editors' personal papers, and interviews with founders, editors, and staff. I will deepen this history by placing it within the wider contexts of New Left underground publishing, publishing in the contemporary women's movement, and traditional scholarly publishing.

Second, this account offers an in-depth ethnographic study of the cognitive structures that inform the practices and processes of feminist academic journals. Serious difficulties arise from attempts to study publishing simply in terms of the product, therefore, my inquiry used the anthropological technique of ethnographic interview and observations.[23] From 1985 to 1990, I visited the offices of *Frontiers, Feminist Studies,* and *Signs,* attended editorial board meetings, and observed how the staffs operated. I was able to study journal files, manuscripts in process, acceptance and rejection letters, readers' reports, and mailing lists. I conducted extensive interviews with thirty-one former and current editors and associate editors, three staff members at *Signs,* two at *Feminist Studies,* and one at *Frontiers.* I conducted follow-up interviews from 1990 to 1993 and also spoke to editors from four new feminist academic journals: *differences: A Journal of Feminist Cultural Studies, Genders, NWSA Journal,* and *SAGE: A Scholarly Journal on Black Women.* During this research I discovered how editorial boards, managing editors, consultants, and staff influence the construction and dissemination of significant research on women, determine scholarly and political criteria, and develop models designed to challenge, transform, and use the traditional university.

Editor is a term that covers a variety of roles and activities in academic publishing. A few of the editors interviewed for this study oversee, or are directly involved with, the physical production of their journals. At times, this includes responsibility for copy editing, proofreading, layout, budget, copyrights, promotion, and distribution. Many of the editors help acquire and develop new projects, edit manuscripts, monitor revisions, and prepare rejections. All of the editors interviewed are directly involved in the evaluation of the scholarly and political merit of research for publication in their journals. Although *Frontiers, Feminist Studies,* and *Signs* use different, although often parallel, titles for these individuals (including editors, editorial board, editorial collective, associate editors, advisory board, and editorial consultants), this study uses the term *editor* to designate any individual officially recognized by a journal as responsible for the evaluation and selection of manuscripts for publication.

My investigation has two concerns: the internal dynamics of the journal (editorial structure, criteria in manuscript selection, and development of alternative forms and conventions) and the external dynamics of the relationship of the journals to the wider women's movement and the university. I have focused particularly on areas where these dynamics intersect (such as the development of scholarly and political criteria for manuscript selection) or clash (such as decisions to maintain independent ownership with a limited audience or sell the journal to a university press with a vastly larger audience). Feminist academic journals attempt to offer a view of reality that differs in scope and emphasis from that presented in traditional scholarship. I have been able to describe the journals' views of reality; however, I am less concerned with establishing the accuracy or inaccuracy of each journal's explanation of reality than in discovering how that explanation defines the parameters of feminist scholarship.

Third, I analyzed the journals' use of academic and community forms, conventions, and structures. This aspect of the study examines the editors' and contributors' use of traditional devices—footnotes, scholarly voice, structure, and style—to communicate and legitimate nontraditional, even radical, content. It also examines feminist experimentation with conventional scholarly publishing forms—forums, notes and letters, symposia, commentaries—to address the immediate and unfolding political issues of the wider feminist movement.

Finally, I provide a cultural analysis of particular controversies in which specific meanings and contours of feminist discourse have been contested or promoted through the journals. Based on information from my informants and a content analysis of the texts, I have selected several key controversies or "cultural dramas" for in-depth analysis.[24] In these case studies I detail how the journals became the localized site in which scholars monitored, negotiated, and debated the terms for the production of new feminist scholarship.

Through intensive interviews and extended observations I have investigated the dynamics of academic publishing from the perspective of journal editors and staff. Following the work of Clifford Geertz, I have sought to explore aspects of this experience from the viewpoint of scholars producing and publishing feminist materials in a nonfeminist, scholarly environment.[25] I have drawn on definitions of culture from cognitive anthropology, the sociology of knowledge, and discourse analysis. In each of these approaches the focus moves beyond an analysis of behavior or texts to an exploration of the knowledge that generates and interprets them and gives them meaning. According to the symbolic anthropologist Ward Goodenough, this cultural knowledge consists of "what one needs to know in order to decide—what is, what could be, how one feels about it, what can be done about it, and how to go about doing it."[26] Such knowledge includes values, beliefs, rules, codes, categories, and assumptions about what is good, bad, believable, and possible. Geertz has called it a "conceptual system of plans, recipes, rules, and instructions for the governing of behavior."[27] Although an analysis of behavior provides a window to systems of knowledge, this definition directs attention to the codes used in the editorial decision to publish, the scholarly and political standards that govern selection, the beliefs that define the nature of the enterprise, and the concepts used in the creation of feminist models within the university.

The basic contentions of the sociology of literature are that knowledge is culturally constructed, maintained, and transformed; inheres in social roles; is differentially distributed in society; and is expressed, sustained, or altered through social interaction. This study examines the social construction of feminist scholarship, the social locations of feminist editors, and the interactions of editor and author, editor and university, editor and feminist communities as they influence the selection, distribution, and conservation of feminist scholarship. In particular, the sociologist Peter Berger's work provides two key concepts for the framework of this work: institutionalization and legitimation. According to

Berger, social institutions originate in behavioral and cognitive human activity that has become cast into predictable, commonly recognized patterns marked by continuity, persistence, and historicity. Institutions are experienced as total and governing because they pattern human activity into stable, predictable, and controlled behaviors and cognition. Legitimation sustains institutions by "explaining or justifying the social order in such a way as to make institutional arrangements subjectively plausible."[28]

The literary critic Stanley Fish has illuminated the processes of institutionalization and legitimation as they function in the scholarly production of literary interpretation. Fish contends that any scholarly analysis of literary meaning is limited by the institution in which it is embedded. This institutionally derived meaning is reproduce by the field's "interpretive communities," one of which is the social network of university book and journal editors, editorial boards, and consultants.[29] And, Philip Altbach cites academic journals as the "main institutional loci for scholarly communication" in this process: "While it is true to some extent that scientific fields develop—and sometimes disappear—on their own, the knowledge dissemination network plays a very important role in determining the nature and focus of fields of study through the creation of journals and the appointment of editors and advisors. Their products are the legitimation of scholarship—perhaps the tip of the iceberg of scientific creativity."[30]

Drawing on her experience as a feminist literary critic, ethnographer, and the former editor of *American Quarterly,* Janice Radway argues that editors, writers, and readers comprise powerful interpretive communities that organize around their texts to determine systems of shared cultural meaning.[31] In this study, I detail how feminist academic authors, editors, and audiences have become an authoritative oppositional interpretive community that uses its scholarly journals to determine the political and scholarly terms on which feminist scholarship is produced.

This project grew out of my long association with the contemporary women's movement as a committed participant and a critical observer. The study is a product of the tension between scholarship and politics. As a feminist, I contend that gender and scholarship are constructed, inherently political, and patriarchal. As a scholar, I am convinced that intellectual detachment provides a useful perspective. For the purposes of this study, I consider myself a passionately engaged but ironically distanced observer of feminist knowledge and institutions.

A number of feminist scholars have called for just this sort of ironic reflexivity.[32] How have feminist institutions challenged or reified patriarchal constructs? Have we focused on particular "women's voices" that generalize the concerns and experiences of middle-class, academic women? What are the inherent and created difficulties in building a viable body of feminist knowledge from within a patriarchal institution? Can we anticipate the real-world consequences of feminist scholarship? Donna Haraway, a feminist theorist, has argued for the use of irony and contradiction in this process of feminist reflection: "Irony is about contradictions that do not resolve into larger wholes, even dialectically, about the tension of holding incompatible things together because both or all are necessary and true. It is a rhetorical strategy and a political method, one I would like to see more honored within . . . feminism."[33]

In claiming acceptance by the academic establishment while participating in feminism's challenge to it, feminist academic journals function as one of Haraway's ironic cultural contradictions.[34] She has argued that we should take pleasure in the confusion of such boundaries and take responsibility in their construction.[35] Feminist academic journals have played a central role in blurring the boundaries between politics and scholarship and in constructing a new feminist knowledge. By placing *Frontiers, Feminist Studies,* and *Signs* in historical perspective, describing the tensions of political and scholarly criteria in their practices, and analyzing the material embodiment of that tension in the scholarship they publish, I hope to illuminate two important forces in contemporary American culture: the women's movement and academia.

Notes

1. James R. Millar, "Publish or Perish: Advice from an Editor," *Social Science Journal* 15 (January 1978): 115–21.

2. Feminists and nonfeminist scholars do not have exclusively divergent arguments concerning the premises of epistemology. Some scholars who are not feminists have begun to question the assumptions of the Western liberal construction of knowledge. For example, challenges to the Enlightenment construction of knowledge can be found in: Michel Foucault, *The Order of Things: An Archaeology of the Human Sciences* (New York: Random House, 1970); H. G. Gadamer, "Hermeneutics and Social Science," *Cultural Hermeneutics* 2 (1975): 307–16; Jurgen Habermas, *Knowledge and Human Interests* (Boston: Beacon Press, 1971); and Peter Berger et al., *The Homeless Mind* (New York: Vintage Books, 1973). Feminist scholars agree on the androcentric and politi-

cal nature of traditional knowledge, but some feminists embrace an empiricist argument. See, for example, Janet Richards, *The Skeptical Feminist* (London: Penguin, 1982); and Jill McCalla Vickers, "Memoirs of an Ontological Exile: The Methodological Rebellions of Feminist Research," in *Feminism in Canada,* ed. Geraldine Finn and Angela Miles (Montreal: Black Rose Books, 1982). The feminist philosopher Mary E. Hawkesworth has detected three models of feminist epistemology: feminist empiricism, feminist standpoint, and feminist postmodernism. Only feminist empiricism accepts the Cartesian tenets of Western liberal approaches; see "Knowers, Knowing, Known: Feminist Theory and Claims of Truth," *Signs* 14 (Spring 1989): 537–39. My categorization of traditional and feminist epistemologies generally characterizes and contrasts their structures of knowledge while acknowledging that these structures are not monolithic, exclusive, or uncontested.

3. Derek Bok, *Beyond the Ivory Tower: Social Responsibilities of the Modern University* (Cambridge: Harvard University Press, 1982), 175.

4. Philip G. Altbach, *The Knowledge Context: Comparative Perspectives on the Distribution of Knowledge* (Albany: State University of New York Press, 1987), 176.

5. Altbach, *The Knowledge Context,* 177.

6. See Rita Mae Kelly, Bernard Ronan, and Margaret Cawley, "Liberal Positivistic Epistemology and Research on Women and Politics," *Women and Politics* 7 (Fall 1987): 11–27; Susan Bordo, "The Cartesian Masculinzation of Thought," *Signs* 11 (Spring 1986): 439–56; Susan Hekman, "The Feminization of Epistemology: Gender and the Social Sciences," *Women and Politics* 7 (Fall 1987): 65–85; Sandra Harding, "Is Gender a Variable in Conceptions of Rationality," in *Beyond Domination,* ed. C. Gould (Totowa: Rowman and Allanheld, 1984), 43–63; Sandra Harding, "The Instability of Analytic Categories of Feminist Theory," *Signs* 11 (Summer 1986): 645–64; Elizabeth Fee, "Is Feminism a Threat to Scientific Objectivity?" *International Journal of Women's Studies* 4 (September–October 1981): 378–92.

7. The feminist philosopher Sandra Harding has noted that there are other feminist scholars who do believe that the Archimedian perspective is valid. These scholars argue that the elimination of masculine bias and a more rigorous adherence to scientific methods will produce an objective, de-gendered perspective. For these scholars, feminist inquiry "represents not a substitution of one gender for the other—one subjectivism for another—but the transcendence of gender which thereby increases objectivity." See "The Instability of the Analytical Categories of Feminist Theory," *Signs* 11 (Summer 1986): 651.

8. For discussions of how knowledge and knower are situated, and so class, race, and gender necessarily structure the individual's claims of knowledge, see Susan Hekman, "From Monism to Pluralism," *Women and Politics* 7 (Fall 1987): 69–71; Donna Haraway, "Situated Knowledge: The Science Question in Feminism and the Privilege of Partial Perspective," *Feminist Studies* 14 (Fall 1988): 575–600; and Hawkesworth, "Knowing, Knower, and Known," 536–37.

9. This definition of politics as a relational distribution of power is drawn from Michel Foucault, *The History of Sexuality,* Vol. 1: *An Introduction* (New

York: Random House, 1980); Donna Haraway, "A Manifesto for Cyborgs: Science, Technology, and Socialist Feminism in the 1980s," *Socialist Review* 15 (March–April 1985): 65–107.

10. Paul Rabinow, an anthropologist, contrasts the critical, activist scholarship in Noam Chomsky's analysis of power with the inherently conservative position in Foucault's treatment of the subject. See Paul Rabinow, ed., *The Foucualt Reader* (New York: Pantheon Books, 1984), 4–7.

11. Barbara Hillyer Davis and Patricia A. Frech, "Diversity, Fragmentation, Integration: The NWSA Balancing Act," *Frontiers* 6 (Spring-Summer 1981): 60–64; Catharine Stimpson, "Women's Studies and the Community: Some Models," *Women's Studies Newsletter* 2 (Winter 1974): 2–3.

12. Marian Lowe and Margaret Lowe Benston, "The Uneasy Alliance of Feminism and Academia," *Women's Studies International Forum* 7, no. 3 (1984): 188.

13. Stimpson, "Women's Studies and the Community," 2.

14. Interview with editor Elizabeth Jameson, College Park, Maryland, May 10, 1985.

15. For a description and history of the younger, radical branch of the contemporary women's movement, see Jo Freeman, "Feminist Organizations and Activities from Suffrage to Women's Liberation," in *Women: A Feminist Perspective,* ed. Jo Freeman (Mountain View: Mayfield Publishing Company, 1989), 541–55.

16. For an account of these alternative education projects, see Charlotte Bunch and Susan Pollack, eds., *Learning Our Way* (Trumansburg: The Crossing Press Feminist Series, 1983).

17. Interviews with editors Estelle Freedman, Palo Alto, June 3, 1985; Rayna Rapp, New York City, October 9, 1986; Ruth Milkman, New York City, October 9, 1986; and Michele Barale, Boulder, January 16, 1985.

18. Nancy K. Miller, "Conference Call," *differences* 2, no. 3 (1990): 76.

19. Joan Landes, *Women and the Public Sphere in the Age of the French Revolution* (Ithaca: Cornell University Press, 1988).

20. Nancy Fraser, "Rethinking the Public Sphere: A Contribution to the Critique of Actually Existing Democracy," *Social Text* 8, no. 3 (1990): 67.

21. Felski, *Beyond Feminist Aesthetics,* 167.

22. Ibid., 289.

23. For explanations of the ethnographic method, see James P. Spradley, *Participant Observation* (New York: Holt, Rinehart and Winston, 1980); James P. Spradley, *The Ethnographic Interview* (New York: Holt, Rinehart and Winston, 1979); David McCurdy and James Spradley, *The Cultural Experience: Ethnography in a Complex Society* (Chicago: Social Research Associates, 1972); Michael Agar, *The Professional Stranger: An Informal Introduction to Ethnography* (New York: Academic Press, 1980). For discussions of the relevance of ethnography to the study of American culture, see John L. Caughey, "The Ethnography of Everyday Life: Theories and Methods for American Culture Studies," *American Quarterly* 34, no. 2 (Bibliography 1982): 222–43; and Murray G. Murphey, "Comment on the Session 'Fieldwork in Modern

America,'" presented at the Seventh Annual Biennial Convention of the American Studies Association, Minneapolis, 1979.

24. The Americanist Gene Wise developed a mode of cultural inquiry called "culture as drama" in which particular social communications are singled out not only for their manifest content but also for their ability to express the underlying cultural themes and conflicts of the social context. For his explanation and use of "cultural dramas," see "When Politics Becomes Cultural Drama: The Irony of Watergate," presented to the American Studies Program, Pennsylvania State University, May 4, 1981.

25. Clifford Geertz, "From the Native's Point of View: On the Nature of Anthropological Understanding," in *Meaning in Anthropology*, ed. K. H. Basso and H. A. Selby (Albuquerque: University of New Mexico Press, 1976).

26. Ward H. Goodenough, "Comment on Cultural Evolution," *Daedalus* 90 (Summer 1961): 521–28.

27. Geertz, "Native's Point of View," 33.

28. Peter L. Berger and Thomas Luckman, *The Social Construction of Reality: A Treatise in the Sociology of Knowledge* (New York: Doubleday, 1966), 74–76.

29. Stanley Fish, *Is There a Text in This Class? The Authority of Interpretive Communities* (Cambridge: Harvard University Press, 1980), 332–33.

30. Altbach, *The Knowledge Context*, 178.

31. Janice Radway, *Reading the Romance: Women, Patriarchy, and Popular Literature* (Chapel Hill: University of North Carolina Press, 1984), 164–222.

32. Jean Bethke Elshtain, "Toward a Reflexive Feminist Theory," *Women and Politics* 3 (Winter 1983): 27–43; Natalie Zemon Davis et al., "Feminist Book Reviewing (a Symposium)," *Feminist Studies* 14 (Fall 1988): 601–22; "Special Issue: Reconstructing the Academy," *Signs* 12 (Winter 1987); Berenice M. Fisher, "Professing Feminism: Feminist Academics and the Women's Movement," *Psychology of Women Quarterly* 7 (Fall 1982): 63–64; Sandra Harding, "Common Causes: Toward a Reflexive Feminist Theory," *Women and Politics* 3 (Winter 1983): 27–43.

33. Haraway, "A Manifesto for Cyborgs," 65.

34. "Editorial," *Signs* 8 (Autumn 1982): 2.

35. Haraway, "A Manifesto for Cyborgs," 66.

chapter one

Feminist Publishing and the Underground Press

It was a good coming together of time, place and personality. Nothing works without a lot of things working. I want to emphasize the timing, 1974 was a good year. The field, there was a "field" but it was still very fresh, so simultaneously we had something to draw on and something to create. It was like the novel, not in the seventeenth century, but in the eighteenth century. It was like American Studies, not in 1941, but in 1955.

Catharine Stimpson, founding editor,
Signs

Most of the scholarly journals concerned with women's studies were created during the first half of the 1970s. Although the *Michigan Papers* broke ground as a monograph series in 1969, the first feminist scholarly journals were both begun in 1972: *Feminist Studies* at the University of Maryland and *Women's Studies* at Queens College. The first issues of *Frontiers,* the smallest and poorest of the nationally recognized journals, and *Signs,* the largest and richest, appeared in the fall of 1975. Dale Spender began *Women's Studies International Forum* in London, and Sherry Clarkson created the *International Journal of Women's Studies* for Eden Press in Canada in 1978.

As Catharine Stimpson explained, it was an extraordinary "coming together of time, place, and personality" for the creation of feminist academic journals. Many factors were at work. The women's movement was peaking in fervor and activity, and its impact extended from neighborhood consciousness-raising groups to the halls of Congress. The burgeoning discipline of women's studies influenced the research of fields far beyond its borders. Feminist publishing had exploded into highly differentiated and distinct genres, creating many feminist presses, publishing collectives, distribution services, and bookstores. The academy was accommodating, audiences available, and individual women willing to commit themselves to the task of publishing a volatile mix of feminist politics and innovative scholarship.

Despite the suddenness of their appearance, feminist publications did not spring from a vacuum. The women who founded these journals were innovators and pioneers. Angrily critical of male supremacist culture and society, feminists challenged all social manifestations of patriarchy, including traditional forms of publishing. But, of necessity, feminists also worked simultaneously with, as well as against, conceptual models, assumptions, and forms of available knowledge. Consequently, feminist editors reworked old publishing traditions in ways influenced by the particular social conditions in which they operated.

The explosion of feminist publishing that occurred during the 1970s drew upon a number of important legacies: the Old Left of the 1930s, the beat publications of the 1950s, the civil rights movement of the 1960s, and, most directly, the underground press of the 1960s. There are also earlier connections to suffragist publishing during the first wave of the women's movement in the nineteenth century. In recent years, feminists who began their political activity in the civil rights and antiwar movements have found much in common with their predecessors in the suffragist women's press who cut their political teeth on abolitionist and social reform movements.[1]

Nineteenth-century abolitionist papers, including the *National Anti-Slavery Standard* of New York, the *Boston Commonwealth,* and the *National ERA* in Washington, D.C., provided some of the earliest forums for discussing women's suffrage. Initially, the fledgling suffragist movement had no publishing tradition of its own, but women had been involved in publishing and editing several established abolitionist papers during the 1840s and 1850s.[2] Suffragists quickly developed a print tradition of their own: Pauline Wright Davis's *The Una* appeared from 1849 to 1855, Amelia Bloomer's *The Lily* from 1849 to 1859, and Elizabeth Cady Stanton and Susan B. Anthony's *The Revolution* from 1868 to 1872. Charlotte Perkins Gilman wrote about feminist issues for thirty years in her newspaper, *The Forerunner;* Lucy Stone and Henry Blackwell edited and published the reformist *Woman's Journal* in Boston from 1879 to 1917; Emily Pitts Stevens published *The Pioneer* in 1869 in San Francisco; and Abigail Scott Duniway began the *New Northwest* in Oregon in 1871.[3]

Despite these women's similar experiences, the legacy of nineteenth-century suffragist publishing has been repressed in history and was unavailable to the founders of the contemporary feminist press. The activities of nineteenth-century women were considered marginal and insignificant to androcentric conceptions of historical scholarship. None of the people interviewed for this study knew much about the publishing models of their suffragist forbearers when they set out to establish their own journals. Excluded from anthologies of historical documents, poorly and rarely archived, and omitted from library collections, nineteenth-century feminist publishing remained a rich but little-explored area of history. Uncovering and restoring this nineteenth-century feminist legacy became one of the central concerns of feminist academic journals. Once they began to recover it, contemporary feminists found their suffragist publishing heritage useful and affirming. As Dale Spender explains in her study of the British suffragist newspaper *Time and Tide*:

> Great strength and great joy can be derived from the knowledge that a little over fifty years ago, many women felt much the same about male power as many women do today. They saw similar problems, sought similar solutions, engaged in similar debates—and encountered similar strategies of male resistance. To know about their existence is to confirm and validate much of our own. And to learn of their 'erasure' from history is to be better informed. To believe that we are on our own, that we have started a protest for which there is no precedent, is to be plagued by doubts, to be vulnerable, to be without models, experience or guidance.[4]

Because of this "erasure," the publishing influence on which the contemporary feminist press relied most heavily was not the nineteenth-century feminist press but the varied and vigorous underground press of the 1960s. Feminist publishing took hold in the last years of the decade and exploded in numbers as the underground press of the sixties waned. Women involved with the New Left learned from the mistakes and successes of the underground press, upon which much of the content and organizational structure of early feminist publications were modeled or to which it was opposed. Consequently, a full understanding of the circumstances that produced the radical feminist press must include an account of its immediate precursor: the underground political press of the 1960s.

The term *underground* referred to the oppositional stance of the press, because the publications were never illegal.[5] Most studies date the birth of the underground press with Art Kunkin's *Los Angeles Free Press* in 1964. Eventually known as the *Free Press (Freep)*, Kunkin's paper promoted a mix of art, drugs, sex, and revolutionary politics. The *Free Press* originated as an eight-page tabloid distributed at a local Renaissance Faire. By 1969, it was a sixty-four-page publication with a paid circulation of a hundred thousand. Although the underground press was diverse in many ways, Kunkin's *Free Press* illustrates a number of its common influences.[6]

The underground press has an impressive heritage, and Kunkin exemplifies its connection with its immediate precursors, the socialist press of the 1930 and 1940s and the bohemian press of the 1950s.[7] Like many of the early editors of underground papers, Kunkin's roots were in the bohemian press and socialist publishing, and he combined these experiences in an explosive mix. He had worked at the *Village Voice,* a Greenwich Village-based paper inspired by the small art and politics magazines that had coalesced around New York's beat scene during the 1950s.[8]

Although they now seem timid, the reporting in bohemian publications such as the *Voice* celebrated political and artistic subjectivity. Favoring the style of the bohemian press, Kunkin rejected the mainstream press's claims of objectivity and balance in news reporting, an opposition carried to its fullest with the *Berkeley Barb,* founded in 1965, which its founder Max Scherr originally planned to call the *Berkeley Bias.*[9] Although the *Village Voice* was devoted to cultural and political radicalism, its cofounders Dan Wolf and Ed Francher "had both always, genuinely, been turned off by the left, by the Communists, the Trotskyites, the socialists, the fronts, the fellow travelers, the hard-core types."[10] Consequently, the radical politics of the underground press during the late 1960s must be traced to another source: Old Left publishing.

Art Kunkin encountered the traditions of the radical left when he began attending socialist study groups and worked at the *Militant,* a Trotskyist Socialist Workers party paper. According to Joseph Conlin, editor of the *American Radical Press,* socialist publishing has been a central feature of political publishing in American from the nineteenth-century *Appeal to Reason* to the contemporary *Guardian.* "At least 600 distinct periodicals were published during the Socialist Party's happiest days. . . . No other facet of radical political activity in the United

States—not strike, not subversion, not demonstration, not oratory—has claimed more attention or time."[11]

Socialist publishing was informed by the theories of Lenin and Gramsci about the revolutionary press as an organizing tool. In *What Is To Be Done?* Lenin argued that a socialist newspaper was an effective mechanism for uniting a geographically dispersed movement: "We have bricks and bricklayers for revolution but the bricks are often so scattered that the enemy can shatter the structure as if it was made of sand, not brick."[12] He believed that both in terms of its readership and its institutionalized network a socialist newspaper would help overcome this fragmentation.

Gramsci believed the socialist press could engender a ruling-class consciousness in the working class. He considered newspapers to be an integral part of the institutional-ideological complex, the "hegemony," that dominated Western Europe. As a whole, he argued, hegemony supports capitalist rule, but institutions such as the press can be penetrated and "colonized" by revolutionary elements. According to Gramsci, a revolutionary press based in the working class "makes the working class think like a ruling class."[13] The revolutionary press would not simply struggle to undermine the hegemonic hold of capitalism, but to gain a position of counterhegemonic authority. Underscoring the activist implications of Gramsci's writings, the cultural historian George Lipsitz explains that

> Dominant groups must not only win the war of maneuver—control over resources and institutions, but they must win the war of position as well; they must make their triumphs appear legitimate and necessary in the eyes of the vanquished. That legitimation is hard work. It requires concessions to aggrieved populations. It mandates the construction and maintenance of alliances among antagonistic groups, and it always runs the risk of unraveling when lived experiences conflict with legitimizing ideologies.[14]

In this "war of position," the oppositional press could use the inherent instability of dominant hegemony to institutionalize and legitimize revolutionary ideologies and consciousness.

Although familiar with socialist publications rooted in such theories, Kunkin and other underground editors often diverged quite sharply in practice. Recalling his Marxist beginnings, he explained his rejection of Marxism's focus on the working class as the only authentic case for revolution: "I was involved with the Socialist Party at that point, and was very fed up with the way all the radical papers were very European oriented. So I had this idea of starting something that would listen to people—listen to minorities, listen to young people. I wasn't locked in theoretically to just being for workers."[15]

Some critics have explained the limited relationship between the New Left and proponents of earlier radical movements as the result of New Left radicalism having been "issued from the gut, not from books."[16] John Downing, an expert on socialist media, offers another explanation, however:

> The mechanics of the McCarthy era sufficed to intimidate and silence . . . the development of socialist politics in its tracks for the best part of a generation. . . . A result of this in the 60s was that good political organization was defined according to a simplified version of anarchism. Instant action, immediacy of feelings, primacy of moral revulsion over political or economic analysis, hostility to structure, abolition of leaders: these were the moods and watchwords that dominated political discourse. They constituted the response of what was for the most part a generation newly exposed to socialist or anti-imperialist or black nationalist or radical perspectives.[17]

Like many socialist publications, the underground press relied on grass-roots support, a shoestring budget, and the ability to maximize its impact with minimal resources. The newly advanced, easy-to-operate, and relatively affordable technology of offset printing expanded political publishing substantially.[18] Editors also optimized their resources by sharing materials and rejecting the use of copyrights. By the late 1960s, the underground press was a large, diverse collection of papers that responded to different geographic communities and political constituencies. By 1969, the peak of radical activity, the underground press had grown to an estimated five hundred papers with 4.6 million readers in the United States.[19] The Underground Press Syndicate (UPS) provided an effective teletype news service that coordinated the efforts and facilities of an increasingly unwieldy and unsteady coalition of publications.

And yet, at the peak of this success, radical activity began to decline. After the repression of the Chicago Seven trial and the violence of the Democratic National Convention and Black Panther shootouts, activists became disillusioned and splintered. Yippies, Abbie Hoffman and Jerry Rubin's Youth International party, hit the streets as "media guerrillas" to perform political theater, and Weathermen turned to increasingly militant tactics like bombing ROTC buildings to "bring the war home."[20] The Black Panthers, the Peace and Freedom party, and the Students for a Democratic Society (SDS) found themselves attacked from outside and fragmented from within. When the SDS split irreconcilably in 1969, a CIA situation report summarized its devastating effect on the underground press: "The 1969 SDS national convention, which split SDS into a number of opposing factions, signalled the downfall of the underground press. Lacking national focus and leadership, each paper was forced to redefine its roles and develop its own political line based on what remained of the radical youth movement, its own readership and financial backers. Most papers vacillated during the ensuing months and many more folded in the process."[21]

What the CIA's report neglected to mention about the demise of the underground press was its own very active role in shutting down radical journalism.[22] At the height of its influence and breadth, underground publishing sustained organizational as well as financial collapse. Its editors and writers took one costly turn that helped lead to the establishment of feminist publishing.

The editors of several leading underground papers—the *Berkeley Barb, Free Press,* and *Rat*—began to fill their pages with sex ads and "dildo journalism" as an attack against censorship and sexual repression.[23] The popularity of these features, and a series of Supreme Court decisions that relaxed the standards of legal obscenity, soon put the press in competition with new underground publications: *The New York Review of Sex, Pleasure, Kiss,* and *Screw.*[24] Sex features began to erode political coverage, but editors claimed that their treatment of sex shattered received cultural notions of sexuality. Despite this defense, the advertisements contributed to a scathing feminist critique of the New Left's glorification of patriarchal politics. According to David Armstrong's analysis of the underground press, "If selling sex was a short-term financial bonanza for the underground press, it was a long-term political failure—one that led directly to the founding of feminist media as alternatives to the underground press itself."[25]

Early in 1969, "The Grand Coolie Damn" by the radical activist Marge Piercy appeared in the underground journal *Leviathan.* Piercy argued that New Left men had created a movement that was a microcosm of the mainstream, which concentrated all power in the hands of men and relegated women to subservient, often invisible, roles. In addition to challenging the prerogative of male activists and the sexual division of labor, Piercy claimed that men in the movement had made violence and domination radical virtues, and such traits did not produce "a more efficient revolutionary, only a more efficient son of a bitch." She concluded, "Sisters, what we do, we have to do together, and we will see about them." [26]

The underground press was filled with women such as Marge Piercy. They were seasoned veterans of radical movements and beginning to assert their leadership abilities, use their organizing skills, and refine their political analysis in service of their own interests. Robin Morgan, another disillusioned, radical woman, was on the staff of the influential New York-based newspaper *Rat*. In her personal account of the experience, she summed up the problem of male-dominated underground newspapers:

> Despite its attempts at genuine muckraking journalism, the underground press had been created and sustained by and for men and male attitudes. As the gentle flower-children style of the middle sixties flared into the confrontation tactics of the late sixties, these male attitudes solidified themselves in Leftist consciousness—being tough, butch, "heavy," and "a street fighter" were now prerequisites for being a radical, male or female. Not surprisingly, most men had a better chance at cutting such a figure than did most women. *Rat* reflected these changes, and began presenting as well a kind of "cultural nationalism" for young white males: rock music coverage, pornography articles, and sex-wanted ads began to clog the pages. . . . the women who worked at *Rat* were angry and had been confronting the men about the paper's sexism and its hierarchy, which employed men as editors and feature writers, women as (usually volunteer) secretaries and bottle-washers who were sometimes permitted to write a short article. I had even warned the *Rat* men that women might take over the paper if there were no change forthcoming. But I was unprepared for the delightful phone call from Jane Alpert. . . . she serenely informed me that the women on the paper seized it.[27]

Important feminist publications had been created as early as 1968 in response to the grass-roots women's liberation movement. However, the feminist takeover of *Rat* in early 1970 was a watershed action that captured a moment in history when women in the left came painfully to reexamine the radical men and radical politics they had worked with so closely. A particularly violent and pornography-filled issue of *Rat*, with articles trivializing women's liberation, so enraged the women on the magazine's staff that they joined with the Redstockings, Weatherwomen, and members of the guerrilla-theater group WITCH to seize the paper and produce a special issue by and about women.

The new feminist sensibility of the collective was summed up in Morgan's "Goodbye to All That." She began by challenging the radical authenticity of leftist men: "We have met the enemy and he's our friend. . . . the counterfeit male-dominated Left." She then proclaimed, "Women are the real Left. We are rising, powerful in our unclean bodies; right glowing mad in our inferior brains; wild hair flying; wild eyes staring; wild voices keening; undaunted by blood we who hemorrhage every twenty-eight days" and ended with the names of twenty-five movement women to be freed—names that later figured prominently in the women's liberation movement.[28]

The feminist issue of *Rat* might have remained one of a handful of token "special women's issues" published and forgotten in the male-dominated underground press had *Rat's* male editors not heralded the return of their paper with a headline that read "The Old *Rat* Is Back" and featured the trademark cartoon rat unzipping his fly. In retaliation, the feminist editorial collective seized permanent control of the newspaper within a week, denouncing its predecessor as an apolitical "pornzine."[29]

Rat was but the first of many feminist takeovers of established underground papers. It was published for another three years under the direction of a feminist collective and then became *Women's Liberation*. But the effort to meld leftist and feminist approaches proved impossible as feminist editors discovered the problem was not simply a matter of male attitudes but rather a matter of inadequate political theory. Morgan remembers, "There was little space left to avoid facing The Awful Truth: that it was the politics of the Left, not solely the men who mouthed them, which were male supremacist. It was the politics, the analysis itself which ignored or patronized more than half the human species."[30] Realizing that women's media should focus fully on women's issues and develop a feminist analysis rather than rely on a derivative leftist vision, radical feminists set out to establish media of their own.

Although feminists left the underground press because they wanted greater freedom to address issues affecting women, the development of the feminist press did not include a complete break with the methods and format of its predecessor. The decade of radical publishing provided models from which feminist editors could imitate, oppose, and fashion their own media. "What took the black and student movements so long to get off the ground was all the time spent figuring out how to communicate nationally. They decided early on against using the mass media, and it was a long time before a network of underground papers emerged. But by 1967–68, when women began organizing for themselves, putting out newspapers and knowing where to distribute them was second nature."[31]

Feminists borrowed and reshaped the publishing forms and traditions of the underground press and its Old Left and beat predecessors. The energy with which they plunged into publishing as a strategy for political action, a vehicle to unify and empower women, and a forum for community debate and development, echoed the Old Left theories of communication that informed the underground press of the 1960s. Along with such practical aspects of publishing as layout, printing, and distribution, feminist editors and writers also followed their underground counterparts by stressing the importance of subjectivity, politically informed reporting, and the integrity of emotion rather than the mainstream claims to dispassionate, objective authority.[32]

Rather than claim value-free journalism, many feminists informed their writing with an explicit reliance on political theory. In early articles, feminists looked most often to the New Left and black power movements for models of effective theories of social change. In the earliest publications, race and class models remained quite common, and occasionally editorial battles between "politicos" relying on class analysis and feminists pursuing an independent analysis destroyed publications. The feminist theory of sexual politics, which viewed women as oppressed by men as a group and brought political analysis to personal relations, finally moved the feminist press beyond a dependence on other metaphors for oppression.

In certain arenas, feminist publishing actually diverged from underground publishing by furthering the values and models of the underground press. Members of the underground press of the 1960s defined their ideal political identity in opposition to the dominant mainstream culture. Although the young, white, middle-class men who dominated the press shared kinship ties, educational backgrounds, and financial privileges with the mainstream culture, they rejected these connections by an early identification with the resurgent civil rights movement. Yet, as the feminist philosopher Berenice Fisher argues, their resistance was contradictory when it came to women: "The radical ideal of political action contained a special obligation for women: compassion and support for male political workers. . . . She can atone for her guilt by giving him her body. She can prove resistance to racism by making love to a man who represents the community. She can realize herself as a political being by conforming to a traditional ideal of womanhood. For both Black and White women . . . the roles of helper nurturer, and lover often served to support male power and privilege."[33] Consequently, feminist applications of a radical ideal of political action would include not only resistance to the American mainstream culture but also resistance to the culture of the male-dominated left.

Similarly, feminists reworked the theory of democratic-anarchism that New Left publishing had used to create its innovative, spontaneous, but often ramshackle structure. Feminists observed that this haphazard organization allowed the line between community-based leadership and media-manufactured celebrity to become very thin. Then, as now, many feminists considered hierarchies and competition central features of "patriarchal culture" and were determined to avoid such structures through meticulous attention to egalitarian structure and process. From the start, many feminist publications were collectively edited and produced, a structure that, in numerous variations, continues to shape feminist organizations. Current feminists consider the early attempts to bring internal structures in line with political visions as problematic and sometimes excessive.[34] However, such collectives retained the dynamic egalitarianism of anarchist-democracy and combined it with close attention to the details of internal process. Despite their attempts to guard against the perceived weaknesses of the underground press, feminists would find that they were destined to face many of the same problems and challenges that plagued their precursors. Limited in resources but significant in influence, feminist publishing quickly grew into a large, varied internecine phenomenon that addressed increasingly complex questions and diverse constituencies. Like the underground press, it reflected the ideologies, issues, tensions, and challenges of its activist movement.

The early feminist press was remarkably prolific. According to Ann Mather's study, between 1968 and 1973, "more than 500 feminist publications appeared in the United States alone. . . . The majority of the American feminist publications were newsletters, although there was 60 newspapers, nine newspaper/magazines, and 72 magazines and journals. They appeared in all but seven states."[35] The breadth of modern feminist publishing was matched by the speed of its development. In nearly each year from 1968 through 1975 pronounced shifts were apparent in sophistication and technique. Each shift was accompanied by a change in publishing forms, content, organization, and theory.

From the earliest days of contemporary feminist awareness, activists used publication as a primary political strategy. In the mid-sixties, this took the form of "memos" from within New Left. But memos quickly evolved into angry manifestos proclaiming the birth of an autonomous radical feminist movement. By late 1968, the radical and reform branches of the women's movement were producing successful newsletters. Radical feminist publishing used newsletters and newspapers to address the split between the New Left and radical feminism until a struggle within the collective that ran the highly successful newspaper *off our backs* revealed tensions between gay and straight staff members that had begun to create factions in the movement.

Reform feminist publications proliferated as newsletters until *New York* magazine spawned *Ms.* in 1972, which led to a variety of moderately successful reform "slicks." Books and theory journals appeared as feminist presses, publishing collectives, and distribution systems were established in 1970. From 1972 to 1975, radical and reform publishing exploded: literary magazines, lesbian publishing, theory journals, national and local newspapers, book review quarterlies, and scholarly books and journals.

Between 1965 and 1968, memos and short, mimeographed articles concerning the status of women sporadically appeared from within the New Left. These early efforts were cheaply printed and often passed around by feminists throughout the New Left publishing network. Written by one or two women, or sometimes anonymously, they addressed men and women within the New Left and spoke within the parameters of that movement's analysis. Often such efforts were trivialized or disregarded, but Mary King and Casey Hayden's 1965 SDS memo led to the irreparable break of radical feminists from the New Left.

> We've talked a lot, to each other and to some of you, about our
> own and other women's problems in trying to live in our personal

lives and in our work as independent and creative people. In these conversations we've found what seems to be recurrent ideas of themes (sex and caste, women and problems of work, women and personal relations with men, institutions, lack of community for discussion). Maybe we can look at these things many of us perceive, often as a result of insights learned from the movement. . . . The reason we want to open up the dialogue is mostly subjective. Working in the movement often intensifies personal problems, especially if we start trying to apply the things we're learning there to our personal lives. . . . Objectively, the chances seem nil that we could start a movement based on anything as distant to general American thought as a sex-caste system.[36]

Although the memo's tone reveals the tentativeness of early feminist challenges, the King-Hayden memo was prototypical of later feminist writings in its attack on the hypocrisy of New Left politics that excluded women, its reliance on a black model of oppression to argue the status of women, and its call to scrutinize personal relationships for political purposes. When King and Hayden read their memo at the national SDS convention in 1965, male radicals responded with "catcalls, storms of ridicule and verbal abuse." The confrontation resulted in feminists walking out of the convention en masse, an action many cite as the moment that New Left men suffered the feminist loss from which they could never recoup.[37]

As feminists began to move out of the New Left and establish their own loosely connected grass-roots organizations, the memo form was replaced by the newsletter, which dominated movement publishing for the next decade. In 1968, feminists had little access to mainstream or underground publications as forums for their concerns. Newsletters were an easy, low-cost, immediate, technically expedient solution to the problem of providing the necessary communication and cohesion for the movement's disparate coalition of grass-roots and national organizations. Requiring minimal editing, community-based, and action-oriented, newsletters were remarkably open to any feminist contributor. Newsletter editors used their publications as bulletin boards for the fledgling movement, to organize grass-roots coalitions for immediate action, and to create a grapevine of information that would be used to organize the movement's geographically dispersed constituency.

Reflecting the radical and reform bases of the contemporary women's movement, the two earliest regularly produced newsletters were Jo Free-man's radical, Chicago-based *Voices of Women's Liberation* and the National Organization for Women's reformist *NOW Acts*. *Voices of Women's Liberation* was connected to a coalition of a number of grass-roots, New Left-influenced women's groups in Chicago and circulated nationally via the inherited distribution networks of the Underground Press Syndicate.[38] The editors of *NOW Acts* spoke to the women's rights branch of the movement, which aspired "to take action to bring women into full participation in the mainstream of American society now, exercising all the privileges and responsibilities thereof in truly equal partnership with men."[39] In accordance with this reformist ap-proach, *NOW Acts* focused on reports concerning discrimination in employment and education, problems of the media's image of women, organized the lobbying of the Equal Employment Opportunity Com-mission (EEOC) and Congress, and, after much internal controversy, abortion rights.

The women's rights branch of the women's movement was interested in attaining equal rights within the existing political system rather than questioning the system itself. Because they relied upon the traditional liberal theory inherent in the American system, the editors of reformist publications had little need to explain their theoretical underpinnings to their white, middle- and upper-middle-class professional audience. Consequently, unlike their radical counterparts, the pages of women's rights publications lacked substantial theoretical discussions. The edi-tors of *NOW Acts* fashioned their publication as a national voice for the women's rights movement and eventually inspired many local ver-sions of itself. In fact, NOW chapter newsletters comprised the bulk of women's rights publications until the arrival of *Ms.* in 1972.

Ms. is often cited as the foremost women's rights publication even though the boundaries between reform and radical feminism have since been heavily traversed by both sides. *Ms.* was introduced as a forty-four-page supplement to the mainstream *New York* magazine in 1971 by Gloria Steinem, a political journalist who specialized in political re-porting at *New York Magazine,* and Pat Carbine, an editor at *Look* and *McCall's*. An immediate success, within a year *Ms.* had a 350,000 circulation and a readership estimated at 1.4 million.[40] The topics that Steinem and Carbine featured reflected women's rights concerns, for example, the Equal Rights Amendment, nonsexist children's books, and legislative recourse in job discrimination. But they also featured more radical issues: lesbian love and sexuality, the effects of poverty on women, and international women's conferences, along with numerous reports on grass-roots women's organizations. However, the inclusion of radical content in *Ms.* was consistently obscured by the mainstream form, structure, and financial arrangement of the publication.

Ms. was an openly commercial venture that considered advertising essential to its success, and a tension between women-as-constituency and women-as-market developed in its pages. Bankrolled with more than a million start-up dollars from the Warner Communications conglomerate and Katherine Graham of the *Washington Post*—and carrying the women's rights movement's aspiration that women be taken seriously in male spheres—Steinem used a slick magazine layout, four-color covers, and the graphics that had been associated with *New York*.[41] In "The Conservatism of *Ms.*" in 1979, the radical Redstockings Pat Mainardi and Kathi Sarachild attacked the popular magazine for its "pervasive class bias," its reliance on feminist media stars, "an obsession with electoral politics," and its focus on sex role "conditioning" rather than on a systemic power analysis.[42] The attack came from the radical branch of the early feminist movement that rejected the goal of attaining "women's rights" within the system in favor of attaining "women's liberation" from the system. Ellen Willis, Sarachild, and Mainardi were New York activists, writers, and editors involved in highly influential radical feminist publishing collectives: the Radicalesbians, the Redstockings, and New York Radical Women.

Before *Ms.* appeared in 1972, feminist publishing was dominated by radical, grass-roots collectives that were populated by women who had been, or still were, involved with the New Left movements of the 1960s. Editors and writers in women's liberationist publications were younger, middle-class, and white. Most had become disillusioned with the civil rights and antiwar movements and had created a loosely structured, grass-roots feminist movement around urban centers and college campuses in New York, Washington, Chicago, Seattle, Boston, and San Francisco. The earliest tensions in radical feminist publishing were concentrated around independent publications run by radical feminists and left-affiliated publications run by politicos. As illustrated in the *Rat* takeover in 1970, New Left sympathizers and radical feminists were divided over the privileging of sex versus class as the primary category of oppression and the use of black power models versus class struggle models for revolutionary change. As Willis, a member of New York Radical Women, has explained the split:

> I joined New York Radical Women, the first women's liberation group in New York City, in 1968, about a year after it had started meeting. By that time the group was deeply divided over what came to be called (by radical feminists) the "politico-feminist split." The "politicos'" primary commitment was to the New Left. They saw capitalism as the course of women's oppression: the ruling class indoctrinated us with oppressive sex roles to promote consumerism and/or keep women a cheap reserve labor force and/or divide the workers; conventional masculine and feminine attitudes were matters of bourgeois conditioning from which we must liberate ourselves. I sided with the "radical feminists." We argued that male supremacy was in itself a systemic form of domination— a set of materials, institutional relations, not just bad attitudes. Men had power and privilege and like any other ruling class would defend their interests; challenging that power required a revolutionary movement of women. And since the male-dominated left would inevitably resist understanding or opposing male power the radical feminist movement must be autonomous, create its own theory and set its own priorities. Our model of course was black power. . . . With few exceptions, those of us who first defined radical feminism took for granted that "radical" implied antiracist, anticapitalist, and anti-imperialist.[43]

No More Fun and Games, published in New York; *Notes from the First Year,* published in Boston; and *Lilith,* published in Seattle, were the first truly independent radical feminist journals produced by the contemporary women's movement without New Left backing. Collectively run, the staffs shared all production and editorial tasks, worked on a small scale, avoided direct links to male organizations, and remained community-based to ensure accountability as well as proximity to feminist ideas and action. Written in the angry, confrontational style of earlier underground press newspapers, these initial radical feminist publications included an extension of the earlier displaced memos: the manifesto. As a form, manifestos were concise expressions of rage and politics that announced newly formed feminist groups. They combined the feminist use of authority based in emotion and experience with the poetics of beat publications and the confrontational pose of the under-ground press. Reprinted since in numerous anthologies and historical collections and considered classics of the women's movement, these early manifestos included the "Bitch Manifesto," the "Fourth World Manifesto," "Sexual Politics: A Manifesto for Revolution," "Politics of Ego: A Manifesto for New York Radical Feminists," "Redstock-ings Manifesto," and "Lilith's Manifesto." The anger, flair, irreverence, and determination of these documents is illustrated in extreme by the "SCUM [Society for Cutting Up Men] Manifesto":

> SCUM—dominant, secure, self-confident, nasty, violent, selfish, independent, proud, thrill-seeking, free-wheeling, arrogant fe-males who consider themselves fit to rule the universe. . . . SCUM is too impatient to hope and wait for the de-brainwashing of millions of assholes. SCUM will not picket, demonstrate, march or strike to attempt to achieve its ends. Such tactics are for nice genteel ladies. . . . if SCUM ever marches, it will be over LBJ's stupid, sickening face; if SCUM ever strikes, it will be within the dark with a six-inch blade.[44]

These heated pronouncements quickly gave way to more substantive articles in radical feminist publications as women's liberationists accu-mulated a core set of issues in keeping with their radical analysis of systemic oppression: lesbianism, prostitution, violence against women, and wages for housework. A considerable effort was made to analyze patriarchy in order to develop feminist theories about the institutional basis of female oppression. *No More Fun and Games,* published by the Cell 16 collective, has all the markings of the early radical pub-lishing movement: an independent, small-group, community basis; a reliance on theory and action; the authority of experience and emotion; the employment of race and class analogies; the systemic analysis of oppression; and opposition to men as a group, whether New Left or mainstream. As an early editorial stated:

> We all felt strongly that our movement must be grassroots, and emerge from the truth of our suffering . . . we did it: we produced a journal, doing all the layout and production ourselves. The Left has officially endorsed "women's liberation" (in order to hold onto their own women). But this is America, and we realize that these are methods of absorption, not a true reflection of changed atti-

tudes. We have done no more than scream, and we were heard. Before us lies the necessity and labor of a thorough social revolution—worldwide, not just in America. Abstract analysis is important, but people are right to look for specific actions. It is our duty to provide an analysis that is so revolutionary, so inescapably true and humane, that women cannot be coopted into the system that formerly enslaved them.[45]

Following the split of the politicos and the radical feminists, a second important factioning beset radical feminist publications as they turned their attention away from the men of the New Left and to the diversification of the interests of the women within their own rapidly expanding movement. The shift in tensions is illustrated in the history of *off our backs*, a national, collectively run newspaper founded in 1970 that continues to dominate radical feminist publishing in the United States. Again, New Left veterans and *Guardian* writers inaugurated *off our backs* (*o.o.b.*) in 1971 with a spread on International Working Women's Day that hearkened to their New Left roots. By the third issue, the staff's radical feminists had carved their own journalistic domain from the material supplied by a growing and vigorous autonomous feminist movement. In addition to factioning along the earlier, politico and radical feminist lines, the *oob* collective also broke along the lines of lesbians and straight feminists. Foreshadowing an important faultline in feminist organizations that would break the movement open a few years later, Coletta Reid recalled her experience of coming out in the collective:

> Most of the women I worked with were surprisingly non-committal. I had expected joy and jubilation, since I was choosing myself, other women, and strength. The non-committal attitude turned into outright hostility whenever I discussed the political implications of my choice. It might have been ok if I had said that my choice was purely personal, that it had no relevance to any other feminist's life. But to suggest that becoming a lesbian might be a happier, more whole way of life for any feminist was too much. In a newspaper article, my politics were identified with those of Normal Mailer—sexual fascism: Mailer required all women to be heterosexual and I required them all to be lesbians. I slowly left . . . or more accurately I was slowly pushed out.[46]

Like many involved in gay-straight splits, Reid's politics were based on an argument put forth in the New York Radicalesbians' statement of lesbian-feminist politics, "Woman-Identified-Woman." Proponents of lesbian-feminist politics argued that lesbianism was a political decision, not just a personal one. Lesbian-feminist politics critiqued the institution and ideology of heterosexuality as the cornerstones of male supremacy. The ideology required a primary commitment to women as a political, economic, and cultural group. "It is the primacy of women relating to women, of women creating a new consciousness of and with each other which is at the heart of women's liberation and the basis for cultural revolution."[47]

The lesbian staffers who left *off our backs* set up two important independent publishing enterprises: Diana Press, a leading publishing company, and the Furies, a forceful, lesbian-feminist theory collective that included Rita Mae Brown and Charlotte Bunch, an organizer. Members of the Furies collective went on to found *Quest,* a theory journal; establish Olivia Records, the cornerstone of the women's culture explosion; and organize Women in Distribution (WIND), a national reprint and distribution service. The tensions of the gay-straight split, the development and influence of lesbian-feminist politics and culture, and the growth of lesbian-feminist publishing fundamentally altered the perspective, questions, definition, and forms of movement publishing.[48]

Radical feminists met the challenge of diversification within the movement with the steadying process of institutionalization: women's centers, rape crisis centers, consciousness raising groups, women's health clinics, feminist study groups, and lesbian support centers. For those involved with feminist publishing, 1970 was a watershed year, as feminists established small presses, publishing collectives, distribution circuits, and bookstores.[49] Diana Press was joined by Shameless Hussy Press, the Feminist Press, Daughters, Inc., and Know, Inc. Reprinting early memos and manifestos, original fiction, forgotten nineteenth-century feminist works, nonsexist children's literature, political theory, and self-help books, feminist presses were usually collectively run, women-only enterprises. Distribution and reprint services such as WIND connected these presses with their primary market outlets: feminist bookstores, women's centers, and the advertising pages of feminist publications. As the sociologists Myra Marx Ferree and Beth B. Hess describe the reifying effect of publishing institutionalization, "as more books are published and reviewed, as more magazine articles appear, as more mention is made on radio and television, as newspaper coverage expands, the movement itself becomes 'institutionalized'; that is, it becomes a 'normal' part of the social landscape."[50]

The stability of feminist institutions provided a base from which feminist publishing mushroomed in number, diversity, and genre from 1972 through 1975. Some of the most enduring works produced by the women's movement, such as New England Free Press's *Our Bodies, Ourselves,* Shameless Hussy's *For Colored Girls Who Have Considered Suicide When the Rainbow Is Enuf,* and Daughters, Inc.'s, *Rubyfruit Jungle,* appeared during this publishing boom.[51] It was a time of feminist momentum bracketed by the residual energy of the sixties' movements and the advent of conservative retrenchment and backlash. In 1973, the *New Women's Survival Catalogue* listed hundreds of feminist organizations; in the 1975 edition, its editors could list only a sampling of the thousands of such organizations.[52]

Radical feminists rose to prominence during the mid-seventies, organizing demonstrations, staging theatrical "zap" actions, shaping feminist theory, establishing rape crisis centers and battered women's shelters, proliferating women's legal and medical self-help groups, and exerting considerable influence over the reform and socialist branches of the movement in an unparalleled era of legislation and social change.[53] Surmounting the opposition of a conservative president, feminists successfully pressured a Democratic Congress to pass the Equal Rights Amendment and the Equal Credit Opportunity Act. Through feminist efforts, affirmative action programs were instituted, rape laws were formed, the EEOC recognized sex as a serious category of discrimination, and *Roe v. Wade* legalized abortion. Although grass-roots feminism had emerged in a number of European and third-world countries, American awareness of international feminism was not evident until 1975, the United Nation's International Women's Year that launched the Decade of the Woman, which resulted in a ten-year World Plan of Action.[54]

During these years of unprecedented feminist strength and influence, the formerly reluctant mainstream media responded with extensive coverage of feminist activities and ideas. In the *New York Times* alone, articles about the women's movement and its concerns increased from 168 in 1966 to 1,814 in 1974.[55] Along with this quantitative increase, mainstream journalists altered the tone and content of their reporting as the women's movement became the topic of serious journalism. Mainstream publishers discovered the lucrative feminist market first charted by Betty Friedan's successful *Feminine Mystique* and set out to acquire a number of feminist press titles as well as develop new works.[56] Whether or not the venture was ultimately purely mercenary or cooptive, the attention of the mainstream press made what had been considered extremist and esoteric in 1969 commonly recognized by 1975.

Faced with growing competition from mainstream publishers, independent feminist publishers expanded their book offerings with radical anthologies, theory works, health manuals, women's almanacs, feminist fantasy and science fiction, lesbian novels, feminist histories, and poetry collections. The spectrum of feminist periodicals expanded to include comic books, literary journals, political journals, and art journals. Rooted in the surge of feminist institutions and fueled by the energy of feminist success at social reform, it was during this proliferation of feminist publishing genres from 1972 through 1975 that feminist scholarly journals were created: *Feminist Studies* and *Women's Studies* in 1972, *Frontiers* in 1975, and *Signs* in 1975.

Notes

1. James P. Dansky, ed., *Women's Periodicals and Newspapers from the Eighteenth Century to 1981* (Boston: G. K. Hall and Co., 1982); David Doughan and Denise Sanchez, eds., *Feminist Periodicals: 1855–1984* (Brighton: Harvester Press Ltd., 1987).

2. Marion Marzolf, *Up from the Footnote: A History of Women Journalists* (New York: Hastings House, 1977), 220.

3. Launched in 1868, Stanton's periodical advocated not only female suffrage, but also the eight-hour workday, prison reform, pacifism, liberalized divorce laws, equal pay, and improved conditions for working women. Although it published only briefly, *The Revolution* was remarkably prophetic, raising issues that would be taken up again a century later. A more detailed description is available in David Armstrong, *A Trumpet to Arms: Alternative Media in America* (Boston: South End Press, 1981), 37–38 and in Lauren Kessler, *The Dissident Press: Alternative Journalism in American History* (London: Sage Publications, 1984), 74–81.

Edited and published by Lucy Stone and her husband, Henry Blackwell, the *Woman's Journal* appealed to moderates who supported the fight for women's voting rights with little social awareness beyond suffrage. It was the longest-running suffrage paper in the nation (1870–1917), with a circulation peak of 4,500 in 1882. See Marzolf, *Up from the Footnote*, 232. For a more complete history of suffrage periodicals and their rhetorical functions, see Martha M.

Solomon, ed., *A Voice of Their Own: The Woman Suffrage Press, 1840–1910* (Tuscaloosa: University of Alabama Press, 1991).

4. Dale Spender, *Time and Tide Wait for No Man* (London: Pandora Press, 1984), 2.

5. The bulk of underground newspapers were not distributed through subscription or newsstands but by street sales. They operated largely on a geographic basis and served the needs of specific communities. These communities were various and diverse but united as a "counter-culture" through their oppositional stance to mainstream American life.

6. Armstrong, *Trumpet to Arms*, 32. An in-depth analysis of Art Kunkin's *Free Press* and its role in establishing the underground press is available in Abe Peck, *Uncovering the Sixties: The Life and Times of the Underground Press* (New York: Pantheon Books, 1985).

7. The tradition of dissident publishing in America claims Thomas Paine's pamphlets, Samuel and John Adams's renegade weekly paper the *Boston Gazette* (1719–98), as well as the *Massachusetts Spy*. *Freedom's Journal* (1827–29) and the *North Star* were black-owned abolitionist newspapers. Utopian communities of the nineteenth century often had their own periodicals, such as *The Oneida Circular* (1851–76), *The New Harmony Gazette* (1825–35), and *The Dial* (1840–44). Armstrong, *Trumpet to Arms*, 33–35.

8. Peck, *Uncovering the Sixties*, 9. The *Village Voice* built its circulation to 130,000, larger than any other commercial or underground weekly in the country. See Roger Lewis, *Outlaws of America: The Underground Press and Its Context* (Baltimore: Penguin Books, 1972), 57.

9. Editors of the underground press rejected as false scientism what mainstream journalists called "objective journalism." The concept of objective journalism was not developed as a means to bring more honest news coverage to the public. It was a technique invented by early cooperative news-gathering associations so their services could be sold to the highly partisan papers of the day, which could not afford to offend any element of readership and assumed a stance of political and moral neutrality. Laurence Leamer, *The Paper Revolutionaries: The Rise of the Underground Press* (New York: Simon and Schuster, 1972), 189.

10. Peck, *Uncovering the Sixties*, 9.

11. Joseph R. Conlin, ed., *The American Radical Press, 1880–1960* (Westport: Greenwood Press, 1974), vii.

12. Peck, *Uncovering the Sixties*, 143–87.

13. John Downing, *The Media Machine* (London: Pluto Press, 1980), 143–87.

14. George Lipsitz, "The Struggle for Hegemony," *Journal of American History* 75 (June 1988): 147–48.

15. Armstrong, *Trumpet to Arms*, 45.

16. Edward E. Ericson, *Radicals in the University* (Stanford: Stanford University Press, 1975), x.

17. John Downing, *Radical Media: The Political Experience of Alternative Communication* (Boston: South End Press, 1984), 48.

18. Offset printing with its multiple publishing centers and inexpensive, easy-to-operate, cold-type composition equipment had made the publishing of small

newspapers financially feasible for anyone with a few hundred dollars and a cause. By sharing expenses and equipment, underground production directors established typesetting centers that were available to all movement papers. A detailed technical description of these technological advances and their effect on underground publishing is available in Robert Glessing, *The Underground Press in America* (Bloomington: Indiana University Press, 1970), 41–45.

19. Peck, *Uncovering the Sixties*, 86.

20. Armstrong, *Trumpet to Arms*, 119–24.

21. Disclosures of the Senate's Select Committee to Study Governmental Operations with Respect to Intelligence Activities revealed that the underground press had been the target of coordinated CIA and FBI campaigns of often-unconstitutional interference with reporting, printing, advertising, and distribution. How these agencies hampered or destroyed papers in the underground press is detailed in Geoffrey Rips, ed., *Unamerican Activities: Campaigns against the Underground Press* (San Francisco: City Lights Books, 1981).

22. Rips, *Unamerican Activities*, 26.

23. Peck, *Uncovering the Sixties*, 211.

24. Such publications were protected by Supreme Court decisions in *Roth v. United States* (1957) and *Memoirs v. Massachusetts* (1966), which defined prurient appeal, community standards and utter lack of redeeming value as the necessary standards for legal obscenity. See Peck, *Uncovering the Sixties*, 211.

25. Armstrong, *Trumpet to Arms*, 55.

26. Marge Piercy, "The Grand Coolie Damn," in *Sisterhood Is Powerful: An Anthology of Writings from the Women's Libration Movement*, ed. Robin Morgan (New York: Random House, 1978), 113.

27. Robin Morgan, *Going Too Far: The Personal Chronicle of a Feminist* (New York: Random House, 1978), 113.

28. Robin Morgan, "Goodbye to All That," in *Going Too Far*, 121–30.

29. Peck, *Uncovering the Sixties*, 215.

30. Morgan, *Going Too Far*, 118.

31. Judith Hole and Ellen Levine, *Rebirth of Feminism* (New York: Quadrangle Books/New York Times Books, 1971), 270.

32. Nineteenth-century feminist periodicals used a similar intimate, experiential rhetorical style. See Susan Schultz Huxman, "The *Woman's Journal*, 1870–1890: The Torchbearer for Suffrage," in *A Voice of Their Own*, ed. Soloman, 99.

33. Berenice Fisher, "Guilt and Shame in the Women's Movement: The Radical Ideal of Action and Its Meaning for Feminist Intellectuals," *Feminist Studies* 10 (Summer 1984): 185–212.

34. Joreen, "Tyranny of Structurelessness," in *Radical Feminism*, ed. Anne Koedt, Ellen Levine, and Anita Rapone (New York: New York Times Books, 1973), 285–300.

35. Ann Mather, "A History of Feminist Periodicals," *Journalism History* 1 (Autumn 1974): 82.

36. Sara Evans, *Personal Politics: The Roots of the Women's Movement in Civil Rights and the New Left* (New York: Vintage Books, 1979), 235–38.

37. Evans, *Personal Politics*, 160–62.

38. *Voices of Women's Liberation* began with a circulation of two hundred in 1968; by the time it folded a year later, its circulation was two thousand. See Hole and Levine, *Rebirth of Feminism,* 271.

39. "N.O.W. Statement of Purpose," in *Sisterhood Is Powerful,* ed. Morgan, 576.

40. Marzolf, *Up from the Footnote,* 243.

41. Armstrong, *Trumpet to Arms,* 246, 243.

42. Redstockings, *Feminist Revolution* (New York: Random House, 1979), 167–73.

43. Ellen Willis, "Radical Feminism and Feminist Radicals," in *The 60s without Apology,* ed. Sohnya Sayres et al. (Minneapolis: University of Minnesota Press, 1984), 93.

44. Valerie Solanis, "The SCUM Manifesto," in *Sisterhood Is Powerful,* ed. Morgan, 577.

45. *No More Fun and Games* 1 (February 1969): 4.

46. Coletta Reid, "Coming Out in the Women's Movement," in *Lesbianism and the Women's Movement,* ed. Nancy Myron and Charlotte Bunch (Baltimore: Diana Press, Inc., 1975), 94–95.

47. Radicalesbians, "Women-Identified-Woman," in *Liberation Now! Writings from the Women's Movement,* ed. Deborah Babcock and Madeline Belkjn (New York: Dell Publishing Co., 1971), 292.

48. Lesbian publications that existed before the seventies usually published in isolation. *The Ladder* (1956–72) featured poetry, fiction, and expository writing and argued for the protection of lesbians under the law and the economic equality of all women. For a discussion of the proliferation and impact of lesbian-feminist publishing ventures, see Clare Potter, "The Lesbian Periodical Index," in *Lesbian Studies,* ed. Margaret Cruikshank (Old Westbury: Feminist Press, 1982); Charlotta Hensley, " 'Sinister Wisdom' and Other Issues of Lesbian Imagination," *Serials Review* 9 (Fall 1983): 7–20; Michal Brody, ed., *Are We There Yet? A Continuing History of "Lavender Woman": A Chicago Lesbian Newspaper* (Iowa City: Aunt Lute Book Company, 1985); and Charlotte Bunch et al., *Building Feminist Theory: Essays from "Quest"* (New York: Longman Press, 1981).

49. Feminist bookstores serve as general meeting places and distribution centers for feminist communities. A list compiled in 1980 includes more than seventy women's bookstores in thirty states, located primarily college towns and large cities. Myrna Marx Ferree and Beth B. Hess, *Controversy and Coalition: The New Feminist Movement* (Boston: Twayne Publishers, 1985), 74.

50. Ferree and Hess, *Controversy and Coalition,* 76.

51. Boston Women's Health Book Collective, *Our Bodies, Ourselves* (New York: Simon and Schuster, 1972); Rita Mae Brown, *Rubyfruit Jungle* (New York: Bantam Books, 1973); Ntozake Shange, *For Colored Girls Who Have Considered Suicide When the Rainbow Is Enuf* (New York: Bantam Books, 1975).

52. Kirsten Grimstad and Susan Rennie, eds., *The New Woman's Survival Sourcebook* (New York: Knopf, 1975).

53. Sayres et al., eds., *The 60s without Apology,* 92.

54. Ferree and Hess, *Controversy and Coalition,* 122.

55. Francesca Cancian and Bonnie Ross, "Mass Media and the Women's Movement: 1900–1977," *Journal of Applied Behavioral Sciences* 17 (January–March 1981): 23, 32.

56. Acquired titles include *Our Bodies, Ourselves, Rubyfruit Jungle,* and *For Colored Girls.*

chapter two

Feminist Publishing
and the Scholarly Press

We were quite suspicious of the university—its structures, its demands, its threat of cooptation—but, then again, we knew it held some sort of possibility for us.

Carol Pearson, member of founding editorial collective,
Frontiers

The women who came together in the early seventies to create feminist scholarly journals were certainly steeped in the political activism of the women's movement and its New Left publishing model. However, as young, untenured faculty and graduate students, they were immersed in the culture of the patriarchal university. Consequently, the women who emerged from the women's movement to found and shape feminist scholarly journals were equally attentive to the academy. As activists and scholars, they secured feminist territory within the university as a basis for more widespread and radical change in the larger academic system. As Florence Howe and Paul Lauter have observed, "Since its beginning, women's studies has had two goals: to develop an interdisciplinary academic program (parallel in some respects to ethnic studies) having distinctive curricula, research concerns, teaching methodologies, and student constituencies; and to implement a strategy for changing the traditional, male-centered academic curriculum . . . and, to some degree, the personnel and structures of colleges and universities."[1]

Feminists cast the tensions arising around these dual purposes into two questions: What degree of reform or radical impulses should be at work in women's studies; and what are the merits of maintaining feminist control of women's studies through autonomous women's studies programs or transforming the entire curriculum through traditional departments? Rarely have feminists questioned the feasibility or desirability of their efforts within the university. Yet the feminist assault on the university's male bastion was neither an arbitrary nor a fated choice, but rather an interaction affected by historical, material, and ideological factors. These sociocultural factors determined the content, politics, and purpose of feminist academic journals.

Women's studies quickly proved a timely and effective way to legitimate feminist ideas within the wider society. Within three years after introductory courses in literature, history, and sociology were established in response to student protest, women's studies grew to nearly five thousand courses and 112 programs across American campuses in 1973.[2] That feminist activism had a swift and dramatic impact on American campuses in the early 1970s has been amply documented.[3] However, impact does not prove causality, as the feminist pedagogian Florence Howe cautioned in the National Institute of Education's evaluation of the impact of feminist scholarship on the traditional curriculum.

> Impact implies causality, but it often proves difficult to establish whether changes on a campus can be attributed to the work of women's studies faculty and students, to the effects of the broader women's movement on and off campus, to changes in the climate of opinion, or even to stubborn material factors like the new female majority in many undergraduate populations. Women's studies is itself a product of such a combination of factors and can, in certain respects, be seen as an agent of change and as a mediator between the factors producing change and the academic community.[4]

The massive infiltration of feminist activists and their ideas into American universities in the early 1970s is certainly a testament to the force of feminist conviction and influence. It must also be understood in terms of an institutional cross-configuration of feminist and university needs at a particular historical moment. The specific contours of this cross-configuration can be sketched out by examining the sociocultural factors that determined the mutual engagement of the modern American university and the contemporary women's movement.

Historically, American universities have never been immune to political movements. Youth movements, student unrest, and political activism have frequented the university campus since its inception. Although Europe has a more consistent history of student politicization, American students rebelled in a variety of ways throughout the eighteenth and nineteenth centuries.[5] The typical late-nineteenth-century student was characterized as "an atheist in religion, an experimentalist in morals, a rebel against authority."[6] Much of the early student protest, such as Harvard's Great Rebellion in 1823 and Yale's Bread and Butter Rebellion in 1828, was aimed at university reform. Yet students were occasionally involved in such larger issues as the abolitionist and temperance movements in American society.

American student protest continued sporadically in the first half of the twentieth century but was confined primarily to isolationists' activity in bohemian enclaves during the 1920s, socialist ferment during the 1930s, and beat-inspired literary and artistic communities during the 1950s.[7] The most dramatic and comprehensive disaffection of large numbers of students from the American consensus was massive student involvement, first in the civil rights movement and later in the anti-Vietnam War movement.

Black college students from North Carolina, South Carolina, Mississippi, and Virginia united with black church leaders and provided the spark that would ignite the civil rights movement of the early 1960s. Forming an umbrella group called the Student Nonviolent Coordinating Committee (SNCC), they were quickly joined by freedom riders. Freedom riders, drawn largely from black southern and white northern campuses, rode buses on interstate routes in the South and were beaten and jailed until they forced the federal government to intervene. Together they formed the basis of the radical student movement. Berkeley's Free Speech Movement (FSM) and its leaders emerged out of the radicalizing experiences of white student involvement in the South.[8] SNCC launched the radical student movement, the FSM brought it to white campuses, but Students for a Democratic Society (SDS) came to embody it. Although Watts, Mississippi, and Haight-Ashbury join Kent State and Jackson State as the settings for turmoil, students were the principal actors, their campuses the center stages, and their underground publications the scripts for the New Left.

In similar fashion, radicalized faculty began to confront the political underpinnings of their scholarship and their universities. As Gene Wise, an American studies institutional historian, recalled in his reaction to the coverage of the 1968 Chicago Democratic Convention, the political urgency of the time seemed inescapable: "My initial response to that event was horror—horror at the grenade launchers, at Mayor Daley and his police, at Hubert Humphrey's efforts at a 'politics of joy' amid the manifest violence outside, at the general breakdown of civility and the siege of insanity. . . . But beyond my horror at what Americans were doing, I was vexed at my own impotence. . . . Here I was a product of years of training in American culture studies, and I had no tools to comprehend what the hell was happening in Chicago in August 1968."[9]

That same year, the annual meeting of the Modern Language Association split over the arrest of the M.I.T. literary scholar Louis Kampf. When he was arrested for hanging radical caucus posters in a hotel lobby, the usually fraternal and decorous convention became the site of an internal revolt that led to Kampf's immediate election as the association's vice president and then its president in 1971.[10] Other radicalized scholars formed the Sociology Liberation Movement (SLM) and called for political action at the 1969 American Sociological Association convention in San Francisco. The SLM presented its research in four "Radical Sessions" allotted by the ASA, sent "Truth Squads" to criticize and expose reactionary scholarship at other sessions, and staged their own radical counterconvention in a nearby church basement.[11] By the time feminists emerged from the SLM's ranks, student activists and their radicalized professors were the vanguard of the revolution.[12]

Feminism flourished around the inherited New Left and civil rights bases of urban centers and major university campuses, which were open, complex systems providing diversity, mobility, and tolerance of adversarial postures. During the early stage of the movement, feminists did not have to assert whether their loyalties were with the institutions within which they taught and studied or to the outside movement that was fundamentally at odds with the university.

Feminists may have inherited this proximity through historical circumstance, but inheritance alone cannot explain why feminists and the university, despite their differences, accommodated each other. The university system provided a demographic and strategic common ground for radical and reform impulses in the women's movement. Demographically, the college structure supplied roles for younger, grass-roots radicals, and older, professional reformists in its multiple gradations of student and professor. Although women were usually denied the security of tenure and full professorial positions, they could be undergraduates, graduate students, instructors, and assistant professors as well as marginal academics.[13] Strategically, radical feminists seeking revolutionary action against the system could work with liberal feminists on reform within the university by using the liberal goals of reform as a radical strategy to revolution. Sally Gearhart, a radical lesbian feminist chairing the Department of Speech Communication at San Francisco State University, explained the benefits of this method:

> Survival of a women's studies program means survival of a bubble of freedom for liberal and radical feminists. The bubble balances precariously between total co-optation by the institution (liberal tilt) and the repression that could occur if it became too overtly threatening (radical tilt). In maintaining a tension between these two dangers, there are territories of agreement among liberal and radical women. From the radical feminist's perspective, the struggle is not so much to make the program itself radical as to maintain the maximum amount of radical input possible. There's good reason, then, for radical feminists to take advantage of the liberal stand for tolerance and individual freedom. The best way to guarantee that radical voices will be heard is to work for a program of variety, full of feminists from all persuasions.[14]

Gearhart's "bubble of freedom" is situated within a more general feminist appeal to tolerance, fair play, and individual freedom in scholarship, which is based on the notion of academic freedom. The ideal right of the scholar to follow an argument wherever it may lead is as ancient as Plato, but as the historians Richard Hofstadter and Walter Metzger document, academic freedom is not an ancient prerogative but an acquisition of relatively recent date, originating in the rejection of the ecclesiastical influence of the denominational colleges that dominated higher education before the Civil War. Since its adoption from the Germans into a formal code in 1915 by the American Association of University Professors as "professorial independence in thinking and utterance," the status and meaning of academic freedom has been intimately connected to, and challenged by, its immediate institutional setting and the wider American social context.[15]

Disputes over the limits of academic freedom have become more complicated since the end of World War II. Scholars have been penalized, dismissed, and denied promotions for "upholding the right to strike, for advocating racial integration, for refusing to testify before the House Un-American Activities Committee, and for supporting the recognition of Communist China."[16] An extensive survey of professors during the McCarthy period reported that almost 20 percent of faculty respondents had become more inclined to avoid controversial topics in their classrooms, speeches, and writings.[17] Even Bertrand Russell was banned from the City College of New York for encouraging extramarital sex and "immoral and salacious doctrines."[18] The political limits of "professorial independence" were tested repeatedly during the 1960s.[19] Although the ideology of open debate within the university has been only imperfectly realized in practice, it is a code that feminists believe can be used to secure some protection from persecution within the academy.[20]

Militancy and separatism have a hearty advocacy in the feminist movement, but, by and large, nonviolent integrationist approaches have been more common. Nonviolent methods of social change include legislation, media influence, economic leverage, alternative institution building, and education. Education as politics, the belief that the oppressed and the oppressor can and should be changed through political enlightenment rather than physical coercion, is the assumption guiding most feminist activism. Equality in education has been a major target of social reform activity in both the nineteenth- and twentieth-century women's movements.[21]

From the earliest stages of the contemporary movement, feminists fought on the battleground of public education for equal educational opportunity, nonsexist textbooks, and implementation of Title IX of the Education Amendments Act of 1972, which prohibits sex discrimination in federally assisted education. As the sociologist Jean Grambs has pointed out, the educational system is "one of the few large bureaucracies that is not only nearby and visible to the public, but available for public manipulation."[22] In a more general sense, feminists recognized that education, whether formal, informal, or in another of its cultural variations, is the process whereby social groups induct their young into its own cultural system. In the last few pages of *Feminine Mystique* (1963), Betty Friedan offered education as the only avenue for redress: "Educators at every women's college, at every university, junior college, and community college, must see to it that women make a lifetime commitment to a field of thought. . . . Liberal education not only trains the mind but provides an ineradicable core of human values. . . . For women as well as men, education is and must be the matrix of human evolution. What is needed now is a national educational program, similar to the G.I. Bill, for women who seriously want to resume or continue their education."[23]

Friedan's reliance on education as a means of social change was proposed at the end of unprecedented, rapid expansion of American public education, an era that had been dominated by the progressive educational programs of nineteenth-century theorists such as John Dewey. According to the proponents of these new programs, complex societies segregate children from the learning environment of the traditional community. Consequently, schools must perform the socializing functions that had previously been the responsibility of the broader community. To do this, schooling had to be much more inclusive and comprehensive than previously imagined in order to compensate for wider social changes and to accommodate, even anticipate, society's needs. Dewey turned to scientific problem-solving as the most effective method of dealing with society's complex problems. Reflecting the mood of Progressivism, experts trained in such skills replaced the parent and community as the main socializing agents of youth. By converting schools into ideal democratic communities, wider social ideals would be realized.[24]

The liberal education tradition inherent in Friedan's recommendation also influenced the civil rights movement that directly affected the more radical branch of the contemporary women's movement. The 1954 Supreme Court decision in *Brown v. Topeka Board of Education* ended legal school segregation and furthered the idea that education was enmeshed with social conscience and should lead in effecting social change. Women involved in the civil rights educational programs and desegregation battles during the 1960s relied on this legacy for feminist purposes during the 1970s. Charlotte Bunch, a theoretician and a former Furie, has described this heritage and her hopes for education as politics:

> I realize that a lot of my approach to politics as education comes from becoming politically aware and receiving my earliest political training in the civil rights movement in the South. Much of my approach to feminist education has been modeled on the Southern Black education model—that combination of being educator/ teacher/activist/ preacher. . . . One of the struggles that goes on with feminists, as it has with blacks, is over our effort to maintain a belief in a different kind of power for change than force and militarism, therefore, education becomes central to political strategy. . . . What is at the heart of feminist education to me is this very concept . . . looking at the world and feeling the need to call forth people's better instincts, to challenge people's ignorance and make them examine it; and to call forth, in particular from women, the ability to do something about the world.[25]

Bolstered by this sort of philosophy, feminists were able to overcome their wariness about establishing a political presence in the university. However, university administrators were not always receptive to student demands for feminist innovations. William McGill was chancellor at the University of California at San Diego and then president of Columbia University during the most tumultuous and combative years of student revolt on those campuses. In his memoir, *The Year of the Monkey*, McGill recalls his reaction to the experiences of 1968–72: "When I first confronted student unrest in 1968–69, I was at first paralyzed with fear, then appalled, then outraged. Toward the end of the year I became an adversary, fighting back and vowing to survive. . . . Sometimes late at night, when the house is still and the slightest sound is audible, I am suddenly awake in the darkness because I think I can hear them chanting again. . . . 'Those bastards are at it again,' I say to myself. 'What can they want now?' "[26]

Given such adversarial postures, why did the university accommodate the demands for women's studies? The reason lies closer to institutional realities than emotional ones. As vigorously as some may have fought curricular innovations, university administrators tolerated, at times even welcomed, women's studies because of particular historical, social, and ideological circumstances that extended far beyond the events in McGill's *Year of the Monkey*.

Throughout history, the American university has been marked by an ideological, material, and demographic expansion that affected beliefs about the nature and the entitlement of higher education. The dramatic growth of higher education in the twentieth century began with waves of older students crowding the university campus after World War II. G.I. Bill-financed veterans not only facilitated a population and demographic expansion on American campuses but also embodied a change in beliefs concerning the general entitlement and use of higher education. The veterans were the most visible aspect of the broadening of college enrollments after the war. The percentage of college-age Americans who attended college was 1.7 percent in 1870, 4 percent in 1900, 14 percent in 1940, and 40 percent in 1964.[27]

The rising rate of college attendance also reflected a more inclusive belief about the economic necessity of a college education for groups such as middle-class males and upper-middle-class females.[28] As Clark Kerr observed in his Carnegie-sponsored study, important shifts in tension accompanied this growth: from elite to egalitarian education, subject-based to competency-based curricula, and autocratic to bureaucratic administration.[29] The shift became even more pronounced when the academic boom mushroomed again after Russia launched Sputnik in 1957, an event that educators used to make a case for the general inadequacy of American education.

During the cold war of the 1950s, enormous private endowments and governmental appropriations dovetailed with the postwar baby boom to create an unprecedented academic expansion that lasted until the mid 1960s. By the time William McGill was squaring off with campus radicals, higher education had come to the end of an era of expanded budgets, increased enrollments and faculty hiring, wider offerings of courses, a substantial building boom, bigger bureaucracy, more state and federal involvement, larger administrations, and closer military and corporate financial ties.

Because context and content are inextricably bound, changes in population, ideology, and economics led to curricular adaptations within the academy. Although administrators have continuously modified the curriculum since the founding of Harvard in 1636,[30] the proliferation of specialized majors and course offerings, as well as the liberalization of elective allotments, characterized what the sociologist David Reisman called the consumer approach of college-marketed curriculum.[31] Student demands to exercise greater choice over more varied and relevant coursework were extensions of a "student as consumer" orientation that developed during the university's massive postwar expansion.

When officials were finally able to turn their attention away from the turmoil of the sixties, they were confronted with the economic realities of the seventies. Ironically, the curricular innovations hard won by radicals in the sixties could be used by administrators to cushion the impact of declining enrollments and escalating financial problems during the seventies. Urban studies, family studies, aging studies, black studies, women's studies, Asian studies, Hispanic studies, ethnic studies, and Judaic studies were available to supplement more traditional courses of study through electives, distributive requirements, concentrations, minors, and certificate programs. These offerings also targeted previously untapped populations for higher education, including a large proportion of older women. Through newly expanded adult education programs, extension center programs, and returning student programs, older women began to attend college, as did a growing percentage of younger women.[32] Administrators often used recently expanded individual studies, independent studies, and interdisciplinary studies programs to allow students to major in areas such as women's studies without committing the university to the permanence and expense of departmental status.[33]

Since the late nineteenth century, departments have become discrete centers of knowledge and faculty specialization within the university structure. The department has developed a powerful, nearly exclusive, role in setting the terms of curriculum. Unless handsomely funded and vigorously defended, it is difficult to launch and sustain coursework outside of the departmental structure.[34] Because it was rarely accorded the financial and intellectual power of departmental status, women's studies struggled outside of the departmental structure. This lack of formal recognition has resulted in unstable, vulnerable programs with precarious futures. Yet, this restrictive and exclusive departmental system allowed chairpersons and faculty in established disciplines to develop and protect women's studies courses under the auspices of their own departments. Exercising their curricular authority and decision making power within the university bureaucracy, sympathetic scholars in the humanities and social sciences developed the early women's studies courses that were later consolidated into women's studies programs.

Thus, a myriad of material, demographic, institutional, ideological, and structural factors helped to bring about the mutual accommodation of the contemporary women's movement and the modern American university. In terms of enrollments and course offerings, women's studies was an immediate success. It grew even during the throes of academic retrenchment and declining admissions.[35] Yet popularity alone cannot sustain courses over the long run. Institutionalization must be accomplished in all of its phases to ensure the longevity of any program of study. Sensing the precariousness of their case within the university, feminist activists quickly moved to translate the popularity of women's studies courses into more concrete concessions: line budget, paid administrators, tenured faculty, major and minor degrees, and university-approved curriculums that fulfill more than electives. By attaining such legitimating devices, an area of study is ensured, as are the necessary stability and longevity essential for developing questions and debates that distinguish the field.

Although departmental status has been rarely achieved, feminist scholars were able to consolidate women's studies courses into women's studies programs, institutes, and research centers. Professionalizing and institution-building activities of early feminist scholars also included development of the traditional ways in which academics recognize intellectual authority: professional associations, disciplinary conferences, and—perhaps most significant—professional journals. By 1977 the National Women's Studies Association had held two national conventions; *Women's Studies Abstracts* provided annotated bibliographies; and commissions, committees, and caucuses grew within established disciplines. Six interdisciplinary journals were also established: *Feminist Studies, The University of Michigan's Papers in Women's Studies, Signs, Frontiers, Women's Studies,* and *Female Studies.* Although the choice of the research journal as a mechanism of intellectual authority and advancement seemed self-evident to the feminist scholars who had been professionalized in academe, scholarly publishing was less a matter of choice than of institutional convention.

During the late eighteenth and early nineteenth centuries, rising literacy rates, the social ascent of the American middle class, and improved, cheaper production methods produced a mass market for books, and publishing was transformed from a cottage industry to a corporate enterprise. With this growth, specialized books and publications were produced to serve wider interests. A partnership between publishing and schooling can be traced to the fifteenth century, but publishing did not become a central feature of academic life until the nineteenth-century revolution coincided with a similarly dramatic upheaval in the American academy during the 1880s.[36]

Important changes in American higher education during the 1880s and 1890s included the rise of research universities, the professionalization of academicians, and the expansion of knowledge and technology into subspecialties. American administrators and faculty reshaped their universities in the image of the highly influential nineteenth-century German system. "The essence of the German university system, which gave it intellectual leadership in the nineteenth century, was the concept that an institution of true higher learning should be, above all, the workshop of free scientific research."[37]

The founders of Johns Hopkins University and the University of Chicago designed their institutions in accordance with the German model, and Harvard, Columbia, and Yale were soon restructured around research activity and graduate schools. Within this context, credentialing mechanisms were created for the emerging class of professionally trained academicians. Research universities played an important role in developing scholarly societies and establishing criteria for admission: specialized research interests and doctoral degrees awarded for original work and scholarly productivity.

Closely related to the development of such societies was Johns Hopkins University's and the University of Chicago's promotion of scholarly journals. Daniel Gilman, the president of Johns Hopkins, established the *American Chemical Journal* in 1878, the *American Journal of Philology* in 1880, and the *Journal of Physiology* in 1881. President William Rainey Harper at the University of Chicago was just as active in promoting scholarly journals; during the first fifteen years of his administration, eleven were launched at Chicago, including the *Journal of Political Economy,* the *Journal of Geology,* the *School Review,* and the *American Journal of Sociology.*[38]

American scholarly journals were modeled on those developed for the newly professionalized "scientific history" in nineteenth-century Germany. The first scholarly historical periodical to survive to the present, *Historische Zeitschrift,* appeared in 1859.[39] The structure of German scholarly journals was consistent with the organization of German universities as centralized, unifying institutions of academic professionalism. Scholarly journals became central to a discipline's professionalism and the principle means of communicating knowledge among scholars.[40] Most of the scholars at Yale, Harvard, and Cornell who united to establish the *American Historical Review* at the turn of the century had studied in Germany and, like the founders of *Historische Zeitschrift,* used the *AHR* to unify and define their emerging disciplines.[41]

Yet German and American journals differed significantly in one respect. Mid-nineteenth-century German historians did not find political convictions inconsistent with scholarly standards; *Historische Zeitschrift* routinely combined academic and political elements in its content.[42] In contrast, most American journals defined themselves as apolitical from the outset.

> The most conspicuous and significant characteristic of the Anglo-American school is its ideal of scholarly impartiality. Scholars advocated neutrality while at the same time holding definite convictions on progress and on the value of democracy. Historians were educated to believe that they should not let present political issues color their interpretations of past events. Although the consensus that supported this view has disappeared as deep cleavages

have occurred within the intellectual community, nothing has replaced impartiality as the official doctrine of English and American historiography.[43]

The American conviction that politics distort scholarship was strengthened when *Historische Zeitschrift* came under Nazi control in 1935 as part of Walter Frank's Reichsinstitute fur Geschichte des neuen Deutschlands. The post-World War II version of *Historische Zeitschrift* has come to resemble its American counterparts in its dedication to "the maintenance of rigorous scholarly striving toward pure, unbiased knowledge."[44]

With the support of major universities, scholarly publishing multiplied in America after the turn of the century. Academic journals were but one of a plethora of research publications that included scholarly books, textbooks, bibliographies, monographs, digests, abstracts, collections of book reviews, literary magazines, annuals, and newsletters. Although journals comprise a narrow category in the classification of scholarly publications, they have become increasingly popular. During the fifteen-year period from 1960 to 1975, scientific and technical journals published in the United States increased by 50 percent: from 2,800 to 4,200.[45] Similarly, the National Enquiry on Scholarly Communication reported an even more rapid growth rate in four humanistic disciplines during the same period.[46] Plagued with the problems of reduced budgets, declining enrollments, and overly tenured departments during the 1970s, administrators and search committees made scholarly productivity a decisive factor in faculty hiring, tenure, and advancement. As a result, the need for publishing outlets in academia intensified just as feminists sought a forum for scholarly academic discourse.

The expansion of academic publishing was marked by increased diversity and specialization. Although still a relatively small area of scholarly publication, the influence of interdisciplinary journals, which have substantially altered the content and form of traditional journals, increased as problems associated with narrow disciplinary specialization resurrected the need for generalist forums.[47] At first, multidisciplinary rather than true interdisciplinarity was common, and most of the new journals were forced to alternate articles from within specific disciplines, for example, publishing one article from history, one from literature, and one from sociology. But "the number of truly interdisciplinary articles have been increasing as studies in this field have become more common and better understood in recent years."[48] For example, based on her belief that a thematic approach encourages more rigorous interdisciplinarity, Martha Vicinus, the editor of *Victorian Studies,* popularized the use of special issues devoted to a theme, a rare occurrence in the late 1960s but a common practice now.[49]

Reflecting the political turmoil of their times, scholarly journals also specialized around ideological and social interests in the 1970s. Pioneers such as *Historia Judaica* and the *Journal of Negro History* (founded in 1916) provided models for publications such as the *Journal of Mexican-American History*[50] Harvard-trained Carter G. Woodson, the son of former slaves, was the second African American to receive a doctorate in history in the United States. His Association for the Study of Negro Life and History began the *Journal of Negro History* as a quarterly that was immediately recognized as a rigorous and respected scholarly publication.[51] The journal included historical and social-scientific articles on African-American life and culture, a "Documents" section that published eighteenth-century materials, book reviews, notes on the profession, and a news column. When Woodson died in 1950, Rayford W. Logan, the association's president, took the journal to Howard University where, despite the dramatic changes in African-American thought and politics, it continues to be a premiere scholarly publication.[52]

Journals dealing with African-American scholarship continued to appear: the *Journal of Negro Education* (1932), *Quarterly Review of Higher Education among Negroes* (1933), *Negro History Bulletin* (1937), *Negro College Quarterly* (1943), and the *College Language Association Journal* (1957). But the richest offering of African-American scholarly journals grew out of the black political activity of 1960s, as well as the attendant appearance of black studies programs, and new publishing enterprises such as Free Black Press, Third World Press, Black Dialogue Press, Jihan Press, and Broadside Press.[53] In 1970 alone, the *Black Academy Review, Black Collegian, Journal of Black Studies, Review of Black Political Economy,* and *Studies in Black Literature* began. Although the *Harvard Journal of Afro-American Affairs* (1965) is credited as the first scholarly journal to reflect the emergent radical politics of the civil rights movement, it is the sociologist Nathan Hare's *Black Scholar* (1969) that most reflected the era's struggle for black scholarly self-determination. Funded soley through subscriptions and published by the Black World Foundation, the journal called for a black cultural revolution: "We recognize that we must re-define our lives. We must shape a culture, a politics, an economics, a sense of our past and future history. We must recognize what we have been and what we shall be, retaining that which has been good and discarding that which has been worthless. *The Black Scholar* shall be a journal for that definition. In its first pages, Black ideologies will be examined, debated, disputed and evaluated by the Black intellectual community." [54]

Scholarly periodicals founded to give expression to leftist political viewpoints include *Past and Present, History Workshop, Telos,* the *Radical Philosopher's Newsjournal,* the *Radical History Review,* and the *Insurgent Sociologist.* Run by volunteer collectives of radical scholars, often with editors who rotated in and out of the job, and, initially, without the prospect of institutional support, these journals went about the task of politicizing the purpose and context of their respective fields. *Studies on the Left,* a journal produced by graduate students in history, began publication at the University of Wisconsin, Madison in 1959. Along with Columbia University, the University of Wisconsin produced "the overwhelming majority of the first two generations of radical historians." [55] Leftist historians of the 1960s were heterogeneous but tended to fall into two camps: younger, activist, countercultural scholars such as Staughton Lynd and Howard Zinn, and more established, traditionally scholarly historians such as Eugene Genovese and Christopher Lasch. Lynd and Zinn had been intensely involved in the civil rights and antiwar movements, had taught at black colleges, and had traveled to Hanoi.[56] They applied their radical viewpoint to their discipline.

> Whatever our social origins, the university is a marvelously effective instrument for making us middle-class men. . . . We become emotionally engaged in the upward scramble, and whatever our rhetoric, in fact let the university become the emotional center of our lives. . . . We ourselves must have a foot solidly off the campus . . . alternate years of full-time intellectual work with years of full-time work for the Movement. . . . Disgorge the bait of tenure, and the problem of making a living can solve itself year-by year.[57]

Similarly, the British historian E. P. Thompson stressed that radical historians must never allow themselves to become completely absorbed by the university. He thought that radical historians had to inhabit "some territory that is, without qualification, their own: their own journals, their own theoretical and practical centers . . . places that prefigured in some ways the society of the future." [58] The younger group of radical scholars created the *Radical History Review* (*RHR*) as a newsletter for the Mid-Atlantic Radical Historical Organization (MARHO). "It grew out of a shared concern among younger scholars, teachers, and students to resist the narrowing boundaries of professional history, the separation of the academy from political concerns, and . . . it has sought to develop a critical history as a means of understanding capitalism as a mode of production and a complex system of social relations."[59]

As a scholarly journal, the *RHR* was soon offering critiques by Raymond Williams, a literary theorist; publishing the work of culture critic Stuart Hall; and monitoring the "political firings" of such Marxist scholars as Bertell Ollman.[60]

Similarly, the *Insurgent Sociologist* originated as a newspaper published by the Sociology Liberation Movement. The *Insurgent* called for a new scholarship that challenged the "value premises, concepts, methodology, and conclusions of establishment sociology," which had, according to the SLM, become an "intellectual prostitute" engaged in "criminal research activities and theoretical legitimations of official violence."[61] Although later editors of the journal characterized this early position as "naive," "underdeveloped," and "unsophisticated," the *Insurgent*'s rhetoric vividly captured the radical scholars' sense of political urgency and its identification with the nonacademic New Left.[62]

In 1972, after the newsletter's subscription list had grown from three hundred to a thousand and its press run to two thousand, the editors Jeff Schevitz and David Colfax broadened the *Insurgent* into a scholarly journal.[63] The existence, and relative success, of such African-American and New Left scholarly journals legitimated oppositional participation in established scholarly discourses. When African-American and leftist perspectives began to be accepted as forms of authoritative, albeit contested, knowledge, it became increasingly difficult for the Archimedean viewpoint to maintain its hegemonic hold in academe.

The creators of *Feminist Studies, Frontiers,* and *Signs* borrowed, reshaped, and made innovations in available conceptual models, assumptions, and forms of publishing. Deprived of their rich nineteenth-century feminist publishing legacy, contemporary feminists reworked the publishing forms of the underground press and its Old Left and beat influences to shape a media of their own. They embraced the explicit emotional and political tone, oppositional stance, technology and distribution system of the underground press. They refined the anarchist-democratic editorial process and structure of their predecessor for their own purposes. However, as Berenice Fisher pointed out, feminists defined their ideal political identity in opposition to the male-dominated left that produced the underground press.

As Casey Hayden and Mary King's memo illustrated, politicizing experiences in the New Left and civil rights movement inspired women to refine their insights in service of their own oppression. The trauma of leaving the left to create an autonomous women's movement is evident in the discourse of the early feminist press. But as the gay-straight split at *off our backs* revealed, feminist editors quickly turned their attention to internal concerns as the women's movement grew and gained political sophistication. Within a few years, feminist media exploded into a multiplicity of forms and genres that required the stabilizing effect of institutionalization: feminist publishing collectives, presses, bookstores, reprint services, and distribution systems.

Feminist academic journals were also shaped by another powerful institution and its publishing form—the modern university and the academic journal. A historically and socially specific matrix of institutional characteristics and needs facilitated the mutual accommodation of the contemporary women's movement and the modern university. The political strategies of feminism and the material needs of the university shaped feminist academic journals powerfully.The individual histories of *Feminist Studies, Frontiers,* and *Signs* are marked by the continued development of the assumptions, concepts, practices, and discourses patterned in this cross-configuration of institutions and publishing forms.

Notes

1. Florence Howe and Paul Lauter, *The Impact of Women's Studies on the Campus and the Disciplines* (Washington: National Institute of Education, 1980), 1.

2. The first women's studies courses appeared in the catalogs of alternate and free universities. The first formally taught course was offered at Cornell University in 1969. History, English, sociology, psychology, political science, and American studies were among the first disciplines to offer women's studies courses in the late 1960s. See Judith Hole and Ellen Levine, *Rebirth of Feminism* (New York: Quadrangle Books/New York Times Books, 1971), 324–25.

3. The concern to transform the university system as well as succeed within it is why so many feminist evaluations of women's studies focus on assessing the impact that the field has had on the university, not just normative evaluations or studies assessing the field alone.

4. Howe and Lauter, *The Impact of Women's Studies on the Campus and the Disciplines,* 38.

5. "Students have been in the forefront of revolutionary movements at least since the appearance of the first German student movement in the early nineteenth century. Thereafter, students played major roles in revolutionary movements in Japan, France, Italy and Russia." Stanley Rothman and Robert Lichter, *The Roots of Radicalism: Jews, Christians and the New Left* (New York: Oxford University Press, 1982), 3.

6. Samuel Eliot Morison, *Three Centuries of Harvard* (Cambridge: Harvard University Press, 1936), 185.

7. As early as 1917, the now-familiar call for intellectuals to lead the resistance to an unpopular American war was voiced by Randolph Bourne in "The War and the Intellectuals," *The Seven Arts* 2 (June 1917): 133–46.

8. Rothman and Lichter, *Roots of Radicalism,* 18.

9. Gene Wise, *American Historical Explanations* (Minneapolis: University of Minnesota Press, 1980), xxiii.

10. Richard Ohmann, *English in America: A Radical View of the Profession* (New York: Oxford University Press, 1976), 27–35.

11. Western Union of Sociologists, "Proceedings of the Berkeley Conference of Radical Sociologists," *Insurgent Sociologist* 1, no. 1 (1969): 3–5.

12. Studies of campus radicalism often focus on the students' participation at the expense of the radicalized faculty, whose work included the influential New University Conference and the Radical Caucus of the Modern Language Association and is documented in Edward E. Ericson, *Radicals in the University* (Stanford: Stanford University Press, 1975). The faculty were principal organizers in the teach-in movement described in Louis Menashe and Ronald Radosh, *Teach-Ins: U.S.A.* (New York: Frederick A. Praeger Publishers, 1967).

13. Between January 31, 1970, and January 31, 1971, the Women's Equity Action League and other women's rights groups brought nearly three hundred complaints of patterns of discrimination against colleges and universities. Many of the challenged universities responded with promises of "vigorous recruitment of females" for academic positions. These early discrimination cases and the universities' responses are chronicled in Hole and Levine, *Rebirth of Feminism,* 321–25.

14. Sally Miller Gearhart, "If the Mortarboard Fits . . . Radical Feminism in Academia," in *Learning Our Way: Essays in Feminist Education,* ed. Charlotte Bunch and Sandra Pollack (Trumansburg: The Crossing Press Feminist Series, 1983), 11–12.

15. Richard Hofstadter and Walter Metzger, *The Development of Academic Freedom in the United States* (New York: Columbia University Press, 1965).

16. Derek Bok, *Beyond the Ivory Tower: Social Responsibilities of the Modern University* (Cambridge: Harvard University Press 1982), 22.

17. Paul Lazarsfield and Wagner Theilens, Jr., *The Academic Mind: Social Scientists in a Time of Crisis* (Glencoe: Free Press, 1958), 194.

18. Bok, *Beyond the Ivory Tower,* 22.

19. The 1960s was a time of struggle over the parameters of academic

freedom. At Rutgers University in 1965, Eugene D. Genovese told teach-in gatherings that he did not fear nor regret a Viet Cong victory in Vietnam, but welcomed it. Genovese successfully overturned his dismissal for the "treasonous advocacy of victory for the enemy." The case is detailed in Menashe and Radosh, *Teach-Ins: U.S.A.*, 210. Appeals to academic freedom did not protect dissident faculty in the James G. Mellen case at Drew University and in the Eldridge Cleaver case at the University of California, San Diego. The issue of academic freedom was effectively circumvented by challenging the dissidents' professional credentials.

20. Further discussion of case studies and general considerations of the political, social, and economic dimensions of academic freedom can be found in Craig Kaplan and Ellen Schrecker, eds., *Regulating the Intellectuals: Perspectives on Academic Freedom in the 1980s* (New York: Praeger, 1983); Lionel Lewis, *Cold War on Campus: A Study of the Politics of Organizational Control* (New Brunswick: Transactions Books, 1988); Steven Olswang, *Faculty Freedoms and Institutional Accountability* (Washington: Association for the Study of Higher Education, 1984); Richard Meisler, *Trying Freedom: A Case for Liberating Education* (San Diego: Harcourt Brace and Jovanovich, 1984); and Jane Sanders, *Cold War on the Campus: Academic Freedom at the University of Washington: 1946–64* (Seattle: University of Washington Press, 1979).

21. Although motivation, rational, and circumstances have varied widely over the years, women have been involved with sex and race reforms in education from the founding of Mount Holyoke Seminary for women in 1834 through the post-Reconstructionist movement of the 1880s to the desegregation activism of the 1960s. See William M. Franch, *America's Educational Tradition: An Interpretive History* (Boston: D. C. Heath and Co., 1967), 213–29.

22. Jean D. Grambs, *Schools, Scholars and Society* (Englewood Cliffs: Prentice-Hall, Inc., 1978), 199.

23. Betty Friedan, *The Feminine Mystique* (New York: W. W. Norton Co., 1963), 355.

24. Henry J. Perkinson, *Two Hundred Years of American Education Thought* (New York: David McKay Co., Inc., 1976), 213.

25. Charlotte Bunch and Betty Powell, "Charlotte Bunch and Betty Powell Talk about Feminism, Blacks and Education as Politics," in *Learning Our Way*, ed. Bunch and Pollack, 305.

26. William J. McGill, *The Year of the Monkey: Revolt on Campus 1968–89* (New York: McGraw Hill Books, 1982), 2. During McGill's administration, "they" wanted and achieved appointments for such radical scholars as the Marxist Herbert Marcuse; politically explicit courses such as those taught by Black Panther Eldridge Cleaver and Angela Davis, a communist; the removal of the military in the form of ROTC and such industrial sponsors as DuPont from campuses; a radical expansion of the curriculum such as the Third College for the Black and Chicano studies at San Diego; the restructuring of university authority to account for student opinion; and the establishment of women's studies courses and programs.

27. Daniel Bell, *Reforming of General Education* (New York: Doubleday, 1968), 105. By the mid 1960s, more than two young men in every five were entering some sort of college, and more than one in five graduated. The proportion was about 25 percent lower for women.

28. Carl Kaysen, ed., *Content and Context: Essays on College Education* (New York: McGraw Hill Books, 1973), 15.

29. Frederick Rudolph, *Curriculum: A History of the American Undergraduate Course of Study since 1636* (San Francisco: Jossey-Bass, 1977), x.

30. "The highly prescribed curriculum of the first American colleges were replaced with a classical curriculum defended by the Yale Report of 1828, then the elective curriculum was adopted by Harvard in the 1870s, and now the many variations of the 1970s," Rudolph, *Curriculum,* ix.

31. David Reisman, *On Higher Education* (San Francisco: Jossey-Bass Publishers, 1980), 105–62.

32. According to Reisman, "for the first time in history, the number of women entering college now exceeds the number of men, although women are less likely to go on for the baccalaureate, and many drop out after two years." See *Higher Education,* 233.

33. Of the 247 women's studies programs listed in the 1986 *National Women's Studies Association Program Directory* as granting undergraduate degrees, 203 award those degrees through independent studies, individual studies, general studies, and interdisciplinary studies.

34. Laurence Veysey, "Stability and Experiment in the American Undergraduate Curriculum," in *Content and Context,* ed. Carl Kaysen (New York: McGraw Hill Books, 1973), 32–34.

35. Florence Howe, *Seven Years Later: Women's Studies Programs in 1976* (Washington: National Advisory Council on Women's Educational Programs, 1977), 7.

36. Lewis Coser, Charles Kadushin, and Walter Powell, *Books: The Culture and Commerce of Publishing* (Chicago: University of Chicago Press, 1985), 7–9.

37. John Brubacher and Willis Rudy, *Higher Education in Transition: A History of American College and Universities, 1636–1976* (New York: Harper and Row Publishers, 1976), 174.

38. Brubacher and Rudy, *Higher Education in Transition,* 188–90.

39. Margaret F. Steig, *Origin and Development of Scholarly Historical Periodicals* (University: University of Alabama Press, 1986), 4.

40. Steig, *Origin and Development of Scholarly Historical Periodicals,* 4–5.

41. Ibid., 47.

42. The nineteenth-century professional historians who published in *Historische Zeitschrift* were similar to twentieth-century feminist scholars in that they subscribed "to a set of standards and to a methodology that did not permit them consciously to adapt their findings to fit their political view. . . . Articles might not differ much in style from those published in political journals, but they differed significantly in their dedication to scholarly standards." Ibid., 5.

43. Ibid., 151.

44. Ibid., 134–35.

45. D. W. King, *Statistical Indicators of Scientific and Technical Communication, 1960–1980* (Rockville: King Research, Inc., 1976), 76.

46. Robert N. Hohwald, "A Morphology of Scholarly Journals," in *Study for the National Enquiry on Scholarly Communication* (Baltimore: Johns Hopkins University Press, 1979).

47. Steig, *Origin and Development of Scholarly Historical Periodicals,* 134–35.

48. Ibid., 134–35.

49. Ibid., 136–37.

50. The *Journal of Mexican-American History* took the *Journal of Negro History* as its model. See "Editorial," *Journal of Mexican-American History* 1 (Fall 1970). Similarly, feminist journals such as *Lilith* and *SAGE* have been created that specifically address the intersection of race, ethnicity, and gender.

51. Walter C. Daniel, *Black Journals of the United States* (Westport: Greenwood Press, 1982), 227, 228.

52. Ibid., 229. For further information on the *Journal of Negro History* see Charles S. Johnson, "The Rise of the Negro Magazine," *Journal of Negro History* 13 (January 1928): 16–17; Frenise A. Logan, "An Appraisal of Forty-One Years of the *Journal of Negro History*, 1916–1957," *Journal of Negro History* 43 (January 1958): 26–33; Sammy M. Miller, "The Sixtieth Anniversary of the *Journal of Negro History:* Letters from Dr. Carter Woodson to Mrs. Mary Church Terrell," *Journal of Negro History* 13 (January 1978): 26–53.

53. Daniel, *Black Journals of the United States,* 363–64.

54. Ibid., 84.

55. Peter Novick, *That Noble Dream: The 'Objectivity Question' and the American Historical Profession* (Cambridge: Cambridge University Press, 1988), 420.

56. Novice, *That Noble Dream,* 428.

57. Ibid., 429.

58. March 1976 interview with E. P. Thompson, *Visions,* 22–23, quoted in Novick, *That Noble Dream,* 459–60.

59. "MARHO Statement," *Radical History Review* 18 (Fall 1978): 172.

60. Michael Merrill, "Raymond Williams and the Theory of English Marxism," *Radical History Review* 19 (Winter 1978–79): 9–32; Stuart Hall, "Marxism and Culture," *Radical History Review* 18 (Fall 1978): 5–16; The Editors, "Political Firings in the University: The Case of Bertell Ollman," *Radical History Review* 18 (Fall 1978): 105–9.

61. "Introduction: Prelude to Radical Commitment," *Insurgent Sociologist* 1, no. 1 (1969): 2.

62. "Introduction," *Insurgent Sociologist* 1, no. 1 (1969): i.

63. "Editorial Introduction," *Insurgent Sociologist* 3 (Fall 1972): 1.

chapter three

Feminist Studies and the Culture of Feminist Scholarship

All of the editors are now well-established professors with all the academic accoutrements. But in the early seventies, before the women's movement had developed an academic branch, the feminist public that supported *Feminist Studies* was far more important than the scholars who produced it.

Claire Moses, manager and editor,
Feminist Studies

Invigorated by the political intensity of campus life and the promise of the feminist movement, activists first conceptualized *Feminist Studies* in 1969. Drawing on women from a consciousness-raising group organized around Columbia University's Women's Liberation Group, a women's studies lecture series at Sarah Lawrence College, and community activists in New York City, a network of feminists discussed the possibility of creating a scholarly journal of high academic quality and community relevance. Such a publication would meet the standards of scholarship but not simply fit into the mold of traditional academic journals. It would also reflect the neglected values, interests, and experiences of women. As the title implied, the content and purpose of *Feminist Studies* would be explicitly political and scholarly.

In fact, as the editor, Claire Moses, explains, every aspect of the journal's content and production was discussed and scrutinized for political implications before the first issue appeared. "It was three years between the planning and the actual publishing of the first issue, as it probably had to be. Networks had to be created; articles had to be found as well as figuring out what kind of paper and printer would be used."[1]

During the early 1970s, feminists were full of ideas for enthusiastic and ambitious projects aimed at cultural reassessment. Not all of the ideas became reality. Often, the success of such projects relied on individuals who stepped forward to take on the tedious, daily, usually unpaid work of translating a good idea into a tangible product. The woman who emerged from the Columbia University, Sarah Lawrence College, New York City network to take on the responsibility of turning a good idea into a feminist scholarly publication was Ann Calderwood. An early editor, Rachel DuPlessis, recalls:

> Around 1969, I remember seeing Ann Calderwood on the steps of Low Library at Columbia. She was talking to a group of feminists about her new idea, a magazine for academic feminists. She saw that one of the things in the feminist effervescence of the time was that feminists were questioning the university, like all things, and saw the seeds of feminist questioning in all the academic fields and its need for an outlet. She postulated the necessity of feminist scholarly publishing from what she saw in the questions of individual women.[2]

Like many activists on the campus periphery in the late sixties, Ann Calderwood frequently crossed the then-permeable line between community activism and university reform. As an M.A. student in history, she organized a lecture series in women's studies at Sarah Lawrence College and helped develop its women's studies curriculum. Yet, unlike many of the graduate students who attended her lecture series, Calderwood did not aspire to an academic career.[3] She preferred to use her skills as an organizer, researcher, publisher, and typesetter for broader political purposes and wider feminist constituencies than the university could offer. As an activist operating in New York's feminist circles, she was involved in grass-roots publishing (Source Book Press), community politics (Human Rights for Women), and feminist archiving (Source Library of the Women's Movement).[4]

Guided by her dual commitment to the university and community activism, Ann Calderwood conceptualized a journal produced by, appealing to, and reflecting the values of university scholars and community activists.[5] Similarly, Calderwood wished to pursue both explicitly political and rigorously scholarly themes in her journal. She envisioned an "open forum for feminist analysis, debate and exchange . . . committed to encouraging analytic responses to feminist issues and analyses that open new areas of feminist research and critique."[6] Financially and institutionally, *Feminist Studies* drew on the traditional university and the community feminist movement but was not beholden to either. Calderwood's journal existed, in those short-lived days of blurred boundaries, in the undefined margin where the university and the community overlapped.

Calderwood published *Feminist Studies* from her apartment on Riverside Drive in New York. Under her supervision, three volumes were published sporadically between 1972 and 1976. She relied on commercial typesetting jobs and private donations to keep herself and her fledgling journal afloat while she served as publisher, editor-in-chief, subscription manager, distributor, typesetter, proofreader, and publicist.[7] "*Feminist Studies* did not begin as a collective endeavor, but was conceived of and heroically edited by one person, Ann Calderwood, from 1971 to 1977," Rachel DuPlessis has said. "The journal has been largely her physical and intellectual creation. . . . For years Ann ran the journal as an out-of-pocket, out-of-apartment operation. She not only helped to solicit manuscripts and scrupulously edited them, she also set the type, handled the subscriptions, and addressed the envelopes."[8]

Such examples of "bravery in the omnicompetent discharge of editorial duties from the conceptual to the detailed, from the philosophical to the practical" were characteristic of small, unaffiliated political and literary magazines, as were financial insecurity and erratic publication schedules.[9] Calderwood handpicked an editorial staff of young feminist scholars and community activists to whom she dispensed manuscripts for review. With a shoestring budget and volunteer help, the journal grew from a typewritten collection of brief essays and articles to a typeset volume of lengthy, influential pieces of feminist scholarship.

A close examination of the journal's development reveals the dual influences of the women's movement and the university on feminist research, the structural feasibility of the journal's marginal affiliation, and how women's studies was constructed and legitimated as a field of study.

The contributors, topics, and style of the first two issues of *Feminist Studies* reflected its editors' intense involvement with the contemporary women's movement. Contributors attracted to the untested journal were an unusual mix of nonacademic activists, reproductive rights workers, civil rights attorneys, and journalists who were published along with graduate students, recent doctorates, newly appointed instructors, and young assistant professors. For many, this was their first publication; for all it was their first publication of feminist research on women.[10]

Although Volume 1, numbers 1 and 2 were clearly scholarly endeavors, they were also similar in topic, argument, values, and style to movement publications in the early 1970s. Early articles such as Linda Cisler's "Abortion: The War Is not Won," Mary Eastwood's "Federal Approaches to Fighting Job Discrimination," Carol Brown's "Sexism and the Russell Sage Foundation," and Erica Harth's "Report from Israel" reflected the editors' interest in movement activism. Topics covered in *Feminist Studies* in 1972 and 1973 include abortion, prostitution, birth control, education reform, motherhood, sex roles, sexuality, working-class women, job discrimination, Israeli, Indian, and South African women, women's studies, women and nature, and Ann Hutchinson. According to the *Alternative Press Index*, all of the subjects except Ann Hutchinson had been covered extensively during those same years in other publications of the feminist community: *Ain't I a Woman?, Everywoman, Goodbye to All That, oob, Other Woman, Second Wave, Women: A Journal of Liberation*, and *Women's Press*. An examination of the contents of *Ms.* during the same period reveals similar consistencies in topic.[11]

The form, purpose, argument, and politics of early *Feminist Studies* pieces were similar to those of publications of the feminist community. The authors all documented and condemned the oppression of women as a group in society; many argued that this oppression was systemic; and all advocated wide-sweeping social change. Even historical essays reflect the authors' concern with the oppression of women. Commenting on the historical research published in *Feminist Studies*, the historian Mary Hartmann noted its "presentist" focus: "Such a preoccupation is 'presentist' in the best sense, since it involves a rigorous and empathetic effort to understand the historical roots of issues that especially touch women today."[12]

The authors shared feminist community writers' enthusiastic advocacy of the contemporary women's movement as the primary vehicle for social change. This explicit advocacy can be seen in the following excerpts:

New educational environments must be designed to eliminate restrictive sex role learning so that girls and boys can be free to explore their full human potential.[13]

> All oppressed people have an interest in using their knowledge to
> end the present exploitation for profit that characterizes American
> society. A feminist input would change the goals of the [Russell
> Sage] Foundation . . . to help in some small way in transform-
> ing the present exploitative system. The author does not think the
> [Russell Sage] Foundation will make these changes voluntarily.
> She merely emphasized that it *could*. Whether it will move at all
> depends on the strength of the women's movement.[14]

> Encouraging men to take care of themselves, without depen-
> dence on the service of women, and to carry their share of the
> responsibility of child raising should be given priority attention by
> both the women's movement and the government.[15]

The form and style of the early articles were somewhat similar to
community publishing in the use of the short, unnoted, speculative essay,
first-person plural narrative, and emotive language. "We no longer have
faith that exemplary action is enough; we believe that we must become more courageous, competent and aggressive in university politics.
Rather than leaving us to take responsibility for our own decisions, that
state instead has preferred to forbid us to act. . . . *We are still owned by
the state.*"[16]

Published in the spring of 1973, Volume 1, numbers 3 and 4 signaled
an important shift in the balance of community and university influence.
Titled a "Special Double Issue on Women's History," it was a collection of selected papers from the first annual Berkshire Conference on
the History of Women held at Douglass College at Rutgers University.
The issue marked the beginning of *Feminist Studies'* long and important
association with the Berkshire Conferences, an association that drew
the journal deeper into academia and shaped its identity as the leading
feminist publication of social history and materialist-feminist analysis.

In March 1973, six hundred scholars attended "New Perspectives on
the History of Women," the first Berkshire Conference on the History
of Women, to share their research. Through the use of her New York
network, Ann Calderwood was able to collaborate with conference
organizers Mary Hartmann and Lois Banner, both assistant professors
of history at Douglass College. The conference papers that Calderwood,
Hartmann, and Banner selected for publication in *Feminist Studies* were
later reprinted in *Clio's Consciousness Raised,* a collection from Harper

Torchbooks. Editor Judith Walkowitz views this affiliation as a reflection of the Calderwood's insight into the importance of the conference: "Ann recognized the field of women's history was at its inception point at the Berkshire Conference and they wanted her journal to be a part of it."[17] But beyond such editorial vision, academic journals and conferences have always been inextricably bound in the development of a discipline because that collaboration guarantees a steady supply of quality submissions for journals, exposure to publishing outlets for conference participants, and promotion of the field. As Claire Moses explains:

> The major problem in the early years was getting good papers to be published in *Feminist Studies*. It's hard to remember exactly how early this was in the development of our field. There was not much work available and, of course, there would never be much work available unless there are journals that would take it. So one is involved in a circle in which researchers aren't working on a field because there's no place to have it published, consequently there is no material to read that has already been published from which you can move on to the next step and do something interesting. The early days of the creation of this new field of study posed a problem for *Feminist Studies* at the time. The best sources for getting good material at the time seemed to have been in both history and literature . . . and the ties into the world of history always connected to the Berkshire Conference.[18]

Ann Calderwood used her affiliation with the Berkshire Conference to fill three special double issues of *Feminist Studies* between 1973 and 1976.[19] The collaboration pulled the journal deeper into academia. The Berkshire Conference, for all its movement fervor, was essentially an institution of the traditional university where scholars presented research using the language, form, style, conventions, and methods of argument recognized by, and intended for, an exclusively academic audience.

Indeed, when compared to articles in earlier issues of *Feminist Studies* the Berkshire papers seem thoroughly scholarly. In the first issues, Ben Barker-Benfield's "The Spermatic Economy: A Nineteenth-Century View of Sexuality" and his "Anne Hutchinson and the Puritan Attitude toward Women," and Sherry Ortner's "Is Female to Male as Nature Is to Culture" were the journal's only lengthy, footnoted, scholarly research articles. That changed dramatically with the publication of the Berkshire issues.[20] All thirty-seven articles published in *Feminist Studies* from the 1973 and 1974 Berkshire Conference on the History of Women were written in a scholarly form and the style of argument acceptable in the humanities. The scholars used a third-person narrative, extensive footnotes, and abstract rational argument instead of the first-person appeals to the authority of emotion and experience found in publications from the feminist community. All but two of the contributors (a writer and a poet) were identified as academics; compared to earlier issues of *Feminist Studies,* assistant, associate, and full professors far outnumbered graduate students, lecturers, instructors, and unemployed Ph.Ds.[21]

In topics and politics, the Berkshire papers were generally similar to works published within the nonacademic feminist movement; they sought to document, condemn, and change the systematic oppression of women. However, the Berkshire papers' particular emphases reflected the important influence of a specific subdiscipline on the construction of feminist scholarly thought: Marxist-influenced social history.[22] The relationship between social history and the construction of feminist scholarly knowledge provides an illuminating case study of how a particular subdiscipline is adapted by a new field and rises to prominence within it.

Although social history was introduced in the United States as one aspect of the "new history" of the 1920s, with roots in nineteenth-century European social reform debates, the approach did not gain wide popularity with American scholars until the 1960s.[23] Scholars then found social history conducive to both the New Left's revival of Marxist materialist analysis as a serious scholarly inquiry and the social sciences' impact on perspectives and methods in the humanities.

Marxist-influenced social historians critically examine how historically specific modes of production determine social conditions. Because their discipline is rooted ideologically and institutionally in the "social question" of the nineteenth century, social historians are often interested in relating modes of production to the history of workers' problems, reform movements, and trade unions. Reflecting the influence of this approach, the Berkshire issues of *Feminist Studies* included "Lancaster Industrial Schools for Girls" by Barbara Benzel, "Women in the Southern Farmer's Alliance" by Julie Roy Jeffries, "Where Are the Organized Women Workers?" by Alice Kessler-Harris, "Feminism or Unionism? The New York Trade Union League and the Labor Movement" by Nancy Shrom Dye, and "The Women's Trade Union League and American Feminism" by Robin Miller Jacoby. Similarly reflecting social historians' interest in nineteenth-century Europe, more than half of the Berkshire issues' articles—twenty-four of forty—were analyses of this era, and nearly a fourth were on Europe.

The social constructs that Marxist-influenced social historians find most useful in understanding gender include the division of labor into public and private spheres, the family as a unit of production, housework and mothering as unpaid labor, and society's control of female sexuality and reproduction. These topics were heavily represented in the *Feminist Studies* Berkshire issues: "Women, Work and Family: Female Operatives and the Lowell Mills" by Thomas Dublin, "Voluntary Motherhood: Beginnings of Feminist Birth Control Ideas in the United States" by Linda Gordon, "Family Limitation, Sexual Control, and Domestic Feminism in Victorian America" by Daniel Scott Smith, "Puberty to Menopause: The Cycle of Femininity in Nineteenth-Century America" by Caroll Smith-Rosenberg, "Prostitution and the Poor in Plymouth and Southampton under the Contagious Diseases Acts" by Judith Walkowitz and Daniel Walkowitz, "Welfare of Women in Laboring Families in England, 1860–1950" by Laura Oren, and "Power of Women through the Family in Medieval Europe" by Jo Ann McNamara and Suzanne Wemple.

Given these consistencies, its understandable that at times the content of *Feminist Studies* resembled neither community feminist publications nor traditional academic journals but rather such Marxist-influenced radical history journals as *History Workshop* (Oxford, England), *Radical History Review* (John Jay College, New York), and *The Journal of Social History* (Carnegie Mellon University Press, Pittsburgh). These journals grew from the socialist movements of the 1930s and 1960s and provided *Feminist Studies* with fruitful models of successfully established, politically informed scholarship. Although materialist-historical approaches emphasize class rather than gender as the primary category of analysis, such approaches enable feminist scholars to learn how women's experience and oppression are shaped by their relation to historically specific contexts. In addition, materialist-historical approaches help illuminate how that relationship is manifested as particular social forms and social institutions, and how those forms and institutions are determined by society's material and ideological underpinnings. *Feminist Studies* editors Judith Newton and Deborah Rosenfelt argue that "a materialist-feminist criticism, in short, a criticism combining feminist socialist and anti-racist perspectives, is likely to assume that women are not universally the same, and that their relations are also determined by race, class and sexual identification." [24]

Perspectives from social history are "presentist," which helped the Berkshire historians use their understanding of how patriarchal underpinnings and their oppressive manifestations were historically changed in order to formulate present strategies of social change. Finally, and most important, as Peter Stearns, a social historian, explains, practitioners in that field pursue explicit political analyses in their work. "There are no social structures which have not arisen from or have been influenced by politics and which, conversely, have not had an effect on the structure of the state or on political affairs. . . . Social history is, therefore, nothing less than 'political history'." [25]

Ann Calderwood's decision to affiliate her journal with the Berkshire Conference on the History of Women profoundly altered the identity, content, and politics of *Feminist Studies*. Through this affiliation, the journal was drawn away from the contributors, forms, and arguments of the larger, grass-roots community and deeper into those of the university. *Feminist Studies* became associated with a newly emerging network of scholars who were establishing institutions and negotiating roles within the university rather than the community. It became identified with a particular discipline (women's history) and a particular politics (socialist feminist) and established itself as the foremost publication of feminist social history. Its influence still lingers. According to its editor, Deborah Rosenfelt, "We don't have a party line, we will publish things from a variety of perspectives and yet. . . . my feeling is that the best analyses are done by people who have a materialist grounding in dialectic/historical methodology." [26]

These changes in *Feminist Studies* reflected how deeply the Berkshire Conference on the History of Women and the field of feminist social history influenced the journal. They also foreshadowed how untenable the journal's location on the community-university margin would become.

How might *Feminist Studies* have developed without its affiliation with the Berkshire Conferences and the strain of the impending community-university split? A glimpse of what direction Calderwood might have pursued can be found in Volume 2, numbers 2 and 3 (1975), which showcased the burgeoning field of feminist scholarship. The success of women's studies was evident throughout the journal's pages: in the variety of scholars and disciplines pursuing feminist perspectives, the predominance of feminist scholarly citations, the number of references to new feminist texts, the reviews of feminist scholarly and trade publications, the mix of conference papers and unsolicited submissions, the blend of community and academic contributors, and the abundance of advertisers for feminist works from university presses, scholarly monograph houses, leftist publications, and feminist community presses. But this rich, stimulating issue was the last published independently under Calderwood's supervision. It was followed by two erratically produced special issues of papers from the Berkshire Conferences in 1975 and 1976, highly influential and often reprinted issues whose strength reflected the success of the conference but not the health of the journal.[27]

Soon after, Calderwood's version of *Feminist Studies* folded, and its audience was left to wonder how a journal as seemingly robust as that embodied in the issues of Volume 2 could suddenly stop publication. Ironically, clues to the impending demise of the original *Feminist Studies* can be found in the very richness of those last issues.

Feminist Studies was conceptualized as a publication of feminist research for academic and community audiences. Indeed, the array of disciplines and the variety of topics represented in its pages were evidence that feminist thought from 1972 to 1976 succeeded in cutting through the boundaries of most traditional disciplines. However, this expansion of feminist influence within the university resulted in an unintended consequence—the creation of a professionalized "culture of feminist scholarship" that attended to, but existed independently of, the community-based women's movement.

The culture of feminist scholarship was differentiated from the community movement not only by feminist scholars' specialized knowledge, but also by their increasing attachment to university forms, codes, networks, and institutions.[28] Through public demonstrations and private negotiations women's studies programs and departments were established. Through texts, bibliographies, curriculum guides, and university curriculum committees their course content was formalized. Through foundation-funded studies and evaluative conferences their standards were codified. Through conference paper selection and editorial decision their canon was delineated. Through professional associations, caucuses, and networks their membership was organized.

According to the historian Burton Bledstein, professionalism "emerged as more than an institutional event in American life. . . . it was a culture—a set of learned values and habitual responses . . . that pointed

individuals in a specific direction—that of career." This professional culture offered the new nineteenth-century middle class "the opportunity
for people to identify themselves without the support of a community
and in absence of the kind of rigid barriers found in Europe." A professional academic culture emerged in 1870 and was fully developed by
1900, competitively configuring the academic profession "according to
a distinct vision—the vertical one of career."[29]

Furthering Bledstein's argument, James Sosnoski, a literary scholar,
explains the connections between the institutional construction of intellectuality and the social construction of gender. Sosnoski argues that
the American scholar's career profile was explicitly designed for the
new gentlemen of the nineteenth century. Success within the structure of
the academy was defined by masculine needs and experience. The ideal
professional scholar "became a composite of masculine traits derived
from the superimposition of the portrayals of exemplary male scholars.
Women working in the academy, in order to succeed in their careers,
had to acquire these traits."[30]

During the first few years of *Feminist Studies'* history, a handful of
unsupported feminist activists working in isolation on American campuses had become an organized field of specialists with recognized
professional associations, conferences, institutes, research centers, networks, texts, and journals. With success and recognition, they were no
longer individual activists working from the community on the periphery of a powerful patriarchal institution, but rather a separate, discrete,
and bounded activist community with concerns of its own inside the
university. Florence Howe, a women's studies pioneer, has discussed
this transformation and publishing's central role in its organization and
development:

> To effect communication a decade ago, we published *Female
> Studies I, II,* and *III,* even before the *Women's Studies News-
> letter,* the antecedent of the Quarterly, was begun in 1972. These
> monographs, filled with course syllabi, bibliographies, and brief,
> encouraging essays about teaching the courses that were to be
> called "Women's Studies," were ordered by a few hundred people,
> many of whom heard about them at the annual meetings of their
> professional associations. The small network was self-sustaining;
> if you came to an annual meeting, you might join it instantly,
> and if that professional association had a caucus or commission,

you might become a name on a membership list and thus receive an informal communication or two through the year. But the
groups, separated often by discipline, remained small enough for
people to know each other's research and teaching interests. A few
interdisciplinary conferences—at the University of Pennsylvania,
for example, at the University of Pittsburgh, and at Sacramento
State University, all before May 1973, as well as the first Berkshire's Women's History Conference—allowed the major pioneers
in each discipline to meet and to feel first hand the attraction of
interdisciplinary scholarship. We are still not clear about the size
of the spurt forward in numbers after 1973, but we do know of
the burgeoning of Women's Studies Programs, even as we also
know of the doubling of percentage of women earning doctorates
during the seventies. In the eighties, there are more of us in the
professions, as there are more of us in Women's Studies.

It is not only size. . . . It is also the burden of information
itself, the growing lists of interested individuals not only in the
United States but around the world, the bulk of knowledge, the
plethora of books and journal articles, the volume of research in
progress, the news about jobs, conferences, institutes, fellowships,
grants, and of course the continued founding of new institutions.
Who is doing research on widowhood? What are the latest statis-
tics about mothers of small children in the workforce? Where are
there fellowships in Women's Studies at the doctorate level? How
might one find people interested in attending a summer institute
on Women and Health? Who would be interested in a new journal
or book?[31]

By 1975, feminist scholars had turned many of their symbolically
radical disciplinary caucuses into the structure acknowledged by the
university: the professional association. Through association activity,
feminist scholars focused their political energy within the university,
"passing on information about jobs and fellowships, lobbying departments for more women faculty, conducting research on women, and
filing formal complaints of discrimination, rather than the community."[32] Soon, Ann Calderwood felt pressure to align *Feminist Studies*
with a professional feminist association.[33]

By 1977, the culture of feminist scholarship was producing its own
specialized publications, which, unlike *Feminist Studies,* were pub-

lished under the auspices of universities and scholarly publishing houses: *Women's Rights Law Reporter* (Rutgers University Law School, 1971), *Women and Literature* (Rutgers, 1972), *Women's Studies Newsletter* (Feminist Press at the State University of New York, 1972), *Women's Studies* (Gordon and Breach Science Publishers, Inc., 1972), *University of Michigan Papers in Women's Studies* (University of Michigan, 1974), *Frontiers: A Journal of Women's Studies* (University of Colorado, Boulder, 1975), *Signs: A Journal of Women in Culture and Society* (University of Chicago Press, 1975), *Psychology of Women Quarterly* (American Psychological Association, Human Sciences Press, 1976), *Concerns* (Modern Language Association Women's Caucus), and *Sex Roles: A Journal of Research* (Plenum Publishing, 1975).

Just as the success of women's studies drew its associations, conferences, and publications deeper into the university, the success of individual scholars within their own fields pulled feminists further into the university structure and its obligations and networks—and away from the activities of the larger community movement. An early editor, the historian Mary Ryan, recalls the effect of the demands of academic work loads on the politics of *Feminist Studies:*

> When we first started the journal, there was more concern to shape the journal and recruit articles which were more political and less academic. And that didn't happen for a variety of reasons. One reason was because we couldn't do it. We were all part time workers with our academic jobs and couldn't really do all of that. And since our contacts were academic, we couldn't recruit people to do that. Somebody with the incredible work load that most feminist scholars have, can't go out and write you an article on topical issues that you want to do.[34]

A number of the contributors to Volume 2, numbers 2 and 3, such as the historian Nancy Schrom Dye, Kate Ellis, a literary critic, and Sherry Ortner, an anthropologist, were emerging as leaders in their fields. In their attempts to secure a feminist presence within the university, they gained scholarly reputations, received academic appointments, earned tenured promotions, and, consequently, found themselves further immersed in the university's time-consuming requirements. Committee work, conference participation, student advising, and classroom teaching keep most academics busy, but "achievement evidenced by publication of scholarly works" is the essential criterion for tenure and recognition in the modern university.[35] To satisfy this criterion, most feminist scholars chose to publish with university-sanctioned academic presses and monograph houses rather than grass-roots feminist alternative presses. University presses also offered larger audiences and press runs, greater financial rewards, and increased university recognition. This further identified the culture of feminist scholarship with the university rather than community because—of all the media industries—publishing is the most characterized by highly differentiated audiences, methods of distribution, and standards of evaluation.[36]

The success of the field created a new market that attracted a number of established, nonfeminist university publishers. The advertisements in the back pages of *Feminist Studies,* Volume 2, numbers 2 and 3 from Harper Torchbooks, Princeton University Press, Stanford University Press, and Columbia University Press reflected the success that the acquisition editors of scholarly houses had recruiting important, definitive books of feminist research. Several of the contributors to the three volumes of *Feminist Studies* produced between 1972 and 1976 published feminist scholarly works with traditional university presses and monograph houses.[37]

Although these authors still chose to publish some of their articles with a community-based journal, they represent the challenge that university presses posed to the domain of *Feminist Studies.* University presses' interest in feminist scholarly books was soon paralleled by that of traditional scholarly journals. Susan Cardinale, a women's studies librarian, has listed 153 scholarly and professional journals that published special issues about women between 1970 and 1975.[38] Traditional scholarly journals require strict adherence to traditional style manuals that do not recognize the manifesto and speculative essay forms preferred by the feminist community's press. Consequently, the publication of feminist research in traditional journals helped delegitimize the use of community forms and styles in the culture of feminist scholarship.

Like most unaffiliated, community-based publishers, Ann Calderwood lacked the capital and structural stability necessary to produce, advertise, promote, and distribute her journal competitively in a scholarly market. Publication in tested traditional journals offered feminist scholars a wider scholarly audience and more substantial academic rewards than publication in a low-circulation, explicitly political publication like *Feminist Studies.* University presses had the financial and structural stability required to publish specialized works that show a profit over an extended publication life, whereas community feminist presses were compelled to rely on immediate returns and quick maximization of profits to survive.[39] Consequently, feminist scholars had more publication offers from university presses than from community feminist presses. By 1977, university presses and traditional journals had usurped *Feminist Studies'* role as the venue of feminist research for scholarly audiences.

Feminist Studies was conceptualized as a journal for and by community and academic feminist audiences. The success of research on the topic and the creation of a culture of scholarship had anchored feminist scholarly publications deep inside the university structure, making *Feminist Studies'* position increasingly untenable. In early 1977, Ann Calderwood recognized this dilemma and, in a letter to Rachel DuPlessis, expressed her dissatisfaction with the almost purely academic route that lay ahead.[40]

And yet the emerging culture of feminist scholarship was not the only challenge to Calderwood's vision of *Feminist Studies* as a community-university publication. Advertisements in Volume 2, numbers 2 and 3 reveal that publishers in the nonacademic feminist community posed a parallel challenge to *Feminist Studies'* position. The issue contained advertisements for *Quest: A Feminist Quarterly* and Diana Press, two of the many new publishing enterprises primarily produced by and for community feminists.

The women's movement had become so widespread and diversified by 1976 that markets appeared that were much more specialized and segmented than when *Feminist Studies* was conceptualized in 1969. The two types of specialized publications that most seriously threatened the journal were nonacademic theory journals such as *Quest: A Feminist Quarterly* (Washington, D.C.), *Chrysalis: A Magazine of Women's Culture* (Los Angeles), and *Heresies: A Feminist Publication of Art and Politics* (New York), and community-based art and literary journals such as *13th Moon: A Feminist Literary Magazine* (New York), *Calyx: A Journal of Art and Literature by Women* (Corvallis, Oregon), and *Womanspirit* (Albion, California).

By the mid seventies, after the fall of Saigon and the resignation of Richard Nixon, American campuses and activist communities were pulling apart. Campus-community tension was further exacerbated by the eruption of gay-straight splits in movement organizations. Increasingly, lesbian feminists felt their concerns to be inadequately represented in the women's movement press, and many created journals and presses. Some of the most respected political theory and creative work of the time was published in lesbian feminist publications. *Quest*, the first, was quickly joined by *Conditions: A Magazine of Writing by Women, with an Emphasis on Writing by Lesbians* (Brooklyn, 1977) and *Sinister Wisdom: A Journal of Words and Pictures for the Lesbian Imagination in All Women* (Amherst, Massachusetts, 1976). Soon lesbian feminist theory became associated with community publications rather than scholarly feminist journals, and the campus-community rift widened.

A genre split appeared in feminist publishing during the same period. The lesbian feminist publishing influence was profoundly apparent in the content of feminist literary magazines, a form of publishing associated almost exclusively with community publishing. Editors of feminist literary magazines absorbed much of the manifesto style and emotional tone found in earlier movement writing. Rationalist, data-based writing began to dominate the style of academic feminist journals as subjective, experiential writing dominated feminist literary magazines. The editors of *Feminist Studies* found that they could no longer stretch their publication to encompass the community-university divisions of audience, content, style, theory, and genre.

Feminist Studies was in the untenable situation of being a scholarly publication that relied on a community publication structure and budget. Although their publications flourished in the mid seventies, editors of feminist literary magazines constantly struggled with burnout, financial instability, erratic publishing schedules, and low circulation.[41] Many managed to survive because they were located in grass-roots political communities that stabilized their tenuous existence. By the beginning of 1977, *Feminist Studies* was burdened by being a nonaffiliated community publication and yet lacking the grass-roots community participation or support of literary magazines.

Recognizing the structural impossibility of her predicament, Calderwood finally abandoned her original community-university vision of *Feminist Studies* and searched for a university affiliation to save the journal. After a year of negotiation with Sarah Lawrence College, Rutgers University, and Haworth Press, her best offer came from the University of Maryland.

When the original *Feminist Studies* ceased publication in 1976, Calderwood and her journal faced similar dilemmas. She was not, nor did she ever aspire to be, an academic working solely within the university structure. As feminist scholarship became increasingly professionalized and credentialed, Calderwood, for all her expertise, was a layperson in a specialized field. After a series of reorganization meetings in 1977, it was decided that *Feminist Studies* would be resurrected and moved from her apartment to the University of Maryland.[42] Calderwood stepped down as editor-in-chief and become the journal's "movement editor" among a collective of specialized academic editors. Just as the history editor would keep in touch with scholars and developments in the field of women's history, so movement editor Calderwood would recruit community contributors and report on movement activism. But the worlds of the community and the university had grown too distinct to support the viability of such a position. Calderwood quickly withdrew from the post and became the journal's typesetter. Shortly thereafter, her disillusionment forced her to leave abruptly and completely. Claire Moses recalls the unhappy ending:

> Ann Calderwood's resignation was entirely unexpected by the editors and it really stunned us. She tried to communicate that it was not done out of anger, and as time has gone by, I have come to believe that perhaps she really couldn't figure out what her place would be in the journal. Even though the editors would have been glad to have her continue as editor-in-chief, she did not want to do that; and I don't think she really knew how to be the kind of movement editor that was a parallel to the history editor. She was not an academic and it was clear that the journal was moving in a more academic direction. I really do think that what she did was something we've seen other people do in other settings, that is, not to let the journal, which had meant so much to her, die. See to it, instead, that there was a new group to take it over; and only then to leave the journal.[43]

Calderwood and the original *Feminist Studies* could not survive between the pressures and powers of the formidable forces of the movement and the university. Yet had *Feminist Studies* not held its untenable position from 1969 to 1976, the university might have totally consumed feminist scholarship under its auspices and the community would have been totally isolated from the academy. After a series of meetings of academics and activists in New York, *Feminist Studies* did return as a highly acclaimed academic journal within the university. But it had an editorial structure, process, and politics that connected it, imperfectly but soundly, with the movement that inspired it. As Claire Moses explains, "We came to peace, in a positive way, with the identity of a more academic journal. At one point, we were discussing whether we'd be political or academic and I remember one associate editor, whom I respect very much politically as well as academically, said, 'What do you mean? We value *Feminist Studies* for your scholarship.' That's what we do, and we do it well; we shouldn't necessarily try to be something we're not. So that meant more acceptance of the academic method."[44]

Even though the editors became deeply entrenched in university forms and structures, the heart of their scholarship remained feminist politics, and feminist politics continued to be defined by the community. The editors of *Feminist Studies* never lost sight of Ann Calderwood's original vision:

> *Feminist Studies* grew out of the women's movement at its early, spontaneous and energetic phase, bringing together political commitment and scholarship. Then merely to assert that women should be studied was a radical act. We are proud of the creation of this generation's feminist speculation, scholarship and theory.
>
> Now that the study of women has become institutionalized, we at *Feminist Studies* feel we must enter a new phase if we are to carry forward our original commitment. We will continue to represent the points of conflict and growth within the women's movement. . . . We welcome serious and engaged writing of a scholarly, critical, or creative nature. We hope to publish theoretical work, review essays, interviews, symposia, manifestos and strategies as well as feminist research.[45]

Notes

1. Interview with editor Claire Moses, Reston, Virginia, May 17, 1985.
2. Interview with editor Rachel DuPlessis, Swarthmore, Pennsylvania, July 18, 1986.
3. Interview with editor Judith Walkowitz, New York, December 11, 1985.
4. Myra E. Barrer, ed., *Women's Organizations and Leaders Directory* (Washington: Today Publication and News Service, Inc., 1976), 35.
5. Mary Ryan, "Preface," *Feminist Studies* 8 (Spring 1982): iii.
6. "Statement of Purpose," *Feminist Studies* 1 (Summer 1972).
7. Interview with Judith Walkowitz, December 11, 1985.
8. *Feminist Studies* 4 (Spring 1978): iii.

9. Ibid.; Mary Biggs, "Women's Literary Journals," *Library Quarterly* 53 (January 1983): 1–2.

10. For an analysis of contributors' university affiliation, degrees, academic positions, and publications, see "Notes on Contributors," and Jaques Cattell Press, ed., *Directory of American Scholars* (New York: R. R. Bowker, Co., 1972–73).

11. *Alternative Press Index,* Vol. 4–5: *1972–73* (Baltimore: Alternative Press Center, 1973); Contents, *Ms.* 4, nos. 1–4 (1972); 5, nos. 1–4 (1973).

12. Mary S. Hartmann, *Clio's Consciousness Raised: New Perspectives on the History of Women* (New York: Harper and Row, 1974), xi.

13. Betty Levy, "The School's Role in the Sex Role Stereotyping of Girls: A Feminist Review of the Literature," *Feminist Studies* 1 (Summer 1972): 40.

14. Levy, "The School's Role," 41.

15. Carol Brown, "Sexism and the Russell Sage Foundation," *Feminist Studies* 1 (Summer 1972): 94.

16. Christine Grahl et al., "Women's Studies: Case in Point," *Feminist Studies* 1 (Fall 1972): 126.

17. Interview with Judith Walkowitz.

18. Interview with Claire Moses.

19. Of the seven issues published under Ann Calderwood, three (including two double issues) were proceedings from the Berkshire Conferences.

20. *Feminist Studies* 1 (Winter-Spring 1973); 3 (Fall 1975); and 3 (Spring-Summer 1976).

21. Of the thirty-five authors published in the Berkshire issues, thirty-one identified themselves as academics, twenty-three at the assistant professor level or higher.

22. For a discussion and application of feminist materialist-historical approaches in the editors' work, see Judith L. Newton et al., *Sex and Class in Women's History* (London: Routledge and Kegan Paul, 1983), and Judith Newton and Deborah Rosenfelt, *Feminist Criticism and Social Change* (New York: Methuen, 1985).

23. Maria S. DePhillis, "Trends in American Social History and the Possibility of Behavioral Approaches," *Journal of Social History* 1 (1967–68): 56.

24. Newton and Rosenfelt, *Feminist Criticism and Social Change,* xxvii.

25. Peter N. Stearns, "Some Comments on Social History," *Journal of Social History* 1, no. 1 (1967–68): 13.

26. Interview with editor Deborah Rosenfelt, San Francisco, May 31, 1985.

27. *Feminist Studies* 3 (Fall 1975) and (Spring-Summer 1976). The only hint that the journal might be in jeopardy is a note on the last page of Volume 2, numbers 2 and 3 in which a handful of individual women were thanked for financial donations that enabled Calderwood to "make publication of this issue possible."

28. For an assessment of women's studies institutions and forms during the early 1970s, see Florence Howe, *Seven Years Later: Women's Studies Programs in 1976: A Report of the National Advisory Council on Women's Educational*

Programs (Old Westbury: Feminist Press, 1977); *Women's Studies Monograph Series*, Vols. 1–8 (Washington: National Institute of Education, 1980).

29. Burton Bledstein, *The Culture of Professionalism: The Middle Class and the Development of Higher Education in America* (New York: W. W. Norton and Co., 1978), x–xi, 288.

30. James J. Sosnoski, "A Mindless Man-driven Theory Machine: Intellectuality, Sexuality and the Institution of Criticism," in *Feminist Institutions: Dialogues on Feminist Theory,* ed. Linda Kauffman (Cambridge: Basil Blackwell, 1989), 65–66.

31. Florence Howe, "The First Ten Years Are the Easiest," in *Women's Studies Quarterly: Index to the First Ten Years 1972–1982,* ed. Jo Baird, Shirley Frank, and Beth Stafford (Old Westbury: Feminist Press, 1984), 1.

32. Alice S. Rossi and Ann Calderwoods, eds., *Academic Women on the Move* (New York: Russell Sage Foundation, 1973), 28.

33. Interview with Rachel DuPlessis.

34. Interview with editor Mary Ryan, Palo Alto, California, June 3, 1985.

35. Press, ed., *Directory of American Scholars,* ix.

36. Lewis Cosner, Charles Kadushin, and Walter W. Powell, *Books: The Culture and Commerce of Publishing* (Chicago: University of Chicago Press, 1982), 36, 68.

37. Authors from Volumes 1–3 who published work on women with traditional scholarly presses include Ben Barker-Benfield, *Horrors of the Half-Known Life: Male Attitudes toward Women and Sexuality in Nineteenth Century America* (Harper and Row, 1976); Susan Groag Bell, *Women from the Greeks to the French Revolution* (Wadsworth, 1974); Nancy Cott, ed., *Roots of Bitterness: Documents of the History of American Women* (E. P. Dutton, 1972); Mary Hartmann and Lois Banner, eds., *Clio's Consciousness Raised: New Perspectives on the History of Women* (Harper and Row, 1974); Gerda Lerner, *The Grimke Sisters from South Carolina: Rebels against Slavery* (Houghton, 1967), *The Women in American History* (Addison-Wesley, 1969), and *Black Women in White America: A Documentary History* (Pantheon, 1972); Cynthia Lloyd, ed., *Sex Discrimination and the Division of Labor* (Columbia University Press, 1975); Jo Ann McNamara, "Marriage and Divorce in the Frankish Kingdom," in *Women in Medieval Society,* ed. Susan M. Stuard (University of Pennsylvania Press, 1976); Elaine Showalter, *Women's Liberation and Literature* (Harcourt, Brace, Jovanovich, 1971); Sherry Ortner, "Is Female to Male as Nature Is to Culture?" in *Women, Culture and Society,* ed. Michele Rosaldo and Louise Lamphere (Stanford University Press, 1974); Judith Stacey, Susan Bereaud, and Joan Daniels, eds., *And Jill Came Tumbling After: Sexism in American Education* (Dell, 1974); and Kathryn Kish Sklar, *Catharine Beecher: A Study in American Domesticity* (Yale, 1973).

38. Susan Cardinale, "Special Issues of Serials about Women," in *Council of Planning Librarians Exchange Bibliographies,* ed. Mary Vance (Monticello, Ill.: Council of Planning Librarians, 1976).

39. According to Coser, Kadushin, and Powell, "The major feature of scholarly publishing is that money can be made on books that sell comparatively few

copies. This is the reverse of trade publishing, where, because of costs involved, money can be lost on books that sell as many as 20,000 copies. Scholarly houses can earn a profit on a book that sells as few as 1,500 copies. . . . The risks in scholarly publishing are therefore minor in comparison with those in the trade market." See *Books,* 57–58.

40. Interview with Rachel DuPlessis.

41. Biggs, "Women's Literary Journals," 4.

42. *Feminist Studies* now operates under the auspices of the Women's Studies Program at the University of Maryland, College Park Campus. The university provides the journal with a faculty line for the manager-editor, as well as office and storage space. Some office equipment is independently owned by the editorial board through *Feminist Studies Inc.,* which is solely responsible for the main costs of staffing, publishing, and distributing the journal.

43. Interview with Claire Moses.

44. Ibid.

45. "Draft of revised editorial statement," in Ann Calderwood to the Editors, February 19, 1977.

chapter four

Frontiers, Signs, and the Community–Academy Split

We asked ourselves, "What was needed? What should we be? We have *Ms.* in the community and we have *Feminist Studies* in the academy. What we need is a translator—a bridge—something to span the widening gulf between the two."

Elizabeth Jameson, founding editor,
Frontiers

In 1975, as *Feminist Studies* faltered, two new feminist academic journals, *Frontiers* and *Signs,* were created. Unlike their predecessor, they operated from within the university-enclosed culture of feminist scholarship but, like *Feminist Studies,* the new journals were forced to address the rapidly widening schism between feminists in the university and feminists in the community.

> Welcome to *Frontiers: A Journal of Women's Studies.* We came together over a year ago to found a journal which we hoped would begin to bridge the gaps between university and community women. It has been a primary aim for us to involve people from the community as well as those from academia. If we are to practice what we all seem to be saying—that the women's movement will eventually fail if it is middle class and academic in its orientation—then we must constantly work to encourage and to use the efforts of our sisters in the "real world."[1]

With this introduction, the new journal's editors[2] acknowledged three important features that had developed in the relationship between feminist scholarship and the women's movement by 1975: (1) a chasm separated feminist scholars from feminists activists in the community; (2) editors of feminist academic journals primarily identified themselves as academics; and (3) feminist academics deplored the loss of their connections to the community. The most authentic and effective political activism was associated with feminists working and organizing in the nonacademic sector of the movement.

The editors of *Frontiers* attempted to realize the failed vision of Ann Calderwood, but with a key difference. *Feminist Studies* began as an unaffiliated, community publication that addressed issues of scholarship. The editors of *Frontiers* positioned their journal as a university-based publication that addressed issues of community activism. Housed on the premises of the University of Colorado at Boulder and supported by a $3,500 grant from that institution, *Frontiers* was firmly located within the university-bound culture of academic feminism. Although the journal was clearly scholarly, complete with footnoted articles, the community posture of its editors was evident in the publication's origins, structure, contributors, style, topics, and intended audience. The editors insistently and pointedly addressed the nonacademic community in the hope that they might transcend the genre distinctions that separated community and university publications.

In their first statement, the editors of *Frontiers* noted that "our sister journals are either scholarly or popularized. We wanted to find a balance between these poles which seem unnecessarily to divide women, because, after all, university women lead real lives in the 'real world,' and women outside the university make valuable contributions to learning. We hope that subsequent issues will contain more articles which cross these barriers."[3] Kathi George, the founding editor, emphasizes that the policy was part of a larger political commitment.

> If we have a political line, it is that we're striving to reach out to the community. Now I don't know what that is called—for instance when you open up the women's studies textbook they classify the varieties of feminism, liberal, radical, socialist, lesbian separatist feminist—we don't necessarily fall into any of those. We have a very strange sort of political line and that is called community outreach. That was a noble goal. And that political goal is the one sort of stable thing that you can see throughout *Frontiers*—whether it is an interview with a nonacademic person, or it is artwork, or it

is poetry, or it is the tone of accessibility in the academic articles we do print. This I think has been what I could say for lack of anything more coherent. . . . this has been our political line.[4]

Another founding collective member, Carol Pearson, elaborates on the journal's original conception of the community and the difficulties inherent in bridging the gap.

I don't think we really had a concrete idea of what "the community" was. I think it was virtue. I think we imagined housewives subscribing from all classes, but in fact we weren't operating on that basis. If we were, we would have been *Ms.* magazine. In practice what it meant was that we wanted to get articles from people who were thinking in a fairly scholarly way but didn't necessarily have appointments in the university—we wanted to break the monopolistic hold of the university on the formulation of ideas. That's the part that was coherent. And not everybody on the editorial board would be actually associated with the university—we knew there were a lot of women who had PhDs who couldn't get jobs, but I think, we also had a romantic idea of reaching the masses. . . . There was also concern with class and that, at least, if we didn't have a lot of working-class women writing for the journal, although we wanted that to happen, the journal would reflect the concerns of working-class women. We used to talk a lot about how to get working-class women to write. . . . I remember we used to go to the coalition of labor unions and stuff like that. . . . How to get the word out; how to get community writing when you don't pay. Academics get rewarded for writing, but other people don't get any reward for publishing in an academic journal.[5]

The editors' imperative to connect with the community was based on more than ideological longing. The origins of *Frontiers* as a politically strategic, grass-roots project paralleled the origins of community journals such as *Quest, off our backs, Big Mama Rag,* and *Lavender Women.* As George recalls:

In the spring of 1974, a group of people, a group of students, started a petition drive to found the women's studies program at Boulder. They got faculty involved, mainly from the English program—Carol Pearson was one of the main founders. And they got together and formed a committee, a real loose sort of ad hoc thing to get women's studies on campus. It was very swift. The first meeting I went to was in April 1974, and by the end of the semester, which was in May, and over the summer we basically had gotten the Program together. A lot of the people who were on the founding committee for the Program said—it really was almost a Judy Garland-Mickey Rooney movie—"Hey kids, let's found a journal!"[6]

As the first director of the Women's Studies Program at the University of Colorado at Boulder, Pearson remembers a different scenario:

The context was starting a women's studies program where the administration basically agreed to have it because they thought the students would riot if they didn't. And they were wrong. Most students didn't really care. But enough of them did. So as a strategy, we figured out we had to get enough in place real fast to be very, very visible so that it would be politically inexpedient for them to close us down. . . . the idea of starting *Frontiers* was part of that visibility effort. It was actually started by a chat with Kathi George.[7]

Whether the program, and consequently the journal, began from spontaneous student protest or strategic faculty organizing, the inclusion of student protest in the folklore of *Frontiers* reveals the importance its editors place on the populist, grass-roots activism of community politics. What is consistent is that the editors remember the journal as being created by a group of activist scholars and students who bonded, established a feminist presence on campus, and defined it in opposition to a university administration perceived as patriarchal and adversarial.

The style, forms, conventions, voice, and language of *Frontiers*' earliest articles reflected the dual influences of academy and community. Submissions were required to conform to the MLA style sheet, with some variations.[8] Although attentive to scholarly conventions and criteria, what mattered to the editors was not strict adherence to accepted academic style, but, as George explains, whether the articles could be read by an audience outside the specialized discourses of the academy.

One of the constant criticisms that I hear from people about some of the other academic journals is, the stuff is great for research, it's great to use, it's making a contribution to the field, but they don't want to read it. They may use it for research, they may refer to it because part of this is just the nature of academia. A person sets up an argument and somebody else rebuts it or refutes it or refines it or one thing or another. What we try to achieve are articles that are accessible and readable to an average intelligent reader who is interested in feminism. We do not want them to be exclusionary. We don't want them to be so academically impenetrable and jargon ridden that people can't sit down and pick up *Frontiers* like a magazine and read it.[9]

In their effort to be "accessible and readable" to both academic and community audiences, the editors of *Frontiers* encouraged mixing forms associated with academic journals and community magazines. They sought "traditional and innovative work from all persons concerned with women's issues" and also welcomed "experiential essays, film and book reviews, exceptional creative work and criticism."[10]

Frontiers' inclusion of manifesto-style essays characterized by first-person narration and calls to action set the new journal apart from the more detached voices and passive constructions of traditional scholarship. In an early article, "Feminism and Fertility," the feminist activist Germaine Greer called her audience to action against inadequate options for contraception:

> Now it's a situation that you're familiar with, so what are you going to do about it? I mean, do you really want that money spent on developing an early abortive agent? Then you'd better go to wherever Searle factories are and start writing on the walls. You'd better start trying to drag the research chemists out of their lairs and ask them what they're doing with the money they're making after selling all those pills. . . . You could ask a lot of questions. And until the questions are being asked loudly, it doesn't matter if they are being asked a bit inaccurately. . . . As long as we make like we're happy with what we've got, what we've got is going to be what we're going to get.[11]

Note Greer's appeal to moral and emotional outrage, her call to action, her use of conversational tone, her explicit advocacy, her identification with her female audience, and her assignment of agency to pharmaceutical companies. All connect her piece with the form and style associated with feminist community publications.

The editorial decision to feature creative work, including personal essays, photo essays, poetry, and science fiction-fantasy, which had become the nearly exclusive domain of community publishing, consciously allied *Frontiers* with nonacademic publications. For example, the editors devoted a special issue to feminist fantasy and science fiction that featured criticism, creative works, and interviews with top authors. Despite its importance to the women's movement, scholarly feminist publications had never adopted science fiction-fantasy, although works of feminist fantasy had been a part of the nineteenth-century and contemporary women's movements. Popular contemporary works included *Woman on the Edge of Time* by Marge Piercy, *The Female Man* by Joanna Russ (who wrote fiction under a pseudonym), *The Kin of Ata Are Waiting for You* by Dorothy Bryant, and *Women of Wonder, More Women of Wonder,* and *New Women of Wonder* by Pamela Sargent. Feminist interest in such work can be gauged from volume, sales, and the attendant feminist fantasy newsletters, organizations, and conventions.[12]

Although this blurring of styles and genres distinguished *Frontiers'* community orientation from other more academically oriented journals, the editors believed that the collective structure and process of the editorial board was their most radical departure from other traditional journals. As the editors Lee Chambers-Schiller and Nancy Mann explain the scholarly implications of their collective structure, "The political process of the editorial board is itself a form of feminist discourse; indeed, it is, in some ways, a microcosm of feminist discourse. For we are privileged to work as a collective, trying to implement our assorted ideas about what constitutes 'feminist publishing.'" Elizabeth Jameson has explained their political motivation: "We were trying hard to be politically correct and egalitarian."[13]

"Politically correct" and "egalitarian" editorial structures had been defined for the women's movement by underground publications of the 1960s. Consequently, like its predecessors and its community cohorts, the *Frontiers'* collective emphasized editorial consensus and job-sharing. The earliest structure required a full consensus on manuscript selection and editorial policy as well as an equitable division of all production tasks. Each member of the collective would select and edit manuscripts as well as prepare bulk mailings, proofread galleys, exchange subscriptions, write rejection letters, and staff the office. The first editorial collective "was made up largely of graduate students and community women—journalist, therapist, or freelance writers for the most part. Only one was a faculty member, the Women's Studies director."[14]

The *Frontiers'* collective was reorganized a number of times in its early history. Each version retained the principle of consensus on manuscript selection but redistributed editorial and production responsibilities. As in the histories of *Feminist Studies* and *Signs,* one woman on *Frontiers'* editorial board emerged to take on the primary organization and promotion responsibilities: Kathi George, a graduate student and former journalist.

The emergence of George as managing editor and eventually editor further assured the journal's community posture. She was a community activist who, although she had an advanced degree, was not interested in a faculty appointment. George embodied the academic-community tension that defined much of the journal's identity. She became the staunchest defender of the its community focus. Charlotta Hensley, another editor, explains, "then there's Kathi and she will claim she doesn't have any real connection to anything, but she's the community, our editor *is* the community."[15]

George and the *Frontiers'* collective recruited activists from the feminist movement in Boulder and Denver to be contributors, consultants, and board members. This community-academy partnership helped develop an unintended "regional" identity for the journal, an identity that had two meanings that were not always applied simultaneously. The journal has been labeled "regional" in terms of its board, contributors, and audience; it was also termed as regional in its content. The original *Frontiers* collective never considered themselves regional in either sense but, as George pointed out, such an identity could be easily inferred from a number of the journal's features:

A lot of people have felt that we were a regional journal. From day one, partly because of the name and a lot because of the location. Because the editorial board was concentrated in Boulder and wasn't a national board, people have felt that we were a regional magazine.

When we first started out, we did use more local authors than we probably should have, simply because getting submissions at all was so tough. We kept tapping our friends and the people we knew who were doing good work and were accessible.

It is partly because of the name; maybe it's because of the dusty, earthy tone cover stock that we've used. Anyway, I know we have that regional aura, or even that stigma, about us.[16]

Indeed, because of its commitment to community authors, its limited funding, and its lack of access to powerful bicoastal feminist networks, eighteen of the forty-three articles published in the first three issues of *Frontiers* were written by students, faculty, and editorial collective members at the University of Colorado at Boulder. Of the remaining twenty-seven, sixteen contributors were based in the Midwest, Southwest, and Far West. Only three contributors from 1975 through 1977 were identified as being based in the Northeast: Jeannine Dobbs of Harvard University, Margaret Culley from the University of Massachusetts, Amherst, and Joyce Jennings Walstedt of the University of Delaware. Later issues reflected a significantly diversified regional base, but *Frontiers* continued to be the only nationally distributed feminist academic journal that consistently published the work of authors and artists from the Midwest, Southwest, and Rocky Mountain states.

Although the first three issues included a variety of national and international topics, including information on India, Korea, China, Belgium, Russia, Germany, Spain, and Austria, *Frontiers* became identified with the American West. It was the first feminist academic journal to devote special issues to women in the West, to Native American women, and to Chicana women.

The editors believe that featuring such contributors and topics, combined with the journal's Boulder-based in-house editorial board, created *Frontiers'* identity as a regional publication. As Kathi George explained, it was a label that the editors wore uneasily:

It is very strange and I don't know why people think of us a regional or a local. . . . I try to deny it or at least try to explain why it isn't factually correct. We are not a regional magazine, we have never been a regional magazine, we publish very few people per volume from the local area. We had a strict policy about local submissions. They get refereed not only by the Board but also by outside referees. We have always had a national subscription base, a national readership, and national submissions. But, in fact, we have still been stigmatized as an in-house journal, a local journal, a regional journal. I don't think we are, but a lot of people think we publish more articles on the West, for instance, than anybody else. That's just hooey. Until we published the Second Oral History Issue [Volume 7, number 1] and "Women on the Western Frontier Issue" [Volume 7, number 3], we'd done squat on women in the West.[17]

Charlotta Hensley's analysis goes a step further:

People on this campus see us as, "Well, that's just our local journal and they're just doing local things and they've got local people on it, and, therefore, they're not scholarly." Well, what is scholarly? Are we too parochial? Do we mean to be parochial? Is there value in somebody being parochial?[18]

These responses stem from the editors' recognition that regionalism implies parochialism—an equation that reveals the persistence of Anglo-European supremacy as an unmarked category in American scholarship. In "The Laying on of Culture," John McDermott argues that university culture is characterized by "the almost uniform hostility to the institutions of local and community life. . . . for these reasons, and for reasons having to do with the demands of the national economy for college-trained persons, the tendency of university experience is to propel the young away from local and community life and toward national life and its institutions."[19]

As Americanist critics have argued, modern studies of American "national" experience have been consistently universalized from studies of New England and West European experience.[20] Similarly, Lawrence Buell, a literary scholar, has analyzed how scholars identify Anglo-Saxonism with American national identity by universalizing New England experience. This experience is then "valorized" while other regional cultures are denigrated as second-rate. "That verdict is echoed by our standard literary histories which present Emerson, Thoreau, Hawthorne, and Dickinson as national literary heros." Buell also observes that "provincial ideology is not just a matter of place, but of race as well. Indeed, regionalism and ethnicity are homologous and sometimes coextensive foundations. Standard accounts of the two overlap to the point of indistinguishability."[21]

Consequently, *Feminist Studies'* reliance on clusters of research on New England and West European women did not stigmatize or label the journal as regional. Similarly, *Signs'* early absence of articles on the

American West did not result in the charge of parochial scholarship. The ancient and entrenched assumption of East Coast superiority enhanced the scholarly status of *Feminist Studies* and *Signs* and denigrated that of *Frontiers.* [22] In the culture of feminist scholarship, to be based in New York connotes national and international scope, to be based in Boulder, Colorado, connotes regional and parochial interest. Consequently, the editors of *Frontiers* bore their journal's identification with regional interest uneasily, understanding the radical nature of publishing scholarship on previously neglected areas of women's experience but suffering the denigration of such scholarship by charges of parochialism.

Perhaps the finest examples of *Frontiers*' ability to produce scholarship that addressed community and regional interests are the journal's two special women's oral history issues. The first (Volume 2, number 2), published under guest editor Sherna Gluck in 1977, is regularly reprinted as an introductory text to women's oral history. The success of the first special issue prompted "Women's Oral History Two" with guest editors Sue Armitage and Joan Jensen in 1983 (Volume 7, number 1). That issue focused on discussions of project design, methodology, and presentation of oral history. Gluck clarified the community's role in developing scholarship on women's oral history: "Women's oral history received its main impetus from grass roots projects like the Feminist History Research Project, the Idaho Women's Project, and the Montana Women's History Project. In what is perhaps the best example of the symbiotic relationship between academic feminist scholars and community feminist researchers, the field of women's oral history blossomed and bore fruit." [23] Susan Armitage explained the political aspect of such scholarship:

> Women's oral histories *are* different, primarily because the interviewers wish to make women historically visible. Those of us engaged in women's oral history share a belief in the importance to women of autonomy and self-definition, both today and in the past. We ask women to speak for and about themselves—about their own work and their own lives, rather than about "history" or the activities of their fathers, husbands, and sons.
>
> Oral history is a basic tool in women's history because the lives, activities, and feelings of so many women have been overlooked and unrecorded. Traditional historical sources such as newspapers and manuscripts generally reflect the lives of middle- and upper-

class urban women, and tell us almost nothing about the lives of working-class, rural, and ethnic women. Because so much of recorded official history is written by and about males, women themselves are the major source for information about women.[24]

The regional contribution of these special issues is most evident in the content of "Women's Oral History Two." Some articles covered familiar settings: a literacy project in London, the world of Jewish immigrant women in New York, and Arab-American women in Boston.[25] However, to demonstrate the journal's commitment to community and regional interests, the bulk of the issue examined less-researched aspects of women's lives in other regions of the United States: elderly women in Colorado, abortion experiences in Montana, Southern Paiute women in northern Arizona, go-go dancers in North Carolina, shipyard workers in Oregon, rural women in Idaho and Arizona, and that of a first-generation American-Japanese teacher in Seattle.[26]

Charges of parochialism and regionalism are but part of the price the editors of *Frontiers* have paid for their commitment to community topics, contributors, and audiences. The publication and its staff share many of the burdens that their unaffiliated community counterparts experience: scarce and unstable funding, work overload and burnout, limited circulation, an erratic publication schedule, inadequate promotional resources, and an uncertain future. The same conditions destroyed Ann Calderwood's version of *Feminist Studies*.

Two stabilizing factors kept *Frontiers* afloat: the continuous, personally financed editorship of George until 1988 and the journal's tenuous sponsorship from the University of Colorado at Boulder. Over the years, *Frontiers* has been drawn increasingly closer, in content and structure, to the stabilizing force of the university, but as Michèle Barale, another editor, explains, the journal's community commitment continues to differentiate it from its peers.

> Some part of me wants to say, "We're still doing what everybody said they were going to do and they didn't do and we kept doing it, damn it. And we were the 'good guys' and you weren't." Another part of me worries, "Maybe they knew something we didn't know." I think we've been true to our ideals [laughs], that's what you say as they march you up to the firing squad. I think that the board saw a vision way back, and I think that vision hasn't gone away. And I think that the easier thing for *Frontiers* would

be to get in and say "OK, we can't be *Signs,* we can't be *Feminist Studies,* but we'll be a second-rate *Feminist Studies,* and at least we'll be doing what everybody else is doing." We haven't done that and I think that's admirable. And I would fear losing that thing that makes us who we are—that we are not intended just for the literati. I certainly am not so blind as to think that we appeal to working-class dykes in Idaho, no way. Not even working-class non dykes in Idaho is my guess. But I think that there is a hope that some of what we publish might appeal, were they to find it. And that part of what we do is to make clear to our readers that the working-class dyke in Idaho and the waitress in Wyoming are part of the concern, and I don't mean a humanistic/feministic concern. I mean just plain "This is what women's studies is about, folks!" And so we continually try to bring that to the fore, even if that's not our audience. And I see that as what the women's movement has tried to do over the years in various clear and unclear and fumbling ways.[27]

The editors of *Frontiers* continued to bridge the gap between community and university by managing to find funding sources year by year. Despite its financial instability and editorial turnovers, *Frontiers* has experienced only minor disruptions in its publishing schedule over the years. *Signs,* its prestigious sister journal, suffered no such liabilities. "Perhaps the simplest thing to say about *Signs* is also the truest: it is an academic journal."[28]

From its inception, the editors of *Signs* sought the recognition, legitimation, and acceptance of feminist scholarship from the academic community. The journal was consciously molded in strict compliance with the university's most rigorous criteria for form, structure, appearance, method, and argument. With *Signs,* the editors produced a journal "operating along standard academic lines—in effect, beating the academics at their own game by illustrating that women's studies was, indeed, a valid academic enterprise."[29] As Joan Burstyn, an associate editor, explains:

The editors intended that *Signs* be as rigorous in its standards as any other scholarly journal. At the time it was founded, there were some people who assumed that any feminist scholarship was trivial, ill-conceived, and badly executed. To combat such stereotypes, *Signs* obtained contributions from established scholars, sought papers that reconceptualized issues, and insured that all studies were accurately and adequately footnoted. This policy proved successful in establishing *Signs* as an equal among scholarly journals.[30]

Signs' scholarly legitimacy not only reflects the hard work of its editors and contributors, but also the status of its originators—the University of Chicago Press. In 1973, the University of Chicago Press published a special issue of the *American Journal of Sociology* entitled "Changing Women in a Changing Society." The issue was so popular and well received that the Press printed an extra three thousand copies and, when these were quickly exhausted by demand, reprinted the issue as a book.[31]

The success of "Changing Women in a Changing Society" did not go unnoticed at the University of Chicago Press, and in early 1974, Jean Sacks, the publications manager, formally proposed the creation of an academic journal devoted to scholarship on women. Members of the Board of the University of Chicago Press were impressed with the success of "Changing Women in a Changing World" but doubted the suitability and durability of a scholarly journal on women for such a prestigious press. Some worried about the quality of submissions for such a journal and questioned its ability to attract acceptable manuscripts. Others feared that such an experiment might prove an embarrassment.[32]

Responding to their objections, Jean Sacks asked the Barnard College scholar and feminist Catharine R. Stimpson to draw up a prospectus that would be circulated to elicit responses from established scholars in a number of fields. In a "Report on Journals to the Board of the University of Chicago Press and Director of the Press," Sacks successfully countered the board's objections with letters of overwhelming support from these scholars.[33] In the fall of 1974, Stimpson was hired as the editor of the new journal, and the University of Chicago Press committed itself wholeheartedly to the development of *Signs,* which appeared as a quarterly in the autumn of 1975.[34]

As a member of the editorial board of the Gordon and Breach Science Publishers' journal *Women's Studies,* Stimpson was one of the few women in 1974 who could claim experience with feminist scholarly journals. She also brought an even broader, less formal expertise to the new journal:

At that point, a lot of it was personal knowledge. What you'd picked up at conferences, by reading manuscripts, by who you knew—there weren't that many people then. Between 1969 and 1974 there had been a number of conferences. We were really self-conscious about what it meant to be doing women's studies, because again and again you saw self-conscious reflection on what it means to be doing women's studies, so that when Jean Sacks asked me to edit *Signs* in 1974 I'd been through five years of discussion and writing about what this meant, what did this enterprise reflect. A focus of that discussion had to do with the founding of the NWSA. I wrote a founding document for it on the theoretical basis of NWSA, "What Matter Mind: A Theory about the Practice of Women's Studies." . . . There was all this ferment. So I was meeting with brilliant people who had been thinking about this, driving in cars thinking about this, drinking tea and eating fried chicken and hot dogs and talking about it—so that our sense of the field didn't come from going into a retreat and brooding. It came from five years of active development.[35]

"What Matter Mind: A Theory about the Practice of Women's Studies" clearly articulates Stimpson's conceptualization of the relationship of feminist scholarship and the traditional university. She argues that American colleges and universities are "repositories of sophisticated knowledge, factories of new ideas" which, unfortunately, have distorted or ignored knowledge about women. This parallels the process that has trivialized women as participants in the academy, which parallels the denigration of female intellect in society at large. Women's studies must take on a political program that would alter not only the knowledge of women but also the "psychological, educational, social, and political context within which knowledge is garnered, passed down, and received."[36]

A year after its first issue, the editors of *Signs* had some observations about "male hegemony" and "the jeopardy of women in academic life":

> When we began, we knew that some portions of the academic and intellectual world looked at the new scholarship about women with suspicion, indifference, or contempt. . . . We must confront a bitter irony: if the number of articles, courses, and books about women is growing, the number of women in academic life itself may not be. Most of us want to act, to paraphrase and quote Adrienne Rich, "for the relief of the body / and the reconstruction of the mind." We will have to be persistent and inventive if we are

to avoid an immediate future in which we will have reconstructed minds but disabled lives.[37]

But the denigration of feminist scholarship and the disabling of feminist scholars were not the only threats facing Stimpson's new enterprise. She worried that the women's movement would be torn apart by internecine battles over the strategic use of the patriarchal university for such a political program. Stimpson argued that women's studies should postpone its role as a "vehicle for any single ideology" and should allow a multiplicity of strategies for social change—one of which would be the prudent use of university and foundation support.[38] Refusing to affiliate *Signs* with the political agendas of any specific faction of the women's movement, she argued that

> A . . . thing that haunted me was the history of twentieth-century revolutions that closed down human possibility. I am about to stop being chair of the MLA committee on academic freedom. I think the Bill of Rights is one of the great documents of human history. I'm an old fashioned liberal when it comes to free speech, human rights and I have an absolute gut horror about totalitarian discourse. . . . My politics always call for the practice of free speech, and I think the lesson of history convinces me I'm right. . . . I think the First Amendment argument is a serious one.[39]

Stimpson's strategy was to achieve legitimacy, and with it institutional power for the political programs of women's studies, by producing a journal of impeccable academic quality under the auspices of one of America's most distinguished university presses. Early indications promised that she would not be disappointed. Published in the fall of 1975, *Signs* amassed a healthy circulation of 8,220 at the end of its first year.[40] The first volume was a hefty one, with almost 1,400 pages, between ten and forty pages of advertisements, and a twelve-page author-title index. Stimpson's strategy was so successful that financial support from the University of Chicago Press was soon augmented by contributions from other powerful institutions: the Ford Foundation, the Lilly Foundation, the Rockefeller Foundation, the Exxon Foundation, and the Department of Housing and Urban Development.[41]

Signs was a journal that had a feminist editorial board and that published politically informed feminist scholarship. As Stimpson observed, "If I thought *Signs* were an ordinary academic journal, I would consider it a failure. I want it to help transform the contemporary study of human life and culture by rescuing it from the culture of male supremacy." The potential power of that transformation was evident in the early issues. The journal showcased the finest works of the new discipline's promising and established scholars. Early articles, which were immediately recognized as influential and originative, included "Capitalism, Patriarchy, and Job Segregation" by Heidi Hartmann, "The Social Relations of the Sexes: Methodological Implications of Women's History" by Joan Kelly-Gadol, "On the Power of the Weak" by Elizabeth Janeway, and "The Female World of Love and Ritual: Relations between Women in Nineteenth-Century America" by Carroll Smith-Rosenberg.

Although such works directly addressed a feminist scholarly audience, it was the editors' professed attention to, and acceptance by, an academic audience that was not feminist that identified *Signs'* position on the community-university continuum. This attention is evident in the editors' manipulation of several textual and structural variables to express the intended identity of their journal.

In the style, form, and language of *Signs,* Stimpson and the other editors consciously and carefully followed the traditional scholarly model.[42] Meticulous attention to accepted academic form was signaled by the inclusion of a full page of citation instructions, admonitions, and examples for footnote form in each issue. Correct citation of authority was so valued that even Stimpson notes that "the authors may have overemphasized some of the scholarly trappings; *Signs* probably prints more inches of notes than other University of Chicago Press journals."[43] Similarly, the editors eschewed the speculative essays, experiential forms, and creative work that *Frontiers* had found so effective as a means of incorporating community interest. Stimpson believed the credibility of *Signs* as an academic journal, and feminist scholarship as a legitimated discipline, relied on a purity of scholarly form.

> We thought about poetry, but the decision not to accept creative work had to do with a sense of the necessity of an identity which was flexible but also pure. Besides, administratively it would have been messy. We got five to six hundred manuscripts a year in every academic field and to add to that—now I respect magazines that do otherwise; for example *Hecate, Feminist Studies* have their poems—but we made our choice and stuck with it. There is one more thing and that is the argument of credibility. We are, I think,

thought to be the most credible of women's studies journals to a certain audience, an academic audience. I've had person after person come in and say *Signs* convinced the dean or department chairperson and the credibility lies, in part, in that purity.[44]

This bid for academic credibility also necessitated the expression of feminist political advocacy in rational rather than emotional language. There was little trace of the manifesto's explicit appeal to moral rage and action. Unlike *Frontiers,* the editors of *Signs* preferred detached, intricately argued, specialized rational analysis—the language that marks the boundaries of modern scholarly discourse. Compared to the quotation from Germaine Greer's article in *Frontiers* on the limitation of contraceptive options, William Bremner and David Kretser's article in *Signs* on the same topic provides a striking contrast in style, voice, tone, and conventions.

In the last twenty years, new contraceptive techniques for females have received wide publicity and use. Over 20 percent of American women in the reproductive age group used oral contraceptives in 1973. Other measures, particularly the intrauterine device, are also very popular. With increasing use of these techniques has come increasing awareness of their hazards. Although the risks for an individual woman using either oral contraceptives or an intrauterine device are extremely small, they are certainly present and have contributed to heightened pressure for alternative means of contraception. An increasingly voiced feeling has been that if there are to be definite health risks associated with adequate contraception, these risks should be shared between male and female partners. . . . The desirability of having a wider range of contraceptive techniques available has become apparent and has led to funding for research along these lines.[45]

Bremner and Kretser differ from Greer in their use of detached tone, their choice of passive voice, their assumption of third-person narrative, their lack of emotional language, and particularly their highlighting of the academically sanctioned "funding for research" as a social change strategy.

Bremner and Kretser's political subtlety was in keeping with Stimpson's attempts to differentiate her journal from nonacademic feminist publications. In one of her most controversial moves she replaced the politically specific term *feminist scholarship* with the politically ambiguous phrase *the new scholarship on women*. "*Signs* was unabashedly an academic journal," she recalls. "It was never designed to be a bridge between the academic and the non-academic community. We said from the beginning that we were going to use academic language. I very deliberately coined the term the 'new scholarship about women' and defended that choice in several editorials."[46]

Indeed, Stimpson's promotion of the phrase was motivated by her belief that practitioners of women's studies were as indebted to the traditional academy as they were to the community women's movement for the nature and content of their field.

> I deliberately chose a term that was overarching, a term that embraced as many methods and as many sources of ideas as possible, because a lot of the ideas that have shaped feminist scholarship, the new scholarship about women, have not come out of the women's movement. . . . *Signs* is an academic journal which understood the links between feminism and ideas about women. But those were not the only links and a term had to be chosen that reflected plurality. . . . What are the sources of ideas about women—the women's movement, feminist theory, individual disciplines, and within the individual disciplines there is a focus on women and then there are other foci. So you have four sources of ideas about women. . . . And I think the job of women's studies is to bring these four sources together in an intellectually coherent program and then to administer it in our institutions.[47]

But feminist scholars, who viewed any catering to university credibility with suspicion, criticized Stimpson's attention to the traditional university's criteria for style, form, argument, and concept. Charges of elitism and cooptation against the journal and its editors were further exacerbated by Stimpson's decision to impose a hierarchical, rather than collective, editorial structure. According to associate editor Burstyn, "Some feminists may have felt the journal was stylistically too conventional; others that it was structurally too traditional."[48]

Aside from debates about the feminist implication of organizational structure, Stimpson's use of the hierarchical structure associated with scholarly journals, rather than the collective structure popular among community journals, further determined *Signs'* location in the spectrum of community-university identification within the culture of feminist scholarship. Stimpson served as editor-in-chief, with clearly demarcated editorial authority. She was supported by two unsalaried associate editors, Domna Stanton from Barnard College and Joan Burstyn from Rutgers University; one salaried managing editor, Sandra Whisler from the University of Chicago Press; and an editorial assistant, Martha Nelson.

Although *Signs* was fueled by volunteer editorial labor, it was financed by academic sources from educational foundation grants, university release time, and the University of Chicago Press. These financial affiliations, coupled with the editors' explicit embracement of scholarly criteria, gave the journal stability, prestige, and access that eluded less academically identified feminist journals. Its reputation attracted forty-three respected scholars for its editorial board, nineteen scholars and writers for its advisory board, and eleven feminist intellectuals to be its international correspondents.

Signs' identity as the preeminent scholarly feminist journal was further determined by its New York location, its national presence, and its international scope. Stimpson expanded the same matrix that had served Ann Calderwood—the Barnard, Columbia, Sarah Lawrence, Rutgers, New York City network of feminist scholars. Stimpson and the associate editors were based at Barnard College and Douglass College at Rutgers. Twelve members of the advisory board were located on the East Coast; eight from the New York network. Twenty-seven of the consulting editorial board were East Coast-based; eleven were from the New York network.

Stimpson considered the New York locus essential to the journal's identity and scope: "It [Barnard] gave us the New York location. A lot of people were coming through and New York was the center of the women's movement: there were feminists, there were feminist theoreticians, foreign visitors coming through, there were some very intriguing intellects. . . . I think in those early days it had to be in a huge urban area with lots of ideas and activity about women."[49]

Stimpson saw New York as the center of the contemporary women's movement. It is also the center of American publishing, a regional consideration that afforded *Signs* the national presence unavailable to the Boulder-based *Frontiers*. According to the sociologist William Powell, scholars working at colleges and universities in the New York area have greater access to scholarly publishers than those elsewhere.

Several things may limit an author's access to a high quality publisher. . . . For the most part, the degree of access that authors enjoy depends on their location in social networks. Academic status is important because it enhances an author's ability to make personal contact with an editor. . . . Other things being equal, academics at geographically peripheral universities will have less access, as will scholars located at less prestigious universities. An important exception to this rule is that academics at less prestigious universities in the New York metropolitan area will profit from their geographic proximity.[50]

The enormous ambition of its editors' vision was signaled by the journal's international scope. For example, the United Nations declared 1976 as the International Women's Year, and Stimpson was able to include U.N. international correspondents as consultants. With University of Chicago Press backing and a Ford Foundation grant, associate editor Stanton attended the first United Nations Congress on Women in Mexico City and traveled to Germany, Italy, and Spain to solicit manuscripts of foreign scholarship.[51]

Stimpson used the New York network further to recruit foreign scholars through U.N. contacts. But it was the publication of papers from the 1976 Wellesley College Conference on Women and Development that secured *Signs'* role "in publicizing throughout the world the work of American scholars, and in bringing the work of foreign scholars to the attention of its readers in the United States."[52] The special issue (Volume 3, number 1) included research, reports, and reviews on women's issues in Argentina, Brazil, Cameroun, Ghana, Guatemala, Israel, Java, Lebanon, Lesotho, Malay, Mexico, Nigeria, Peru, Turkey, South Africa, and the West Indies.

In other issues from 1975 through 1977, *Signs* paralleled *Feminist Studies* in publishing research on West European subjects. Unlike its feminist contemporaries, *Signs* also published the work of many feminist scholars who were not Western. By late 1977, when *Frontiers* was struggling into existence and *Feminist Studies* had finally regrouped at the University of Maryland, *Signs* had become the premiere American publication of feminist scholarship and was avidly vying for the same role in an international forum.

Stylistically and conceptually, *Signs* attended to the university from within the newly professionalized culture of feminist scholarship. Because it was created by one of America's most prestigious university presses, it is not surprising that the journal is identified with a university. Perhaps the surprise is how palpably radical its contents were under such circumstances. Early articles examined the intersection of racism and sexism (Diane K. Lewis, "A Response to Inequality: Black Women, Racism and Sexism" [Volume 3, number 2]); violence against women (Rochelle Semmel Albin, "Psychological Studies of Rape" and Edward Shorter, "On Writing the History of Rape" [Volume 3, number 2], and Judith Herman and Lisa Hirschman, "Father-Daughter Incest" [Volume 2, number 4]; capitalism and patriarchy (Linda Gordon, "A Socialist View of Women's Studies" [Volume 1, number 2], Mary Jo Buhle, "Socialist Women and the 'Girl Strikers,' Chicago, 1910" [Volume 1, number 4], and Heidi Hartmann, "Capitalism, Patriarchy, and Job Segregation by Sex" [Volume 1, number 3, part 2]); reproductive control (Mary Chamie, "Sexuality and Birth Control among Lebanese Couples" [Volume 3, number 1]; Bremner and Kretser, "Contraceptives for Males" [Volume 1, number 2], and Catherine Watson, "Review Essay: Abortion" [Volume 2, number 3]); prostitution (James Brundage, "Prostitution in the Medieval Canon Law" [Volume 1, number 4]); power (Volume 1, number 4, a special issue); women in poverty (Susan A. Hertz, "The Politics of the Welfare Mother's Movement: A Case Study" [Volume 2, number 3]); and the nature of power ("Viewpoint: Power and Powerlessness" [Volume 1, number 1]).

Many articles offered harsh and systemic analyses that rivaled treatment of these topics in community publications. *Signs* provided a forum of institutional authority that presented a number of feminist critiques of women's oppression and experience. Stimpson's bid for academic legitimacy and institutional power was successful, but, as she explained in "Women as Knowers," she was not blind to the limitations of her strategy. "Unless higher education has the wit and will to change utterly, which it cannot do unless American society changes, it will continue to be easier to footnote an article about the history of child care than to insist that universities have enough child care facilities to enable men and women to combine professionalism, affectionate parenting, and more than a dab of domesticity." [53]

Complicated by the quickly changing, dual contexts of an embattled community movement, and a retrenched university system, Stimpson's dilemma—how to keep a scholarship of activism and social change from becoming confined to the boundaries of the text and isolated within the discourse of a few specialized scholars—became a challenge that editors of *Signs, Feminist Studies,* and *Frontiers* wrestled with for the next ten years.

Notes

1. "Letter to Our Readers," *Frontiers* 1 (Fall 1975): iv.

2. The founding *Frontiers'* Editorial Collective included Kathi George, Renee Horowitz, Elizabeth Jameson, Carol Pearson, Alanna Preussner, Mary Rohn, and Marilyn Sawin. For the purposes of this study, members of the collective are identified as "editors."

3. "Letter to Our Readers," iv.

4. Interview with editor Kathi George, Boulder, Colorado, January 14, 1985.

5. Interview with editor Carol Pearson, College Park, Maryland, May 12, 1985.

6. Interview with Kathi George, Boulder, Colorado, January 21, 1985.

7. Interview with Carol Pearson.

8. Interview with Kathi George, January 21, 1985.

9. Interview with Kathi George, Boulder, Colorado, January 15, 1989.

10. "Manuscript Policy," *Frontiers* 2 (Spring 1977): ii.

11. Germaine Greer, "Feminism and Fertility," *Frontiers* 1 (Spring 1976): 17.

12. Newsletters include *Windhaven: Toward a Feminist and Humanitarian Fiction* (Seattle) and *The Witch and the Chameleon: Feminist Science Fiction Magazine* (Hamilton, Ontario).

13. Lee Chambers-Schiller and Nancy Mann, "Draft *Frontiers* letter to Vol. 8, no. 3" (unpublished), 3; interview with editor Elizabeth Jameson, College Park, Maryland, May 10, 1985.

14. Chambers-Schiller and Mann, "Draft of letter to Vol. 8, no. 3," 5.

15. Interview with editor Charlotta Hensley, Boulder, Colorado, January 21, 1985.

16. In separate interviews, Charlotta Hensley and Kathi George voiced unsolicited concern over the identification of their journal as "regional." Each believed that some administrators at the University of Colorado at Boulder had misidentified *Frontiers* as a regional, local, or in-house journal. In addition, they were concerned that some portions of the general feminist academic audience had misinterpreted their journal as regional. Interview with Kathi George, January 21, 1985.

17. Interview with Kathi George, Boulder, Colorado, January 17, 1985.

18. Interview with Charlotta Hensley.

19. John McDermott, "The Laying on of Culture," *Nation*, March 10, 1969, 296–301.

20. Jay Mechling, "If They Can Build a Square Tomato: Notes toward a Holistic Approach to Regional Studies," *Prospects IV: An Annual of American Culture Studies* (1979): 59–77.

21. Lawrence Buell, "The New England Renaissance and American Literary Ethnocentrism," *Prospects X: An Annual of American Culture Studies* (1985): 411–12, 413–14.

22. Kathi George referred to this phenomena as an "East Coast/West Coast sorority" that bypasses her journal. Interview with Kathi George, January 21, 1985. This sentiment was echoed at the Third National Conference of Women in

Print, Berkeley, May 31, 1985. During the workshop "An East Coast/West Coast Bias," *Calyx* editor Margarita Donnally complained that feminist publishers in the Midwest suffer from funding shortages because they are peripheral to the "power circles" on each coast.

23. Sherna Berger Gluck, "Women's Oral History: The Second Decade," *Frontiers* 7, no. 1 (1983): 1.

24. Susan H. Armitage, "The Next Step," *Frontiers* 7, no. 1 (1983): 100.

25. Jane Mace, "Women Talking: Feminism and Adult Literacy Work," 38–43; Sydney Stahl Weinberg, "The World of Our Mothers: Family, Work, and Education in the Lives of Jewish Immigrant Women," 71–79; and Evelyn Shakir, "Syrian-Lebanese Women Tell Their Story," 9–13.

26. Elizabeth Jameson and David Lenfest, "From Oral to Visual: A First-Timer's Introduction to Media Production," 25–31; Dine Sands, "Using Oral History to Chart the Course of Illegal Abortions in Montana," 32–37; Lucille Jake, Evelyn James, and Pamela Bunte, "The Southern Paiute Woman in a Changing Society," 44–49; Phaye Poliakoff, "The Pebble Lounge: Oral Histories of Go-Go Dancers," 56–60; Corky Bush, "Telling Our Life Stories," 80–83; Katherine Jensen, "Woman as Subject, Oral History as Method," 84–86; Mary Aickin Rothschild, "Using Oral History to Find the 'Common Woman': An Arizona Project," 87–90; and Sue Davidson, "Aki Kato Kurose: Portrait of an Activist," 91–97.

27. Interview with editor Michèle Barale, Boulder, Colorado, January 16, 1985.

28. Catharine R. Stimpson, "The Making of *Signs*," *Radical Teacher* (1980): 23.

29. Linda Kirby and Cristine C. Rom, *"Signs," Serials Review* 5 (October–December 1979): 5.

30. Joan N. Burstyn, "A Journal of One's Own: *Signs* in the Evolution of Women's Studies, 1975–1980," paper delivered at the annual meeting of the Organization of American Historians, Los Angeles, April 1–4, 1981, 11.

31. Burstyn, "A Journal of One's Own," 4.

32. Ibid., 4.

33. Ibid., 17.

34. According to *Signs'* editor Barbara Gelpi, the journal was treated so well at the University of Chicago Press that it was nicknamed "the Princess" by the Journals Division of that press. Interview with Barbara Gelpi, Palo Alto, California, June 3, 1985.

35. Interview with editor Catharine R. Stimpson, New Brunswick, New Jersey, August 5, 1985.

36. Catharine R. Stimpson, "What Matter Mind: A Theory about the Practice of Women's Studies," *Women's Studies* 1, no. 3 (1973): 307, 308

37. "Editorial," *Signs* 1 (Summer 1976): vi.

38. Stimpson, "What Matter Mind," 308–9.

39. Interview with Catharine R. Stimpson.

40. Burstyn, "A Journal of One's Own," 1.

41. Ibid., 7.

42. Catharine R. Stimpson, "Editing *Signs,*" *Bulletin of the Midwest Modern Language Association* 12, no. 1 (1977): 37.

43. Kirby and Rom, *"Signs,"* 6.

44. Interview with Catharine R. Stimpson.

45. William J. Bremner and David M. Kretser, "Contraceptives for Males," *Signs* 1, no. 2 (1975): 387–88.

46. Interview with Catharine R. Stimpson.

47. Ibid.

48. Burstyn, "A Journal of One's Own," 11.

49. Interview with Catharine R. Stimpson.

50. William W. Powell, *Getting into Print: The Decision Making Process in Scholarly Publishing* (Chicago: University of Chicago Press, 1985), 182, 205.

51. Burstyn, "A Journal of One's Own," 6.

52. Ibid., 7.

53. Catharine R. Stimpson, "Woman as Knowers," in *Feminist Visions: Toward a Transformation of the Liberal Arts Curriculum,* ed. Diane L. Fowlkes and Charlotte S. McClure (Alabama: University of Alabama Press, 1984), 23.

chapter five

Defining the Political Parameters
of a Feminist Scholarship

The emergence of a distinctive feminist academic community, in some way different from the other feminist "community," creates all kinds of tensions. . . . We know that we want to have a movement of political purpose as well as of academic purpose and not feel our lives pulled apart as we're being identified with one or another of two communities—we wish the communities were one.

Claire Moses, manager and editor,
Feminist Studies

The broader, nonacademic feminist movement was—and has remained—the source of political authenticity for the editors of *Feminist Studies, Frontiers,* and *Signs.* Although all three journals are now firmly entrenched within the university, the realization of feminist movement goals through politicized scholarship continues to motivate them: "the point of our work is to change the world. Like women's studies generally . . . feminist criticism began with the assumption that we make our own knowledge and are constantly remaking it in the terms with which history provides—and that in making knowledge we act upon the power relations of our lives [and] radically challenge modes of thinking that are dominant in our world."[1]

By combining the political analyses they cultivated as activists with the scholarly standards they inherited as young academics, the editors of *Feminist Studies, Frontiers,* and *Signs* challenged one of the most deeply ingrained modes of thinking in academia: the liberal ideal of value-free scholarship. In the university, and in the larger American culture, the domain of the political and the domain of the scholarly are still constructed in a dichotomous relationship that posits political relevance and scholarly quality as antithetical.

In contrast, feminist criticism, along with other contemporary modes of criticism, asserts that all scholarship is based on ideological assumptions about power relations. The denial of politics in scholarship is itself a political act that has material consequences.[2] "Feminist theory, for the most part, assumes that our experience of history, even history of our own lives, is constructed, is a story we [feminist scholars] tell ourselves, is ideological, and it assumes that ideologies are political, that they sustain or challenge relations of power."[3]

Unlike traditional academic journals, their editors have deliberately situated *Feminist Studies, Frontiers,* and *Signs* within the cultural tension that exists between the realm of the scholarly and the realm of the political. But the journals are operating in a larger cultural meaning system so pervasive and embedded in language that it is impossible to transcend the power of its constructs totally. Consequently, when interviewed for this project, the editors of *Feminist Studies, Frontiers,* and *Signs* found that they could only discuss their positions within the tension between the scholarly and the political by assigning specific attributes to each domain.

The limitation of language that tended to dichotomize these domains in discussion of manuscript selection is much less evident in the text of the journals, where political and scholarly attributes are usually mutually dependent and interactive. These attributes are organized into a "spectrum of scholarly and political criteria" recognized by the larger culture of feminist scholarship and applied in the practices and processes of feminist academic journals. The criteria that the editors associate with the scholarly domain are those that most academic editors use: "quality of presentation" and "contribution to knowledge."

Quality of presentation includes stylistic considerations of structure, organization, clarity, grammar, and logic. The journals require that authors use accepted academic forms of presentation in submitted manuscripts as defined by the *Chicago Manual of Style* for *Feminist Studies* and *Signs* and by the Modern Language Association Style Sheet for *Frontiers.* But stylistic problems do not preclude manuscript selection; a skilled editor can help restructure a poorly presented piece of research. More important than stylistic concerns is the work's contribution to knowledge, which involves evaluation of the argument's complexity, sophistication, and originality as well as how the topic and approach are "embedded in the current debate and discussion of various critical issues in the field."[4] Such qualities are often elusive and only tacitly shared in academia but are easily recognized by the broader, largely nonfeminist, academic culture in which the journals are situated.

It is the political, rather than the scholarly, criteria that feminist editors use that differentiate their journals from others. The editors of *Feminist Studies, Frontiers,* and *Signs* tolerate the expression of a wide range of political viewpoints when reviewing manuscripts for publication. They eagerly solicit manuscripts that contain "strong statements," "contrasting views" and "controversial stances."[5] But such political diversity is firmly within the parameters of a single encompassing political criterion: "feminist." "Feminist" is the preeminent political criterion for the editors because it marks the outermost boundaries of their enterprise and distinguishes it from all other scholarly publications.

> The first cut in manuscript selection for publication in *Feminist Studies* is easy. . . . Some manuscripts were obviously sent to the wrong place because they are not feminist or barely feminist or something like that.[6]

> In terms of manuscripts, if there's no feminist perspective . . . things that were scholarship but had no consciousness of feminism, of gender inequality let's say, but were simply reporting—that is not very interesting scholarship to *Signs*.[7]

> Of course, a *Frontiers'* piece has to be good . . . to be well thought out, sophisticated . . . current to the field. And, of course, feminist.[8]

The meaning and use of the term *feminist* and the question of what comprises feminist scholarship provide the basis of a central, ongoing discussion that has filled the pages of the journals since their inceptions. No encompassing definition of *feminist* or *feminism* can fully account for the range of theories and applications produced within the discipline. Rather, feminist scholarship is made up of dynamic constituent attributes that mark the outermost boundaries of its purviews. The constant renegotiation of those boundaries, as well as the meanings and application of their identifying attributes, have been debated in a number of forums by the editors, authors, and audiences of the journals.

In the early 1980s, the journals featured a series of debates about the continued relevance of a particular attribute long associated with feminism—the belief that "the personal is political." A highly esteemed feminist scholar, Jean Bethke Elshtain, had just published *Public Man, Private Woman* in which she criticized the use of classical Western images in feminist critical thought.[9] In a commentary initiated by Judith Stacey, an editor of *Feminist Studies,* Elshtain was criticized as representing a dangerous new direction in feminist scholarship that Stacey called the "New Conservative Feminism." The writing Stacey identified and criticized was by established and esteemed feminists and included Elshtain's *Public Man, Private Woman,* Betty Friedan's *The Second Stage,* Carol McMillan's *Women, Reason and Nature,* and Alice Rossi's *A Biosocial Perspective on Parenting. Feminist Studies* cited all the authors as examples of self-identified feminists whose reactionary formulations repudiated a central, definitive constituent of feminism known as "sexual politics" and its epigram "the personal is political." [10]

Kate Millet originated the term *sexual politics* in 1970. It is radical feminism's representation of the idea that "woman" and "man" are historically constructed social categories institutionalized within public and personal relationships of power. It asserts that acceptance of these categories and institutions as natural or universal ideologically obscures the reality of women's systematic oppression in society. Sexual politics maintains that the systematic domination of women by men is institutionalized in all aspects of public and personal life. All arenas of female experience—whether located in the boardroom, the factory, the kitchen, or the bedroom—are shaped by gendered relations of power.

This insight came under renewed scrutiny during the conservative resurgence of the 1980s. The New Right claimed personal and family issues as its own and advocated a return to traditional family structures and restricted gender roles. New conservatism coincided with a crisis in feminist personal life in the 1980s. Feminists who had managed to create alternate living structures for themselves during the experimental atmosphere of the 1960s found it increasingly difficult to maintain those structures during the more reactionary 1980s. Some feminists who had delayed child-bearing in the 1970s found that they had only temporarily circumvented the sexual division of labor inherent in society's methods of child-rearing. Still others found themselves worn down by the demands of continually living against the grain of the dominant culture.[11]

Such public backlash and private frustration found voice in the works of Elshtain, Friedan, McMillan, and Rossi. In *Public Man, Private Woman,* Elshtain argued that political scrutiny collapses the boundaries between public and private life, erodes both realms, and leaves each vulnerable to the forces of bureaucratic capitalism and totalitarian socialism. She called for an end to the feminist politicization of family and personal life and the creation of "social feminism" that would preserve the nurturing ethics of family life and ultimately transform public life into an "ethical polity." [12]

Stacey, however, rebutted that any analysis devoid of sexual politics is not authentically feminist because it essentializes women, inverts the meaning of feminism, and loses "the capacity to analyze the social processes through which individuals, cultural forms, and social systems are engendered." She argued that "an attack on sexual politics is an attack on the radical core of feminist thought and practice" and "initiates a new and conservative terrain of struggle over what feminism will mean in the next historical period." [13]

The struggle for that terrain continued in a special issue of *Feminist Studies* that featured "Guilt and Shame in the Women's Movement: The Radical Ideal of Action and Its Meaning for Feminist Intellectuals" by Berenice Fisher. Fisher questioned the personal moral code implicit in feminism as it relates to the movement's ideal of political action, "a politics that both fears and emphasizes judgement of individual adequacy (whether one is a good enough, radical enough feminist) and takes it as a main way to keep the movement on course, misconstrues the role of judgement, narrows our range of political options, and weakens our sense of our own capacities to employ them." [14]

In "Is Personal Life Still a Political Issue?" Barbara Haber argued that the 1980s' crisis in political and personal life required heterosexual feminists to reflect on the structures of their private lives and "take the responsibility for restoring the critique of the family and personal life to its primary position in feminist debate." [15]

Frontiers' commitment to the continued relevance of "the personal is political" never waned. As part of their effort to address the experiences of community women, the editors regularly presented political analyses of personal issues. By 1980, the journal had published five theme issues devoted to the politics of the private sphere: "The Politics of Reproduction" (Volume 1, number 2); "Therapy from Feminist Perspectives" (Volume 1, number 3); "Woman as Victim: Sexual Violence and Battery" (Volume 2, number 1); "Mothers and Daughters" (Volume 3, number 2); and "Equal Opportunity Addiction: Women, Alcohol, and Drugs" (Volume 4, number 2).

Signs indicated its growing concern over the politics of the personal by organizing two symposia on the subject. The summer 1979 issue (Volume 4, number 4) featured "Viewpoint: On *Of Woman Born*," which examined public and private accounts of motherhood. The autumn 1981 issue (Volume 7, number 1), "Viewpoint: On 'Compulsory Heterosexuality and Lesbian Existence': Defining the Issues," debated the political meaning of lesbian identity. Like *Feminist Studies, Signs'* special attention to personal politics was heightened by the New Right's appropriation of the family and sexuality. In "The Sexual Politics of the New Right: Understanding the 'Crisis of Liberalism' for the 1980s," which appeared in the journal's spring 1982 issue, Zillah Eisenstein defined the New Right's challenge to feminism: "In a fundamental sense, the sexual politics of the New Right is implicitly antifeminist and racist: it desires to establish a model of the traditional white patriarchal family by dismantling the welfare state and by removing wage-earning women from the labor force and returning them to the home. . . . The New Right assault is aimed at feminism precisely because it is women's liberal feminist consciousness about their rights to equality that is the major radicalizing force of the 1980s."

The debate over the meaning and limits of "the personal is political" eventually erupted into what has come to be known as the "sexuality debates" in the academy and the "sex wars" in the community. Participants in the sexuality debates, with the use of the journals, pushed the epigram into the deepest recesses of human psyche—the interconnections between responses to sexual pleasure and sexual danger. An unexpected and insular debate, the conflict was rooted in two seemingly compatible critiques that originated in the late 1960s. One analyzed how patriarchy shapes female sexuality into dominant or submissive relations of power. Proponents extended their analysis of male domination of female sexuality to include rape, degrading images of women in advertising, the myth of the vaginal orgasm, and pornography. A second critique explored constructions of female sexuality free of patriarchal distortion. This perspective pursued alternative concepts and expressions of female sexuality and erotica.

Initially, the search by one critique for female sexual protection and the other for female sexual pleasure were not considered exclusive positions. Throughout the 1970s, *Feminist Studies, Frontiers,* and *Signs* published essays representing compatible analyses from both groups. As late as 1982, *Feminist Studies* confidently published a comprehensive review by editor Martha Vicinus, who summarized literature featuring both critiques' conceptions of sexuality. Commenting on Vicinus's review, B. Ruby Rich observed that "she could not have known that her article would appear simultaneously with the disappearance of the landscape it described." [16]

The conflict was unexpected but not unforeseeable. Although both critiques shared the same origins, the group organized around issues of male sexual domination became the more public and influential of the two. Eventually known as the antipornography critique, it grew in membership, visibility, and influence through the strategic boycotts and educational work of organizations such as Women Against Pornography (WAP) and Women Against Violence Against Women (WAVA). By 1980, the antipornography critique had gained hegemony over the movement's interpretation of "the personal is political" while the alternate critique increasingly but unobtrusively challenged accepted notions about the nature and limits of female sexual pleasure.

Despite its authority, there was some uneasiness about the antipornography critique and its strategies. Given the sexual conservatism of the 1980s, antipornography feminists were uncomfortably aware of their surface resemblance to New Right censors and carefully attended to differentiating their ideas about sex and power from those of conservative groups. The New Right, Moral Majority, and other conservative interests had focused on a number of personal and family issues in the 1980 conservative electoral landslide. The simultaneous loss of feminist influence in the wider society, coupled with the crisis of personal life that many feminists experienced, foregrounded the oncoming split. Ironically, the threat to antipornography feminists came from inside, rather than outside, the contemporary women's movement.

The sex wars were publicly initiated when the community-based art journal *Heresies* challenged the antipornography critique by publishing a special "Sex Issue" in 1981.[17] The issue pointedly celebrated mixing female sexual pleasure with sexual danger by depicting in image, argument, and verse all forms of "politically incorrect sex," including sadomasochistic practices, butch-femme roles, and violent pornography. Although the concern seemed obscure concern from an outsider's point of view, the *Heresies* declaration of the sex wars is important because it illustrates how feminist critics often move to the margins of accepted social practices in order to view them at their most basic. The periphery of society enables feminist critics to gain a unique vantage point on patriarchal constructions of sexuality, "an intersection of the political, social, economic, historical, personal, and experiential." [18]

In 1982, the spring following the *Heresies* "Sex Issue," the sex wars erupted at a conference at Barnard College: "The Scholar and the Feminist IX: Toward a Politics of Sexuality." The conference has since been recognized as the event that "provides a convenient before-and-after landmark delineating the terrain of feminism and sexuality." [19] The event featured forty participants who represented a wide variety of analytic perspectives on sexuality, including the two polarized critiques that had evolved from the radical insights of sexual politics. A few panels featured discussions of the connection between sexual danger and sexual pleasure.

Three prominent antipornography organizations, Women Against Pornography, Women Against Violence Against Women, and New York Radical Feminists, formed an ad hoc "Coalition for a Feminist Sexuality and Against Sado-Masochism" to denounce publicly the conference participants whom they considered proponents of antifeminist sexuality. Among other tactics, the coalition produced and distributed a leaflet entitled "We Protest," which named and condemned specific individuals and organizations as proponents of sadomasochism, pornography, prostitution, adult-child sexual relations, and butch-femme sexual role-playing—all practices the coalition considered perpetuations of patriarchal power relations.

As is often the case with such seemingly parochial factioning in the women's movement, the conference had real-world repercussions. Fifteen hundred copies of the conference diary of planning notes, panels, and events were confiscated by Barnard's administration, and the Helena Rubenstein Foundation withdrew its financial support of the conference. Participants named as "sexually marginal" in the leaflet were "disinvited to feminist panels and conferences; projects in which they were even marginally involved were blacklisted." [20] In response to the "We Protest" leaflet, three hundred participants and members of the feminist scholarly community signed a petition condemning the "uses of McCarthyite tactics to silence other voices." [21]

The Barnard confrontation produced a split in the movement that had bearing on the culture of feminist scholarship, its conferences, and— ultimately—its journals with a degree of intensity and passion not often seen in academic circles. As the editors of *Signs* described the emotional, political, and intellectual importance of the confrontation,

> This latest political split . . . has been painful for participants and observers alike. . . . At times many of us have wished that the debate would simply fade away, or magically resolve itself, without our having to take personal stock of our confusion about sexuality, violence, pornography, and power. But when feelings run so high, on so central a political concern, there is, we sense, more than a mere factionalization, personality conflict, or a natural process of organizational subdivision at stake. The debates and their intensity signal important issues that come at a critical moment in the history of our movement.[22]

Kathi George, characteristically, put the matter more succinctly: "People doing work on sexuality were bombed out of the water by Barnard. It was a powerful piece of politics."[23]

The original "We Protest" leaflet and the countering anticensorship petition became the two defining documents of the Barnard confrontation and were archived by their publication in the spring 1983 issue of *Feminist Studies*. Editor Rayna Rapp recalls:

> We sat in my apartment late on a Sunday afternoon. How well I remember it. I felt very responsible, because Judy [Walkowitz] and I brought it up. Judy had been on the planning committee of the Barnard Conference, and I had signed the petition protesting the leaflet. We said, "Well, it would be important to give this some coverage." We agreed with the petition against censorship, but in order to show why that document was right, we had to show the scurrilous nature of the offending leaflet. So we created an archive by publishing both documents.[24]

Although the publication was well-intentioned, Carole Vance, who organized the Barnard Conference and was its keynote speaker, later pointed out that the editors of *Feminist Studies* underestimated the transformative power engendered by publishing such documents in an academic journal: "This is not an academic debate which has no repercussions in the real world. This is not a document from an ancient feminist dispute, an interesting datum. . . . Publishing the leaflet had increased the scope of damage, now to national and international levels . . . imagine yourself named, with the leaflet now in libraries to be read by employers, colleagues, and students."[25]

Mixing the political immediacy of the women's movement with the scholarly detachment of the academy complicates the role of feminist editors in the culture of feminist scholarship. To be a feminist editor one must assume a number of available postures: participant, arbiter, archivist, and legitimator. One must also simultaneously immediately participate in and distance oneself from the feminist debate. The editors of *Feminist Studies* responded to the Barnard Conference controversy as participants and arbiters, momentarily suspending their roles as archivists and legitimators. By publishing the "We Protest" leaflet, even as a means of criticism, they recorded, legitimated, preserved, and disseminated a document that associated specific individuals with culturally "suspect" sexual practices. Rapp stresses the importance of reflexive editorial processes in such decisions:

> We had a lot of political discussion about it *after* the fact. We should have discussed it differently prior to publication. Editorial process—everything comes out of the editorial group discussion and we didn't have that beforehand. I don't know what we would have ultimately decided, but I suspect we would have published a summary report of the conference rather than the documents. Or we might have called the women who were named in the document and said, "Your name is named in this document which we are publishing as a protest against it, how do you feel about that?"[26]

The editors immediately published an apology, critical responses by those named in the leaflet, and excised the offending pages from remaining copies of *Feminist Studies*.[27] Yet the damage had been done. Commenting on the general tenor of the debate, B. Ruby Rich observed, "If journals and conferences prove too rugged an environment for productive growth, then perhaps the late 1980s will bear witness to a revival of consciousness-raising groups among women."[28]

Feminist Studies' decision to act as a public forum for the Barnard controversy paralleled external pressure at *Signs* and internal pressure at *Frontiers* to also take sides in the debate. Barbara Gelpi, who edited *Signs* during its tenure at Stanford University from 1980 to 1985, recalls:

> We did the "Viewpoint" forum on the sexuality debates as a response to the many requests that we take a stand about the Barnard Conference. We didn't think that was appropriate; we realized that we hadn't even been at the Barnard Conference. But we realized that participants from both sides of the controversy wanted to use

the journals as a forum for airing their differences. Sexuality was a big and divisive issue at the Humbolt NWSA Conference and more generally among feminists. Carole Vance, who had connections with *Feminist Studies* and *Signs* came to us and said, "Now what about this? We need to get these issues out."[29]

The editors of *Signs* decided not to involve the journal in the controversy, but instead provided "a means of stepping back and assessing the debates themselves."[30] Given their different histories and intentions, it is not surprising that *Signs* would deem it inappropriate to criticize the politics of either camp in the sexuality debates, whereas *Feminist Studies* felt compelled to take a stand against the "We Protest" leaflet. *Signs'* editor Estelle Freedman compared the political perspectives of the two journals: "Compared to *Feminist Studies* there is much less of the political in *Signs, Feminist Studies* has much more of a concern with contemporary politics and *Signs* tends to step back and try to do scholarship that we make politically relevant in the editorial, or we try to get authors to speak to current issues in feminist scholarship. . . . I think that we at Stanford have opened *Signs* up to more political concerns than previously, but I still think relative to other journals *Signs* is less political."[31]

In this case, the academically inclined *Signs* was not alone in pushing for a more distanced and intellectual examination of the debate. Commenting on the Barnard confrontation for the radical community newspaper *off our back*, Claudette Charbonneau argued that "without a clear understanding of the intellectual foundations and meanings of our movement, we will be stranded. Very simply, we need to hang onto ideas. 'The Scholar and the Feminist IX: Towards a Politics of Sexuality' at Barnard abdicated that responsibility. Midway through, I realized that they had thrown out the 'feminist' promised in the title. By the end . . . they succeeded in throwing out the 'scholar' as well."[32]

In an attempt to fill the void, *Signs,* in "Forum: The Feminist Sexuality Debates" (Autumn 1984), tried to deescalate and depolarize the controversy by moving it from the heated realm of political confrontation to the cooler one of intellectual discourse. The forum dissected and critically examined the philosophical foundations of both critiques of sexuality, which led to a reexamination of the assumptions and terms long associated with "the personal is political." Ann Ferguson, a feminist philosopher, argued that the opposing critiques represented the polarized and inadequately realized legacies of early feminist radical and libertarian concepts of sexuality. Irene Diamond, a political scientist, and Lee Quimby, a literary scholar, connected that inadequacy to the language of "control" adopted from Marxism by the early women's movement to construct its concept of sexual politics. They argued that anchoring the feminist discourse in the language of sexual control is problematic because such language is "devoid of the ambiguities and richness of human experience." The Berkeley sociologist Ilene Philipson continued with an examination of the inherited ahistorical, universalized understandings of patriarchy used by the antipornography critique and of the sexual repression used by its opponents.[33]

This initial, necessarily tentative, attempt by *Signs* to examine the ideological complexities underlying the Barnard confrontation opened an explicit reconsideration of the meaning of the term *feminist*. A flood of research followed, and *Frontiers* published a special issue in 1986: "Sex, Sexuality, Contraception, Abortion, and Reproductive Technology" (Volume 9, number 1) that featured editor Michèle Barale's extensive review of the new literature: *Powers of Desire: The Politics of Sexuality* by Ann Snitow, *Pleasure and Danger: Exploring Female Sexuality* by Carole Vance, and *Coming to Power: Writing and Graphics on Lesbian S/M* by Samois.[34]

The same work was featured in 1986 in *Feminist Studies* in a review essay by the film critic B. Ruby Rich, illustrating that there is no longer a hegemonic hold on the interpretation of "the personal is political" in the culture of feminist scholarship. Throughout the sex wars, the journals were intimately involved in renegotiating the meaning of that concept—from the Vicinus essay of 1980, through the archiving and arbitration of the Barnard confrontation, to the initial translation of that confrontation into reasoned feminist reformulations of sexuality, and then to the retrospective review essays of the now-reestablished discourse.

More often, the editors and their readers debated attaching the term *feminist* to other existing or emerging sociopolitical approaches. In the late 1980s, the journals debated the affiliation of "feminist" with poststructuralist criticism. Generally, incorporating French poststructuralist theories into the journals paralleled the theories' introduction into wider American feminist circles. Specifically, the debate emerged in each journal in a manner that reflected the journal's position within the community-academy polarity.

Feminist poststructuralism has social roots in the 1968 Paris uprisings and intellectual roots in the work of Simone de Beauvoir. It has a sizable nonacademic following in France but found its way into the women's movement in the United States through academic networks, particularly those working in literary theory and the romance languages. The term *poststructuralism* represents a range of critical approaches developed during the 1970s and 1980s from the work of Jacques Derrida in deconstruction, Jacques Lacan in psychoanalysis, Julia Kristeva in semiotics, Louis Althusser in Marxism, and Michel Foucault in historiography. These approaches vary considerably, but all contend that individual and social meaning is constructed in language. Social meaning is neither unified nor fixed, but an ever-changing plurality arbitrarily attached and contingent upon its discursive context. Language does not simply reflect social reality, it constitutes social reality. Because it has the power to constitute reality but has no fixed meaning and is always open to challenge and redefinition, language becomes a site of political struggle. As Chris Weedon, a feminist poststructuralist, explains, "Once language is understood in terms of competing discourses, competing ways of giving meaning to the world, which imply differences in the organization of social power, then language becomes an important site of political struggle."[35]

Like feminism, poststructuralism does not recognize—and hence transcends—society's dichotomy of public and private realms of experience. It provides models for scholars who want to challenge the existence and authority of hegemonic realities, like patriarchy, that confine them. It confers academic legitimacy to "those limited, awkward, and often idiosyncratic artifacts that are the chief evidence of women's past."[36] Poststructuralism analyzes how the cultural category *woman* is socially constructed as a derivative and defining complement to that of *man*. Consequently, poststructuralism became a critical approach of great scholarly and political interest to feminist scholars. The approaches most publicized in American feminist circles are those of Hélène Cixous, Luce Irigaray, Julia Kristeva, and Monique Wittig. Although they differ significantly in some respects, each follows the assumption that *woman* is an arbitrarily unified invention of the dominant symbolic order.[37] These theoreticians agree that the individual identity *woman* and the collective identity *women* are cultural fictions that define the centrality of their binary complements, *man* and *men*. Mary Poovey, an American poststructuralist, explains the problem of attaching "feminist" to an ideology based on this assumption: "if a 'woman' is falsely unified, and if one's identity is not given . . . by anatomy, the 'woman'—or even women—cannot remain a legitimate rallying point for political actions. Real historical women have been (and are) oppressed, and the ways and means of that oppression need to be analyzed and fought. But at the same time, we need to be ready to abandon the binary thinking that has stabilized women as a group that could be collectively oppressed." [38]

Editorial decisions about when, how, and whether to include post-structuralist work are important to this study because they illuminate the relative political and social positions of *Feminist Studies, Frontiers,* and *Signs.* The ensuing debates reveal not only the process by which a new ideological approach is negotiated into the feminist scholarship but also make explicit which particular constituent attributes of "feminist" must be satisfied for an approach to be included under its rubric.

According to Kathi George and Charlotta Hensley, the editors of *Frontiers* took exception to the exclusivity of poststructuralist approaches.

> Unless it is done brilliantly, it represents the worst tendencies in academic feminism—the stuff that is so arcane, so abstract, so self-absorbed—we viewed it very critically.[39]

> The core publications in women's studies are defined by the academy, *Frontiers* envisions an audience that can be made up of anyone interested in feminism. Can our articles be picked up and understood by a scholar, a student, a community woman using a public library, a newsstand? Can they all read the journal and learn something from it? That we are not so turgid that you have to understand each discipline's defining jargon. A discipline like sociology changes its terms every five years, you couldn't pick up one of their journals and read it even if you wanted to. So we keep ourselves far from the jargon. That's our attention to the community.[40]

Once again, the reservations of *Frontiers* echoed community under-standings of the political obligations of the culture of feminist scholar-ship. The journalist Cara Gendel Ryan admonished feminist intellec-tuals to remember that although they produce knowledge essential to revolutionary practice, the language in which this knowledge is often reproduced creates conditions of domination and exclusion. Early post-structuralist analyses were so abstract, ahistorical, and removed from women's everyday experiences that they raised another of Ryan's concerns: "Intellectuals . . . must expand the scope of their theoretical work by going out into the world to study what they can never learn from theory alone: the concrete conditions of oppression: the specific forms of suffering and exploitation."[41]

Inclusion of poststructuralist work in the pages of *Feminist Studies* followed the path that brought the critique to the attention of American feminist scholarship in general. A special issue celebrating the thirtieth anniversary of Simone de Beauvior's existentialist classic *The Second Sex* was followed in 1981 with an issue that introduced the analyses of Cixous, Irigaray, and Kristeva. It was a contentious introduction because semioticians such as Cixous have argued that the term *feminist* is itself "parasitic upon phallogocentric thought" and should be avoided.[42]

Initially, the editors of *Feminist Studies* published very few poststructuralist pieces, in part because the journal was known for its contextualized and materialist approaches to literature but also because poststructuralist language is too highly specialized for interdisciplinary audiences. However, by the mid 1980s theoretical models drawn from Derrida and Lacan had so influenced feminist literary criticism that *Feminist Studies* editor and contributor Barbara Christian worried that poststructuralism had become the field's "authoritative discourse."[43]

As the influence of poststructuralist approaches grew throughout the 1980s, *Feminist Studies* monitored the "fitful" relationship of deconstruction and feminism in such articles as the literary scholar Annette Kolodny's "Dancing between Left and Right," in which deconstructionists were characterized as "rejecting the historicizing and contextualizing practices of feminism . . . thereby blunting their ability to maintain a critical discourse with real-world engagements."[44]

By 1986, however, the impact of poststructuralist criticism in feminist academic circles in the United States compelled the editors of *Feminist Studies* to publish a special issue to present interpretations, applications, and criticisms in which the attachment of deconstruction to feminism was variously described as "useful and clarifying," "misapprehending and contradictory," and "ambivalent and tense."[45]

Given its international connections, its receptivity to highly abstracted scholarship, and its elite status, *Signs* was much more open to poststructuralist analysis than *Frontiers* and *Feminist Studies* and showcased work by Cixous, then little-known in the United States, in its first issue. In fact, the association of *Signs* with French poststructuralist theory was so well established that poststructuralists approached the journal during the divisive Psych et Po-Mouvement de Liberation des Femmes split in the French women's movement.[46] Asked to take sides, *Signs* again opted to withdraw to the role of archivist and presented an overview of the debate rather than to defend either side. As Barbara Gelpi recalls:

> When the group "Psychoanalyse et Politique" [Psych et Po] was copyrighting the name "Mouvement de Liberation des Femmes," *Questions Feministes* circulated a petition and asked *Signs* to sign it. As with the Barnard petition, we didn't sign, because we felt that we didn't know enough about the issues and we didn't like acting as the forum for one group without hearing from the other. We didn't sign, but we did do a "French Issue" and have published other discussions of the French Question. And though it was taken at that time, because Hélène Cixous was on our board, that *Signs* favored Psych et Po, actually we didn't. We didn't then know the politics of it at all. Learning the issues required a lot of homework.[47]

The special issue on "French Feminist Theory" appeared in 1981 and included translations of, and introductions to, the works of Kristeva, Cixous, and Irigaray. Two critical pieces—one by French theoretician Christine Fauré and another by Susan Mosher Stuard, an American feminist—were also included. The commentaries by Fauré and Stuard in *Signs,* and by Rabine, Poovey, Christian, and Kolodny in *Feminist Studies,* reveal how poststructuralist perspectives bring constituent attributes of feminist scholarship into serious contention:

> Feminism is a visionary politics which declares that a theory is only as good as its practice. To become theoretically sophisticated about how gender and racial hierarchies structure both knowledge and cultural institutions imposes upon us the responsibility to act in the world to dismantle institutionalized inequities. If respectability is achieved at the cost of this visionary politics, then feminist inquiry is rendered an empty, enervated exercise, essentially timid and accommodationist . . . theory devoid of activist politics isn't feminism, but rather pedantry and moral abdication.[48]

A feminist scholarship works to alter the condition of women and make a difference in the world. Violating that goal brings into question whether poststructuralism can be amended to the social change goals of feminist scholarship. Because poststructuralist work is highly abstract, written in specialized language, considers the cultural category *woman* inauthentic, is not interested in the chronological history of public events, and disavows political closure, feminist scholars continue to debate whether it can be affiliated with feminist scholarship without substantial revision.

Such efforts to ascertain and refine the meaning and use of the term *feminist* through debate in the pages of the journals produce much more exacting connotations than those applied behind the scenes in the processes and practices of the journal. The acts of manuscript selection, revision, and editing call for a broader, less nuanced understanding of the term. According to Barale, the central questions include: "Is the article interested in the story of women? Does it analyze women's reactions to their various cultures? The way women live in it. The way they react to it. The way they understand it. The way they write about it. The way they paint it."[49]

Based upon extensive interviews with editors, staff, and consultants; observations of editorial board meetings; and analysis of editorials, reader reports, rejection letters, and policy statements, four attributes place a submitted manuscript within the journals' broadest definition of "feminist":

1. Gender is the primary category of analysis in the argument.
2. The argument emphasizes the relations of power between women and men.
3. The argument centralizes women's experience in a way that does not objectify, victimize, romanticize, or overgeneralize women.
4. The argument is remotely or directly interested in affecting social change.

This analysis examined not only why certain manuscripts were accepted for publication, but also why other manuscripts were considered unsuitable. Consequently, discerning these criteria involved an analysis of both accepted and rejected manuscripts. Although confidentiality prohibits the inclusion of titles, references, or excerpts from specific rejected manuscripts, readers' comments, or rejection letters, representative editorial comments include: "overgeneralizes experience of women," "needs to distinguish more clearly between women and feminists," "a glorifying and superficial portrait of women," "discomfitted by its romantic approach," "denigrates women," "uncritically accepts all of the old male myths . . . including amoral individualism," "sentimental and politically repressive depiction which reinforces gendered roles," "fundamentally elitist in its emphasis," "lacks awareness of race," and "needs political context."

Editors also insist that this broadly defined feminism must be placed, explicitly or implicitly, within the context of other relations of power, which include race, class, and sexual identity. At *Signs*, Barbara Gelpi says the editors understand that "there are other political questions within manuscripts. Classism, racism, heterosexism. They make inadequate and unsophisticated scholarship. I've never rejected an author simply because of racism or heterosexism, but because these factors make for inadequate reporting of facts, unsophisticated analysis or ignorance concerning the complexity of the issues an author has taken on." [50]

The importance of these attendant political criteria has been argued at various points in the history of each journal. The community-minded *Frontiers* has consistently underscored the diversity of female experience by devoting entire issues to the "Native American Issue," "Women on the Western Frontier," "Chicanas in the National Landscape," "Feminism in the Non-Western World," and the pioneering "Lesbian History Issue." For *Feminist Studies,* the use of race, class, and sexual identity was furthered by publishing "Racism and Feminism: A Schism in the Sisterhood" by the philosopher Margaret A. Simons (Volume 5, number 2); "What Has Never Been: An Overview of Lesbian-Feminist Literary Criticism" by Bonnie Zimmerman, a lesbian literary and film scholar (Volume 7, number 3); and "Race, Class, and Gender: Prospects for an All-Inclusive Sisterhood" by Bonnie Thornton Dill, an African-American theorist (Volume 9, number 1).

Signs regularly reviewed new scholarship on race and racism, featuring such articles as "A Response in Inequality: Black Women, Racism and Sexism" by Diane K. Lewis, an anthropologist (Volume 3, number 2) and self-examinatory pieces such as "The Costs of Exclusionary Practices in Women's Studies" (Volume 11, number 2). The editors also examined the political implications of sexual identity by publishing the classic "Compulsory Heterosexuality and Lesbian Existence" by lesbian feminist poet and scholar Adrienne Rich in Volume 5, number 4, and a Viewpoint response, "On 'Compulsory Heterosexuality and Lesbian Existence': Defining the Issues," in Volume 7, number 1.

The inclusion of these attendant political criteria has been argued in various points in the history of the journals. The use of race, class, and sexual identity was derived from the concomitant civil rights-black power, gay liberation, and New Left social movements of the 1960s and 1970s.[51] The history of the inclusion of these political criteria in feminist scholarship is a long and contentious one, just as it was in the broader feminist movement.

In 1980, *Feminist Studies* published an article by Kolodny, "Dancing through the Minefield: Some Observations on the Theory, Practice and Politics of a Feminist Literary Criticism," which called for more a diverse and "playful" pluralism in the development of a feminist literary criticism.[52] The piece won the Modern Language Association's Florence Howe Award in 1981 but prompted a number of critical responses that were published in the fall 1982 issue of the journal. Elly Bulkin, editor of the community-based *Conditions,* criticized Kolodny and *Feminist Studies* for presenting " 'a feminist literary criticism' without reference to the work of women of color and/or identifiable lesbians."[53] Rena Grasso Patterson, a New York feminist academic and activist, criticized *Feminist Studies* for helping Kolodny legitimate the "false universalization" of white, middle-class social consciousness in feminist scholarship. Patterson offered a more inclusive definition of feminism developed by Barbara Smith, an African-American lesbian scholar, as a touchstone for future feminist scholarly criticism: "Feminism is the political theory and practice that struggles to free *all* women: women of color, working-class women, poor women, disabled women, lesbians, old women, as well as white, economically-privileged heterosexual women. Anything less than this vision of total freedom is not feminism, but merely female self-aggrandizement."[54]

Kolodny countered that Bulkin and Patterson's criticisms "are directed not so much at my essay per se, as at some imagined monolith of established white feminist criticism within academe. . . . 'Dancing Through the Minefield' thus provides them an occasion for addressing persons and issues that are simply beyond (or unrelated to) that essay's intentions."[55] She was correct in pointing out that more explicitly exclusionary work had certainly been published in the past. Thus the charges may have been arbitrary to the scope of Kolodny's argument, but not to the timing and visibility of her article's publication. Heated debates over the importance of addressing issues of race, class, and sexual identity in feminist scholarship had just disrupted the 1980 National Women's Studies Association (NWSA) Conference, where, in the wake of the gay-straight splits, the editors of *Feminist Studies, Frontiers,* and *Signs* were confronted with charges that lesbian contributors and content were underrepresented in their publications.[56]

The Second Annual NWSA Convention at Indiana University in Bloomington was a strife-ridden and contentious event where the issues of race, class, and sexual identity dominated the proceedings. A special convention issue of the NWSA's *Women's Studies Newsletter* was filled with charges and rebuttals concerning the prevalence of racism, elitism, and heterosexism at the convention.[57] The gay-straight tension was so intense that the Lesbian Caucus successfully sponsored a resolution through the NWSA General Assembly:

> *1981 Convention-Related Resolutions* (6a): Be it resolved that the Convention Program Committee and Coordinators arrange for autonomous lesbian space at the NWSA Conventions in terms of housing and meeting facilities as alternatives available to the many lesbians attending the Conventions who want them. Of course, space must be provided for dialogue between lesbians and non-lesbians.[58]

Within such a polarized context, it is not surprising that the journals were targeted for how they addressed race, class, and lesbian issues.

Over the years, *Feminist Studies* had given ample space to class analysis and had been attentive to the early work on race, but Claire Moses acknowledges that the journal was properly taken to task on its lack of lesbian content.

> It [the NWSA confrontation] was a meeting in which *Feminist Studies,* along with other academic journals, was criticized for its lack of lesbian materials, authors and articles. For years *Feminist Studies* did not publish much material on lesbianism, separatism, or issues related to exploring women's own history of "women-identifying"—I'm searching for a word that resonates with Adrienne Rich's sense of "lesbian continuum"—We did not publish in that field and were taken to task for it. But, it would have been an even more painful experience for me to represent the journal in that exchange if we hadn't already started to deal with it. I was able, at that time, to talk much more about our future plans. The person who organized the meeting was Elly Bulkin, an editor of *Conditions,* and the person who jumped up to take

Feminist Studies in particular to task was Bonnie Zimmerman, both of whom have since published wonderful work with *Feminist Studies*. Both do wonderful work, and we've been very pleased to publish them.[59]

At *Frontiers* the reaction was different. Kathi George felt that the criticism of her journal was most unfair. In her opinion, this was another case of *Frontiers'* invisibility in relation to the more prominent feminist academic journals—alternately ignored by the culture of feminist scholarship when it comes to submissions and then lumped in with the more influential journals for criticism of publishing practices. In fact, because of the editorial freedom allowed by *Frontiers'* size and community posture, the journal had been the first to integrate content on lesbians, women of color, and class.

Judith Schwarz was invited to guest edit a special issue of *Frontiers* on Lesbian History—the first of its kind in 1979, a much cited and used issue. We had terrible trouble putting this issue together but overall I am very happy with it. I am happy from the political point of view that we were the first academic journal to really go out and do a whole issue devoted to lesbian concerns. As a historian I loved it. . . . there were three very good methodological essays by Lillian Faderman on who is hiding lesbian history and Frances Doughty on doing biography, and we had a very decent bibliographical essay about how to find sources. That was a first for the field and we thought it was a real contribution. I still think that this issue holds up very well, I think that the questionnaire on issues in lesbian history that Judith Schwartz compiled at the beginning . . . was a wonderful piece. It included all kinds of very different and interesting people who we couldn't get articles from, but at least we were able to include their voices and their points of view in a sort of mosaic compilation. Overall, I'm not unhappy with the lesbian history issue, but there were a lot of problems with it.[60]

The "problems" of producing the issue underscore a common tension between the predominantly heterosexual academic editorial boards and lesbian content.

What was difficult about this issue was the question: Who is judging what is historically lesbian and what isn't. For instance, we had a lot of trouble with some of the articles that went into this issue, because some of the straight editors believed that some of the authors were simply reading lesbian content into history. There were things that the guest editor wanted to go in because they had a political point to be made that the editorial board in Boulder simply couldn't swallow. It was the first time we really got into some heavy fights. Nasty fights—"I'm going to take my name off this issue if you do this, or you don't do this"—sort of stuff.[61]

Working in the now-established field of lesbian feminist criticism, Zimmerman views the historical mutability of sexuality and sexual identity as the "special problem" that still characterizes the field: "to state that Mary Wollstonecraft 'was' a lesbian because she passionately loved Fanny Blood, or Susan B. Anthony because she wrote amorous letters to Anna Dickinson, without accounting for the historical circumstances, may serve to distort or dislocate the actual meaning of these women's lives (just as it is distorting to deny their love for women)."[62]

The *Frontiers'* Lesbian History issue was widely indexed, cited, and acclaimed as a breakthrough publication, yet the tensions surrounding a predominantly heterosexual editorial board deciding what was or was not authentic lesbian history produced ambivalent reviews. The issue's reprint and back-issue order rate, however, indicates it was a particularly useful library and classroom resource in those early years.[63] Although publicly praised, Barale recalls that the editorial board was privately "trashed" as "those straight women who tried to take over lesbian history. . . . It was a blow. I don't know if the problems of process were as damaging as the trashing afterwards. It was unexpected. In 1979, perhaps our neck was stuck out and the axes were ready—there was a lot of anger and here was a chance to focus it."[64]

Although *Signs* was less committed to diverse content than the community-minded *Frontiers* (it did not publish a special issue on lesbian scholarship until 1988), Catharine Stimpson agrees that timing rather than content accounts for the NWSA confrontation.

I got mad, and I rarely get mad in public. You can accuse me of whatever you want, but don't you dare do it without some facts. . . . I think they were wrong. We had some problems with early reviews . . . but I have nothing to apologize about in terms of the treatment of those women in *Signs*. I think it was off the wall for several reasons: one is, when you're self-consciously marginal, the anger that this creates needs to be articulated. Women's Studies is ideologically generous and can be manipulated. Consciously and unconsciously. There really are ideological cleavages about what it means to be a feminist. And the fear of selling out and being co-opted. The fear of getting soft and sucking up to the status quo. A third difficulty is an old one which is the unhappy truth that it is easier to attack your sister. People will listen to you attack *Frontiers, Feminist Studies,* and *Signs*—are people going to listen if you attack *Newsweek?*[65]

It is safer to "hit your sister," especially in times of cultural conservatism. Even though feminist journals see themselves as renegades with a "toe-hold" in the university, their position on the margins of a powerful patriarchal institution can be used as a conduit into the university. If the journals help define feminism's academic arm—the discipline and content of women's studies—as it will exist and be recognized by the university, then it matters greatly that the journals remain accessible and accountable to community influence. Kolodny argued that "real change can occur only when there are pressure groups without and responsive power-brokers within. Although, individually, each of us can be at only one place at a time, together we must be everywhere."[66]

The unique position of feminist academic journals in the university but not truly of it allows the women's movement to enter and influence a powerful patriarchal institution. Peter Berger argues that institutions codify and pattern human activity and human experience.[67] Feminist academic journals pattern human experience at the cognitive level and codify the discipline of women's studies.

The patriarchal university ambivalently recognizes women's studies as a legitimate authority that defines and interprets gender-based human experience. As a result, the political and scholarly criteria that editors of *Feminist Studies, Frontiers,* and *Signs* use are not idle abstractions but powerful constructs that shape and define the discipline's parameters and applications. Aware of their participation in this process, editors are, like Mary Ryan, highly reflective about their responsibilities:

The editor has a role in shaping a field. I think we have shaped feminist scholarship through the work we do with authors and through the standards we set by the work we publish. We play a role in shaping a whole discourse by defining topics which are worth pursuing, not always intentionally, and setting standards, and in the criticism that the editors and reviewers give. Editors shape the kind of work we publish and, therefore, shape the kind of work we get. Consequently, there will be internal reference to other work we've published in the journal, and the questions we've raised.[68]

Consequently, the participation of an externally based political movement in monitoring the content and processes of the journals ensures the process of accountability. Yes, it is easier to hit your sister than *Newsweek,* but, in a sense, that is why the journals exist—to make it easier for the movement to exert pressure on patriarchal institutions that would otherwise be beyond their grasp, especially in a reactionary context when dominant culture media has declared their concerns irrelevant in the "post-feminist" era.[69]

But to rely on internal confrontations to effect external change is inherently dangerous. In her review of lesbian personal narratives, Zimmerman recalled Sara Evans's history of early movement experiences to caution against regulating the behavior of "sisters" rather than that of the patriarchy: "One critical weakness that developed during the early years of the women's liberation movement was 'A preoccupation with internal process—an effort to live out the revolutionary values of egalitarianism and cooperation within the movement itself—took precedence over program or effectiveness [which] . . . drove parts of the women's movement into ideological rigidities, and the movement splintered as it grew.' "[70] Internal confrontations are not adequate substitutes for directly challenging patriarchal institutions. Yet by keeping the journals politically accountable (even through arguably arbitrary symbolic acts like the NWSA confrontation or the Kolodny commentaries), confrontations reproduce some form of community participation in reshaping patriarchal institutions.

Although editors cannot avoid differentiating the domain of the political from that of the scholarly in abstract discussion of manuscript selection and revision, politics and scholarship are dynamic, often embedded, principles in journal practices. Political and scholarly criteria are, on rare occasions, clearly polarized for the editors in the process of manuscript selection. There are unusual circumstances when the editors must evaluate work on underrepresented political interests that have been excluded from the university and, consequently, have not enjoyed the privilege of achieving the level of critical sophistication that results from long-term scholarly discourse. In such cases, the editors must weigh the cost of violating scholarly standards against the benefit of moving feminist scholarship in new political directions.[71]

More often, *Feminist Studies, Frontiers,* and *Signs* seek to publish work that approximates the ideal that furthers standards of rigorous scholarship and goals of effective politics. Feminist scholarship has many such intersections, and debate over which combinations of scholarly rigor and political relevance most closely approach this ideal has always been a central issue. Such debates reinforce the editors' convictions that various forms of domination are interconnected in women's lives, and any analysis that ignores these relations of power produces inaccurate and incomplete scholarship. Consequently, whenever possible, the editors prefer to publish work on gender that includes an explicit or implicit consideration of the attendant power relations of race, class, and sexual identity.

Once the editors of *Feminist Studies, Frontiers,* and *Signs* successfully incorporated the inherited political interests of the broader feminist movement into their "spectrum of political and scholarly criteria," they had to create ways to continue to attend to the developing political interests of the women's movement. The dominant publishing form of academic journals—the footnoted scholarly article—could not quickly and directly address these interests, which were immediate and unfolding. The scholarly process of manuscript review, selection, revision, and publication takes months, even years. In order to address the ongoing political interests of the feminist movement in a direct and timely manner, the editors of *Feminist Studies, Frontiers,* and *Signs* had to translate immediate community concerns into the cognitive and temporal distance of scholarly articles, as well as develop experimental forms to better suit the political immediacy of the contemporary women's movement.

Notes

1. Judith Newton and Deborah Rosenfelt, eds., *Feminist Criticism and Social Change* (New York: Methuen, 1985), xv.

2. The liberal hegemony of academic knowledge has been similarly challenged by other criticisms. Marxist analyses of the production and social uses of scholarly knowledge in a number of humanistic and social scientific disciplines can be found in Bertell Ollman and Edward Vernoff, *The Left Academy: Marxist Scholarship on American Campuses* (New York: McGraw-Hill Book Company, 1982). Of similar profound impact is the influence of poststructuralist critiques of knowledge by Jacques Derrida, *Writing and Difference,* trans. Alan

Bass (Chicago: University of Chicago Press, 1978); Michel Foucault, *Power/ Knowledge: Selected Interviews and Other Writings, 1972–1977,* ed. Colin Gordon (New York: Pantheon, 1980) (selected interviews and writings, 1972– 77); and the emerging colonial discourses of Edward Said, *Orientalism* (New York: Vintage Books, 1979). For incorporation of these new critiques into the culture of feminist scholarship, see "Special Issue 'Textual Politics: Feminist Criticism,'" *Diacritics* 5 (Winter 1975); "Special Issue 'Feminism and the Critique of Colonial Discourse,'" *Inscriptions,* nos. 3–4 (1988); and Biddy Martin, "Feminism, Criticism, Foucault," *New German Critique* 27 (Fall 1982): 3–30.

3. Judith Newton and Judith Walkowitz, "Preface," *Feminist Studies* 9 (Spring 1983): 3.

4. Interview with editor Deborah Rosenfelt, San Francisco, California, May 31, 1985.

5. Interview with editor Mary Ryan, Palo Alto, California, June 3, 1985; interview with editors Rayna Rapp and Ruth Milkman, New York, October 9, 1986.

6. Interview with editor Judith Stacey, Berekely, California, June 16, 1985.

7. Interview with editor Estelle Freedman, Palo Alto, California, June 3, 1985.

8. Interview with editor Kathi George, Boulder, Colorado, January 15, 1985.

9. Jean Bethke Elshtain, *Public Man, Private Woman: Women in Political and Social Thought* (Princeton: Princeton University Press, 1981).

10. Judith Stacey, "The New Conservative Feminism," *Feminist Studies* 9 (Fall 1983): 559–84.

11. Stacey, "The New Conservative Feminism," 575.

12. Ibid., 565.

13. Ibid., 570, 557.

14. Berenice Fisher, "Guilt and Shame in the Women's Movement: The Radical Ideal of Action and Its Meaning for Feminist Intellectuals," *Feminist Studies* 10 (Summer 1984): 205.

15. Barbara Haber, "Is Personal Life Still a Political Issue?" *Feminist Studies* 5 (Fall 1979): 421.

16. B. Ruby Rich, "Feminism and Sexuality in the 1980s," *Feminist Studies* 12 (Fall 1986): 525–62.

17. "The Sex Issue," *Heresies: A Feminist Publication of Art and Politics* 12 (1981).

18. Carole S. Vance, *Pleasure and Danger: Exploring Female Sexuality* (Boston: Routledge and Kegan Paul, 1984), 16.

19. Rich, "Feminism and Sexuality," 536.

20. Carole S. Vance, "Notes and Letters," *Feminist Studies* 9 (Fall 1983): 591.

21. The leaflet "We Protest" by the Coalition for a Feminist Sexuality and Against Sadomasochism was distributed outside the conference by women wearing t-shirts imprinted with the coalition's name. The leaflet specifically criticized four groups: No More Nice Girls, Samois, the Lesbian Sex Mafia, and feminists who endorse butch-femme roles.

22. Estelle B. Freedman and Barrie Thorne, "Viewpoint: Introduction to the 'Sexuality Debates,'" *Signs* 10 (Autumn 1984): 102–4.

23. Interview with Kathi George, July 14, 1989.

24. Interview with Rayna Rapp, New York, October 8, 1985.

25. Vance, "Notes and Letters," 591.

26. Interview with Rayna Rapp.

27. After meeting in June 1983, the editorial board of *Feminist Studies* wrote individual apologies to the women named in the "We Protest" leaflet, solicited their personal statements, and printed all of the responses it received. This incident, its genesis, and its ramifications, became the focus of discussion among the editors for much of the spring and summer of 1983.

28. Rich, "Feminism and Sexuality in the 1980s," 537.

29. Interview with editor Barbara Gelpi, Palo Alto, California, June 3, 1985.

30. Freedman and Thorne, "Introduction to the 'Sexuality Debates,'" 104–5.

31. Interview with Estelle Freedman.

32. Claudette Charbonneau, "Commentary: Sexual Confusion," *off our backs* 12 (June 1982): 29.

33. Ann Fergusen et al., "Forum: The Feminist Sexuality Debates," *Signs* 10 (Autumn 1984): 106–35.

34. Michèle Aina Barale, "Body Politic/Body Pleasured: Feminism's Theories of Sexuality, a Review Essay," *Frontiers* 9, no. 1 (1986): 80–89.

35. Chris Weedon, *Feminist Practice and Poststructuralist Theory* (New York: Basil Blackwell, Inc., 1989), 24.

36. Susan Mosher Stuard, "The Annales School and Feminist History: Opening Dialogue with the American Stepchild," *Signs* 7 (Autumn 1981): 137.

37. Weedon, *Feminist Practice and Poststructuralist Theory*, 27.

38. Mary Poovey, "Feminism and Deconstruction," *Feminist Studies* 14 (Spring 1988): 62.

39. Interview with Kathi George, January 17, 1985.

40. Interview with editor Charlotta Hensley, Boulder, Colorado, January 17, 1985.

41. Cara Gendel Ryan, "Intellectuals and Political Action," *Heresies: A Publication on Art and Politics* 20 (1985): 78–79.

42. Helene Vivienne Wenzel, "The Text as Body/Politics: An Appreciation of Monique Wittig's Writings in Context," *Feminist Studies* 7 (Summer 1981): 270–71.

43. Barbara Christian, "The Race for Theory," *Feminist Studies* 14 (Spring 1988): 67.

44. Annette Kolodny, "Dancing between Left and Right: Feminism and the Academic Minefield in the 1980s," *Feminist Studies* 14 (Fall 1988): 455.

45. The issue devoted to deconstruction is *Feminist Studies* 14 (Fall 1988). Because of the materialist-historical inclination of a number of its editors, *Feminist Studies* published fewer semiotic and deconstruction analyses and was more critically reflexive about the politics of poststructuralism than *Signs*, its sister journal. *Signs*, which is further entrenched in the university, better connected with international scholarship, and more receptive to decontextualized literary studies, published works by Julia Kristeva as early as 1975 (Volume 1, number 1), and Helene Cixous in 1976 (Volume 1, number 4).

46. Since May 1968, the French feminist movement, the Mouvement de Libération des Femmes (MLF), had gone through a series of volatile controversies that resulted in an ideological and structural factioning over the issue of feminine difference. The most developed analysis and advocacy of difference took place in the group "Psychoanalyse et Politique [Psyche et Po]." Although many French feminist groups opposed Psyche et Po's notion of difference, the publishers of the journal *Questions Feministes* led the most systematic attack on the idea of biologically based attributes of masculinity and femininity. When Psyche et Po legally registered the name "Mouvement de Liberation des Femmes" as its own in 1978, the French feminist movement went to court, and American feminist journals were asked to take sides in the controversy. See Claire Duchen, *Feminism in France* (London: Routledge and Kegan Paul, 1986).

47. Interview with Barbara Gelpi.

48. Kolodny, "Dancing between Left and Right," 461–64.

49. Interview with editor Michèle Barale, Boulder, Colorado, January 16, 1985.

50. Interview with Barbara Gelpi.

51. The use of race, class, and sexual orientation was furthered through pieces such as Margaret A. Simons, "Racism and Feminism: A Schism in the Sisterhood," *Feminist Studies* 5 (Summer 1979): 384–401; Bonnie Zimmerman, "What Has Never Been: An Overview of Lesbian Feminist Literary Criticism," *Feminist Studies* 7 (Fall 1981): 451–76; and Bonnie Thorton Dill, "Race, Class and Gender: Prospects for an All-inclusive Sisterhood," *Feminist Studies* 9 (Spring 1983): 131–50. The most explicit published reference to the use of these attendant criteria in manuscript solicitation is found in Mary Ryan, "Preface," *Feminist Studies* 8 (Spring 1982): iii–v.

Frontiers featured a continuing discussion of these criteria in Barbara Smith, "Racism and Women's Studies," *Frontiers* 5 (Spring 1980): 48–49; Leila J. Rupp, " 'Imagine My Surprise': Women's Relationships in Historical Perspective," *Frontiers* 5 (Fall 1980): 61–69; Margaret Cruikshank, "Looking Back on Lesbian Studies," *Frontiers* 8, no. 3 (1986): 107–9; and Sylvia Gonzales, "Toward a Feminist Pedagogy for Chicana Self-Actualization," *Frontiers* 5 (Summer 1980): 48–50.

Signs consistently addressed the emerging literature in review essays on race (Volume 4, numbers 2 and 4; Volume 7, numbers 1 and 2; Volume 8, numbers 1, 2, and 4; Volume 9, numbers 1 and 2; Volume 10, number 4), on class (Volume 4, numbers 2 and 3; Volume 5, number 3; Volume 7, number 4; Volume 8, numbers 2 and 4; Volume 9, number 1; Volume 10, numbers 1, 3, and 4), and on sexual identity (Volume 9, number 4; Volume 1, number 2; Volume 5, number 4; Volume 8, number 4).

52. Annette Kolodny, "Dancing through the Minefield: Some Observations on the Theory, Practice, and Politics of a Feminist Literary Criticism," *Feminist Studies* 6 (Spring 1980): 1–25.

53. Judith Kegan Gardiner et al., "An Interchange on Feminist Criticism on 'Dancing through the Minefield,' " *Feminist Studies* 8 (Fall 1982): 636.

54. Gardiner et al., "An Interchange," 655–59.

55. Ibid., 667.

56. Although the NWSA Bloomington meetings are accurately characterized as particularly "strife ridden," such struggle and conflict are, in part, inherent in the NWSA's structural commitment to decentralization, inclusivity, and egalitarian participation. For a more complete analysis of NWSA's political ideals and structural innovations, see Robin Leider, "Stretching the Boundaries of Liberalism: Democratic Innovation in a Feminist Organization," *Signs* 16 (Winter 1991): 263–89.

57. Special plenary session on lesbian content in feminist academic journals at the Second National Women's Studies Association Conference, Indiana University, Bloomington, May 1980.

58. "Special Convention Issue," *NWSA Women's Studies Newsletter* 7 (Summer 1980): 22.

59. Interview with editor Claire Moses, Reston, Virginia, May 17, 1985.

60. Interview with Kathi George, January 17, 1985.

61. Ibid.

62. Bonnie Zimmerman, "What Has Never Been," in *Making a Difference: Feminist Literary Criticism,* ed. Gayle Greene and Coppèlia Kahn (New York: Methuen, 1985); cf. June Howard, "Feminist Differings: Recent Surveys of Feminist Literary Theory and Criticism," *Feminist Studies* 14 (Spring 1988): 179.

63. The *Frontiers'* Lesbian History Issue sold out in three months and was hailed as "a wonderful piece of newly emerging lesbian history." See Carol Anne Douglass, "Review: *Frontiers'* Lesbian History," *off our backs* 10 (August–September 1980): 18–19. For a fuller account of the controversies involved in the production of this special issue, see "To Our Readers," *Frontiers* 4, no. 3 (1979): i.

64. Interview with Michèle Barale, Boulder, Colorado, January 21, 1989.

65. Interview with editor Catharine Stimpson, New Brunswick, New Jersey, August 5, 1985.

66. Kolodny, "Dancing between Left and Right," 462.

67. Peter Berger and Thomas Luckmann, *The Social Construction of Reality* (New York: Doubleday, 1966), 60–64.

68. Interview with Mary Ryan.

69. Deborah Rosenfelt and Judith Stacey, "Review Essay: Second Thoughts on the Second Wave," *Feminist Studies* 13 (Summer 1987): 341–42.

70. Bonnie Zimmerman, "The Politics of Transliteration: Lesbian Personal Narratives," *Signs* 9 (Summer 1984): 679.

71. The weighting of scholarly and political criteria in manuscript selection is not done in a mechanistic or formulaic manner by the editors. The editorial boards and collectives meet several times a year to discuss manuscripts under consideration and, on occasion, vigorously debate the scholarly and political merits of specific submissions, with widely varying outcomes. Although individual editors disagree on the appropriate weighting of political and scholarly content in the journals, only one editor, Kathryn Pyne Parsons of *Feminist Studies,* has resigned on the basis of such disagreement.

chapter six

The Politics of Scholarship in the Production of Feminist Knowledge

In 1974, I sat in a hot little room in a shack on the side of a mountain with an Olympia typewriter and a telephone. . . . I woke up one morning and the format for the journal was in my mind. I said, "We have to have review essays, we have to have articles, we have to have book reviews, we have to have viewpoint." It was later refined, but the essential concept appeared like a vision one morning.

Catharine Stimpson, founding editor,
Signs

Questions concerning the content of feminist scholarship cannot be fully understood without examining the academic publishing forms that its expression employs. Scholarly forms are literary structures that presuppose an ideal organization or pattern of expression for content. Conventional form precedes, and consequently predetermines, the content and meaning of the work. The conventional form most readily identified with academic journals is the noted, scholarly article.[1]

The scholarly article is a concise but in-depth examination of a topic that "presents original research or analysis, but is always predicated on the authority or disputation of previous published research."[2] Its tone is "calm, deliberate, measured," its logic "ordered by the relationship or chronology of ideas or events," and its structure dictates that its author demonstrate "familiarity with the previous scholarship on the topic, suggest an original thesis, present supporting evidence, and point to the significance of the proposition advanced."[3] As a definitive scholarly form, the journal article dates from Germany in the nineteenth century:

In the pages of, *Historische Zeitschrift,* the scholarly article achieved its preeminence as the core of the scholarly historical periodical. Written on a single topic, the result of scholarly investigation that is documented and not tied to any other publication, the article is a distinct scholarly form. The first volume of *Historische Zeitschrift* contained several pieces that were clearly articles. . . . other pieces were just as clearly not articles. . . . this mixture resulted from [editor] Sybel's desire to meet the needs of professional historians, to whom the articles were primarily addressed, and to influence a larger public politically, the purpose of essays. Ultimately these intentions proved incompatible, and during the early years of *Historische Zeitschrift* the essay gradually disappeared from its pages [because] . . . the desire to reach a nonscholarly public acted as a major deterrent to scholarly contributors.[4]

Predicating original research on the authority or disputation of previously published research and acknowledging sources originated when scholarship consisted mainly of biblical exegesis, "Scholars dealt with sacred texts, and dealt with them reverently, pushing their own ideas off into the margins."[5] Footnotes or endnotes are designed to substantiate claims, connect the thesis to an established body of work, expand on the main argument, and acknowledge scholarly debts. Some feminist literary critics argue that such conventions represent a "masculine" voice, and that women need to create new "feminine" forms. The editors of feminist academic journals, however, believe that notes are neither inherently "masculine" nor empty form. Catharine Stimpson, for example, has argued the political importance of acknowledging intellectual debts. "We would permit almost anything to be said about political points of view as long as it met certain rhetorical standards. Originality, cogency, respect for the past scholarship—it was very important to us that it respect the past scholarship. Not out of pedantry, but out of respect for the women who suffered to do it. You leave Mary Beard out of a footnote, you are not just being sloppy, you are demeaning Mary Beard."[6]

Scholarly forms and conventions help produce legitimated and thorough scholarship on women but are less useful in addressing the immediate, unfolding, often unexpected events of the contemporary women's movement. In-depth, predicated discussions do not easily accommodate exploratory or impressionistic analysis. Feminist scholars are often in the position of trying to challenge, rather than reify, the authority of received knowledge. In such cases, they have no published body of work to call into service because their work is often groundbreaking and unprecedented.

The publishing process itself also exacerbates the limitations of inherited scholarly forms. Editors at an established journals such as *Signs* consider hundreds of submissions. The process of manuscript review, selection, revision, and publication takes months, even years. The journals' publishing timetables—three times a year or quarterly—render full-length, in-depth, timely responses to movement events nearly impossible. Editors often find that space in each issue is fully committed six to eighteen months in advance of publication.[7]

For editors of *Feminist Studies, Frontiers,* and *Signs* to address the ongoing political interests of the feminist movement in a direct and timely manner they must create alternative forms for their journals and reinterpret the meaning and uses of conventional scholarly forms. Such deviations from convention are designed to augment, rather than replace, a reliance on noted, scholarly articles, editorial statements, and book reviews. *Signs* and *Frontiers,* for example, have used an innovative "Archives" section designed to publish retrieved documents in the history of women without editorial comment or discussion. Although initially used to publish only recovered historical documents, the editors eventually expanded the form to preserve current movement documents.

The editors of *Feminist Studies* created an abbreviated, theoretical essay, "Commentary," to allow response to controversial developments within feminism and the wider society. In structure, tone, and political purpose, "Commentary" hearkens to the political essay of early feminist academic publishing and the manifesto of underground publishing. The use of first-person voice is typical, as is the assignment of agency, the appeal to emotional and political authenticity, and the call to action. A "Commentary" response to Margarete Sandelowski's analysis of feminist reactions to infertility, for example, charges that: "She [Sandelowski] asks us to empathize with the infertile woman's desire for children. But if we love children, we must surely protest against the inadequacy of prenatal care, medical services, and child care that are available to much of our population. Sisterhood is indeed powerful, but only if it integrates empathy for individual suffering into a commitment to solidarity and struggle."[8]

The editors of *Frontiers* began to use their own versions of "Commentary" in 1991 to pointedly condemn, caution, evaluate, and recommend political positions. "Commentary" has enabled the editors to initiate immediate critiques of urgent political events—the rise of the New Right, developments in international feminism, and notions of multiculturalism.[9]

Along with instituting new section of their journals, the editors of *Feminist Studies* and *Frontiers* continue to encourage the submission of work in community forms. In "A Word to Prospective Contributors," the editors of *Feminist Studies* state that "creative work, particularly poetry and art; and reports from the women's movement, such as manifestos, position papers, and strategies for change are . . . categories of material which we are also happy to consider."[10]

Because of their reputations as academic publications, *Feminist Studies* and *Signs* receive very few manifestos, position papers, and strategies for change; most community content is published in the form of poetry. But, as Rayna Rapp, an editor of *Feminist Studies*, concedes, academic journals marginalize community forms of expressions. "If you look at the contents of the journal, it is a scholarly journal . . . and these things are almost snuck in through the back door."[11]

Frontiers has been more successful in integrating a number of community forms, including photo essays, creative essays, and personal histories, to complement its scholarly articles. In addition, *Frontiers* has consistently treated creative community expressions, such as the music of Meg Christian and Linda Tillery, as topics of serious scholarly analysis.[12]

Despite such efforts, most editors are not "entirely satisfied" with the capacity of experimental and community forms to integrate current political interests into their journals. They have also reinterpreted the purpose and scope of conventional—but auxiliary—sections of academic journals. *Signs* selected the traditional review essay as a means of introducing and legitimizing feminist scholarship, for example. In Joan Burstyn's opinion, doing so lent credibility to new, sometimes startling, information: "When I became the associate editor, Catharine had in mind already that there would be a section that would deal with reviews of the field, but the exact format of it and how it would be done, that was something I did a position paper on and suggested what we might do. In retrospect, those review essays in those first years turned out to be totally crucial for women's studies."[13]

Academic journals often include a section that acts as a professional bulletin board and lists conference announcements, calls for papers, job listings, and research exchanges. *Frontiers, Feminist Studies,* and *Signs* expanded this section to include announcements of political events, calls to action, updates on organizing efforts, and short topical statements or rebuttals.[14] In addition, *Signs'* "Comment and Reply," *Feminist Studies'*

"Notes and Letters," and *Frontiers'* "Reviews and Responses" publish lively exchanges that are political as well as scholarly in nature between authors and readers.

Yet editors still need a publishing device that can effectively address the immediate political interests of the women's movement and remain an integral part of their journals. The section used most often for this purpose is the symposium, another recognized scholarly form. *Feminist Studies* and *Signs* regularly present symposia in which competing political and scholarly perspectives are debated. As useful as it has been, Rayna Rapp and Carol Nagy Jacklin are uncomfortable with what they consider the form's inherently confrontational structure:

> *Feminist Studies* is faced with a problem. . . . there has to be a way to have serious feminist political debate, but the forms inherited either from the classical, straight, male academic world or many of the ways that debates have surfaced in feminist academic journals have not been entirely satisfactory. We have yet to develop a good form in which you debate political issues in a way that doesn't make one person the "expert" and everybody else the "angry challengers." I'm against the notion that there is one position and then there's the calling of what's wrong with it, rather than some way of putting all the possibilities out in a more collaborative fashion, and then fighting about it. I'm not against fighting about it. But I don't think we've found a way to publish serious political debate.[15]

Often *Signs* creates a cross-disciplinary dialogue among feminists simply by publishing articles from a variety of disciplines on adjoining pages. This symposium, however, is an example of a more truly interdisciplinary exchange, as it allows the perspective and knowledge of scholars from a range of fields to bring into focus different aspects of the same issues. Here, too, this meeting of ideas generates real controversy: *are* there meaningful sex differences in female and male moral development? Interesting as well is a related question: does the style of this forum itself represent a new academic "voice," a break from the male-dominated tradition of confrontational debate? The reader will have to decide.[16]

The editors have yet to settle on a publishing form that integrates unfolding political debates into the pages of the journals in a direct and timely manner, and yet they have managed consistently to integrate the unfolding political concerns of the broader feminist movement into their scholarship. They do so by adapting standard academic conventions, forms, and codes for feminist purposes. Yet in doing this, the culture of feminist scholarship must address the immediate and evolving political interests of the broader feminist movement with cognitive and temporal distance.

This process can be better understood through a careful analysis of how the community-based "women's culture" movement was negotiated into the culture of feminist scholarship. In their spring 1980 issue (Volume 6, number 1), the editors of *Feminist Studies* published the journal's first scholarly political debate—a symposium entitled "Politics and Culture in Women's History." Ostensibly, the symposium was a discussion of the concept of the nineteenth-century "female homosocial world" described in Carroll Smith-Rosenberg's influential essay "The Female World of Love and Ritual: Relations between Women in Nineteenth-Century America," which had been published in the first issue of *Signs* in 1975. But the symposium was equally a result of the editors' need to initiate discussion of women's culture, a hotly contested emergent politics within the contemporary feminist movement of the late 1970s. Annette Kolodny has observed that the confidence of feminist scholars "is rooted not so much in any definitive understanding of the past, as it is in our need to call up and utilize the past on behalf of a better understanding of the present." Or, as Claire Moses explains, "Yes, we're talking about the nineteenth century, but we're also talking about ourselves." [17]

Smith-Rosenberg's article, based on a modest sampling of letters and diaries written between the 1760s and the 1880s from thirty-five families, put forth a seemingly innocuous assertion: from "at least the late eighteenth through mid-nineteenth century, a female world of varied and yet highly structured relationships appears to have been an essential part of American society." The key phrase, which later caught the attention of feminist scholars, was *female world*, which Smith-Rosenberg depicted as an exclusively female subculture characterized by intense love and devotion. She argued this was a single-sex world that did not dichotomize genital and platonic love, as well as a homosocial world that emotionally and intellectually complimented a rigidly segregated heterosexual world.

This "world of women" did not automatically produce feminism, but, according to Smith-Rosenberg, raised a question: "Can feminism develop outside a female world?"[18] The timing of *Feminist Studies'* symposium to revive Smith-Rosenberg's argument five years after it had been published would seem belated and arbitrary had the culture of feminist scholarship not been attending to developments in the broader feminist movement.

The assertion that feminist political interests could be furthered through the creation of a separate female world was one of the ideas that lesbian feminist theorists developed during the gay-straight splits in the contemporary American woman's movement. A feminist and female counterculture that expressed and embraced the idea of female difference was an outgrowth of both lesbian-feminist and radical-feminist theory. The counterculture thrived and attracted gay and straight participants from a variety of feminist political perspectives. Eventually known as "women's culture," it celebrated the "female aesthetic" in art, music, dance, poetry, and spirituality and was quickly institutionalized as women's festivals, concerts, theaters, and record companies.[19] It was a feminist counterculture almost exclusively expressed in community forms and community-based publications.

"Women's culture draws inspiration from the heart and body as well as from the conscious mind. The focus of this culture is on women's experiences and expression . . . as they are different from men's."[20] Housed in the Los Angeles Woman's Building, the "nucleus of women's culture," *Chrysalis* (begun in 1976), became the definitive women's culture publication. Filled with free-form illustrations, personal essays, stories, and poetry, *Chyrsalis* reflected the alternative culture's focus on female artistic, creative, personal expression, spirituality, and intuition. According to Ruth Iskin, the journal's founder,

> Women's culture as it has emerged in the seventies is the expression of women's experiences, ideals and goals for themselves and the world. When feminism reemerged in the seventies, it brought to the forefront a recognition that Western culture mostly represented a partial point of view dominated by men's experiences in a role-divided culture and society. . . . Simone de Beauvior discusses how women's lives, with their mindless daily chores, do not provide for the kind of daring and adventurousness necessary for exploring and creating important innovations. It certainly

has hampered women from contributing fully. On the other hand, women's traditional way of life has had a positive impact in providing a nourishing source for women's creations.[21]

Feminist academic journals contrasted sharply with women's culture journals in their rationalist forms and conventions, nonseparatist politics, patriarchal university setting, and placement on the rational-instrumental, rather than the intuitive-expressive, side of society's dichotomy. When *Chrysalis* first appeared, the original editors of *Feminist Studies* realized that new territorial boundaries were being negotiated and identifying choices had to be made. Responding in 1976 to a letter from Rachel DuPlessis concerning the future of *Feminist Studies*, Adrienne Rich wrote:

> I think it would be a tremendous loss for *Feminist Studies* to stop publishing. It has always been one of the most interesting movement journals despite its largely academic and scholarly orientation. . . . I do agree that a broadening of approaches is needed, perhaps more symposia, more creative work, maybe now and then an interview. . . . neither *Signs* nor *Chrysalis* should be any kind of threat to *Feminist Studies;* on the contrary, I believe that the more options for publishing there are, the more stimulation to good new work and thought.

When *Chrysalis* appeared, *Feminist Studies'* literary editor Rachel DuPlessis wrote to a contributor in 1976 that she believed that *Feminist Studies* would have to accommodate women's culture in order to survive: "the possibility is STILL strong that we may close up, fold, disband end the journal. There is to be a big meeting on this very subject in New York City in about a month, to discuss the financial and intellectual status of the journal. I think there is a need for *Feminist Studies*—especially a *Feminist Studies* which is not so thoroughly academic, but continues to branch out into cultural theory, creative work, poetry, and possibly such cultural discussions as symposia and review articles."

Instead of integrating the forms and concerns of women's culture, however, feminist academic journals were defined in opposition to it. As *Signs'* editor Estelle Freedman points out, "There is a scholarly and literary split in feminist publishing with the literary and the artistic not tied to the universities. *Signs, Feminist Studies* and *Frontiers* are university-affiliated, and community journals like *Chrysalis, Common*

Lives/Lesbian Lives, and *Sinister Wisdom* are not." [22] The founding editors of *Frontiers, Feminist Studies,* and *Signs* felt compelled to make choices that limited the representation of women's culture in their pages. *Signs* would only publish women's culture content when it was presented in accepted scholarly form, hence the journal's acceptance of Smith-Rosenberg's piece. *Frontiers,* by contrast, attempted to integrate the forms with photo essays, special issues, poetry, and creative essays. *Feminist Studies* found it difficult to integrate the forms and conventions of women's culture and preferred to publish poetry and the occasional personal essay under the direction of DuPlessis.

Feminist Studies editor Mary Ryan has explained why women's culture countered both the scholarly form and the editors' feminist politics: "There is a pretty strong lack of sympathy with cultural feminism among the editors. That's not where our views are, because in a fundamental way we look more toward social and materialist things and have a stronger sense of gender as more complex than just female experience. Despite that, I think we're extremely receptive to things written from that point of view. If we could get it. We get very little of it. Cultural feminism is usually presented in a nonacademic way or it goes to journals related to the arts." [23]

Consequently, women's culture material primarily appeared in feminist academic journals in the form of occasional poetry and personal essays. When women's culture began to transcend the boundaries of these community forms and move into the main body of feminist scholarship, editors felt seriously compelled to address its political and scholarly implications.[24]

The journals are part of a complex tension between the community and the university. Although often postured as "gate-crashers" in the university, feminist editors simultaneously function as gatekeepers. Their journals use the interpretive authority conferred by their participation in the university to legitimate feminist knowledge through rationalist codes. Therefore, movement phenomena such as women's culture are not absorbed uncritically into feminist scholarly discourse, but must be mediated through academic criteria and conventions. The success and controversy surrounding Smith-Rosenberg's article, for example, prompted the editors of *Feminist Studies* to organize a symposium where associate editor Ellen DuBois and consulting editor Temma Kaplan criticized the concept of a "female world" and Gerda Lerner, Mari Jo Buhle, and Smith-Rosenberg herself, all historians, defended it. It is important to note that the symposium's participants all debated the terms and territory of a female world without directly addressing women's culture. Instead, the issue was cast to the temporal distance of the nineteenth century and the cognitive distance of academic understandings of the term *women's culture*.[25] And yet, the immediate political relevance of singling out a women's culture that celebrates female difference was inescapable; an emergent and contested area of the broader feminist movement had been initiated into the discourse of the culture of feminist scholarship.

The *Feminist Studies* symposium on Carroll Smith-Rosenberg confined its discussion to the political and scholarly implications of women's culture perspectives in the field of history, but women's culture had entered and influenced a wide array of disciplines involved in the study of women.[26] Working in the field of moral development theory at Harvard's Graduate School of Education, Carol Gilligan published "In a Different Voice: Women's Conceptions of Self and Morality," in a 1977 issue of the *Harvard Educational Review* (Volume 47, number 4).

Gilligan argued that "women and men possess different moral sensibilities" based upon their different socialization experiences. For men, this socialization process creates "a self defined through separation"; for women, "a self defined through connection." Thus, women develop a moral imperative based on a contextualized responsibility to self and others, whereas men develop a moral imperative based on universalized rights of the individual. Gilligan contrasted her findings with those presented in Lawrence Kohlberg's classic study of moral development in young men. She concluded that moral development theory, which relies only on male experiences, results in theory that normalizes the experiences of males and defines female experience as deviant rather than different.[27]

The editors at *Feminist Studies* interpreted Gilligan's work as a liberal manifestation of women's culture and connected it directly to the debate over Smith-Rosenberg's use of "separate spheres": "Cultural feminism is tied to what we used to call lesbian feminism or radical feminism. I mean, certainly the dominant work from that perspective is tied to a certain kind of celebration of female difference. You get it in other things that are much more liberal, like Gilligan. It is not surprising that *Feminist Studies* would initiate a discussion on Gilligan. There is a caution along those lines that is relatively unique to *Feminist Studies* and the other academic journals," observes Judith Stacey.[28]

The journal published a critical commentary by Judy Auerbach among others, "On Gilligan's *In a Different Voice*," in its spring 1985 issue (Volume 11, number 1) because the editors were "concerned with the potentially antiegalitarian implications of work that valorizes difference" and were worried that Gilligan's work in particular "has lent itself too easily to popularization by those wishing to defuse its feminist insights." Indeed, the material consequences of arguing and celebrating female difference concerned many feminist scholars. Participants in the commentary criticized what they thought were scholarly and political ambiguities in Gilligan's argument, but they were really concerned that "in the absence of an alternative explanation for the root of . . . difference it is easy to fall back on psychological/reproductive determinism and renewed rationalizations for gendered separation of spheres."[29]

Like *Feminist Studies'* editor Judith Stacey, the editors of *Signs* also saw Gilligan as part of the continuing negotiation of the emergent politics captured by Smith-Rosenberg.

> Ten years ago, Carroll Smith-Rosenberg gave us a new understanding to this separation of spheres when she argued that it had made possible psychologically sustaining relationships among women and had been congruent with strong bonds of female friendship, affection and love. As interpreted by Smith-Rosenberg, and many historians who wrote after her, the separation of spheres could offer advantages as well as disadvantages. . . . It could sustain a distinctive women's culture which embraced creativity in domestic arts, distinctive forms of labor, and particular patterns of nurturing relationships. For the last decade, a rich literal and lively debate among historians have explored the nuances of this nineteenth-century ideology.[30]

The heightened intensity of the debate from the early to mid 1980s can be seen in the fact that in 1983 *Signs* featured Gilligan's work in a favorable review by the sociologist and psychotherapist Jessica Benjamin, who stated: "Gilligan's research stands among the significant revisions of traditional scholarship that change the face of that scholarship as well as of feminist thought."[31]

When *Signs* featured Gilligan's work again in 1986, much had changed. "In a Different Voice" had been widely reprinted, published as a book, reviewed, and popularized, having been twice featured in *Ms.* magazine, which named Gilligan "Woman of the Year." *In a Different*

Voice was no longer simply one of many significant revisions of traditional scholarship, it was now, according to *Signs,* an important and influential "encapsulation" of one of the two "central concerns of feminist thought during the five years of our editorship." According to the *Signs'* editors, Gilligan "encapsulates" the "quest for values which can be described as essentially female," values that provide "alternatives to the abstraction and competitiveness associated with male dominance."[32]

In the *Signs'* symposium, Gilligan was again faulted for both her scholarship and her politics. Critics claimed that she lacked a shared sample, procedures, and scoring with Kohlberg, and a "reliable objective scoring system" for her own categories of moral development.[33] She was criticized for overgeneralizing her sample of white, middle-class, ivy-league women as the defining female voice. It was an inattention, according to the critics, that obscured the way race and economics might alter her findings.[34] Politically they cautioned against reifying patriarchal bifurcations of man-reason and woman-feeling. They charged that Gilligan inferred gendered behavior to be biologically determined, an idea that echoes the nineteenth-century idea of the cult of true womanhood. That idea was based on romantic and intuitive "truths" of gender stereotyping—the sort of romantic, biologically based "truth" that, according to the critics, led to anti-Semitism in Nazi Germany and racism in the suffragist movement.[35]

Gilligan countered by claiming that her critics "essentially accept the psychology I call into question—the psychology that has equated male with human in defining human nature and thus has construed evidence of sex difference as a sign of female deficiency, a psychology that, for all the talk about research design and methods, has failed to see all-male research samples as a methodological problem."[36] But Zella Luria from the Department of Psychology at Tufts University summarized the fundamental political challenge that the popularity of Gilligan's scholarship posed:

> What is it that we want today as women and as feminists? That is not a question about evidence but about goals. Do we truly gain by returning to a modern cult of true womanhood? Do we gain by the assertion that women think or reason in one voice and men in another? Gilligan's view focuses on the characteristics of the personality, the situation is only a vehicle for the expression of the reasoning personality, whether that be caring or abstract. The

same rationale has often been used to shunt people into the "appropriate" job. Surely Gilligan and I want one voice that allows both men and women a variety of differentiated responses. Anything else is a step backward.[37]

Indeed, this step backward occurred less than a year later, when the discussion of women's culture in academe crossed into the U.S. District Court of Chicago and was misused as testimony in a landmark sex-discrimination case brought against the world's largest retailer, Sears Roebuck and Company. The Equal Employment Opportunity Commission (EEOC) brought suit against Sears in 1979 when it discovered that, despite instituting an affirmative action program, 74 percent of Sears's noncommission jobs were held by women, who received only 40 percent of promotions to commission jobs. In addition, 61 percent of applicants for full-time sales jobs were women, but only 27 percent were hired as commissioned salespeople. Because workers who received commissions could make more than double than those who did not, Sears's sex-segregated sales force constituted a major occupational gender gap in pay. Citing qualitative and quantitative evidence, the EEOC attributed the statistical discrepancy to discrimination on Sears's part.[38] The case seemed routine. The EEOC had achieved out-of-court settlements in similar cases involving AT&T, General Electric, and General Motors; it was the last major antidiscrimination case brought by the government against a large corporation.

When the case went to court in 1984 and 1985, two feminist historians, Rosalind Rosenberg of Barnard College and Alice Kessler-Harris of Hofstra University, were brought in as opposing expert witnesses.[39] Duplicating the women's culture controversy, they presented conflicting testimony about whether gender difference in job preferences, or sex discrimination in employment practices, most accurately account for the exclusion of women from higher-paid commissioned sales jobs. Using the ideas developed by proponents of women's culture theory in historical scholarship, Rosenberg defended Sears's hiring and promotion practices:

> The assumption that men and women have identical interests and aspirations regarding work is incorrect. Historically, men and women have had different interests, goals, and aspirations regarding work. Because housework and child care continue to affect women's labor force participation even today, many women

choose jobs that complement their family obligations over jobs that might increase and enhance their earning potential. Men and women differ in their expectations concerning work, in their interests as to types of jobs they prefer or in the types of product they prefer to sell, and in the continuity of their participation in the labor force. It is naive to believe that the natural effect of these differences is evidence of discrimination by Sears.[40]

Kessler-Harris countered that Rosenberg's claim that women choose noncompetitive, low-wage jobs out of domestic interest avoids dealing with the complex ways in which discrimination is institutionally and socially manifested.

A segregated labor force cannot be explained as a result of women's "choice." . . . Choice can be understood only within the framework of available opportunity. In the past, opportunities to women have been conditioned by society's perceptions of women and assumptions about them. Thus, women have been hired into limited numbers of jobs and discriminated against in the work force generally. The resulting profile of "women's work" has been perceived to be what women choose. . . . Where opportunity has existed, women have never failed to take the jobs offered. . . . Failure to find women in so-called "non-traditional jobs" can thus only be interpreted as a consequence of employer's unexamined attitudes or preferences, which is the essence of discrimination.[41]

At the heart of the courtroom debate was the difference versus equality controversy that had been generated by the contested field of women's culture. That an ideology based on the insights of a radical community phenomena would eventually be used to defend Sears Roebuck and Company was beyond the expectations of its feminist originators but not its critics. When the judge acquitted Sears in 1986, he described Rosenberg as a "highly credible witness" and agreed with her opinion that "the overall tendencies of many women" is "to see themselves as less competitive."[42]

Many feminist scholars criticized Rosenberg for using feminist scholarship to damage the material conditions of working women. In retrospect, however, these people overstated her effect. A dramatic repositioning of federal policy, rather than a lone historian's testimony, shaped the outcome of the Sears's case.

Under the Reagan administration, the EEOC dismantled statistically based systemic discrimination cases and rechanneled its resources to individual discrimination complaints. The Sears complaint had been initiated at great expense under the Carter administration but came to trial under EEOC chair Clarence Thomas during the Reagan administration. Thomas substantially reallocated EEOC personnel and funds from the Sears case to individual discrimination complaints. In light of such policy changes, the significance of Rosenberg's testimony is not that it substantially determined the outcome of the Sears case, but that it provoked debate inside and outside of the academy over the use of scholarship for politics, and equally profound, the politics of scholarship.[43]

In December 1985, when both Rosenberg and Kessler-Harris addressed the Columbia University Seminar on Women and Society, the audience was openly hostile to Rosenberg's position.[44] That same month, at the annual meeting of the American Historical Association, the Coordinating Committee of Women in the Historical Profession and the Conference Group on Women's History passed a series of resolutions in response to the case: "We . . . are deeply concerned by certain circumstances and issues raised in the 1984–85 trial of a 1979 EEOC case against Sears Roebuck. In the trial . . . a respected scholar buttressed Sears' defense against charges of sex discrimination. . . . We believe as feminist scholars, we have a responsibility not to allow our scholarship to be used against the interests of women struggling for equity in our society."[45]

Having been a central forum for the women's culture debate for years, feminist academic journals were quick to respond. The editors of *Feminist Studies* believed "rarely had the stakes been so high in a scholarly debate" and immediately prepared and published a critical commentary in the summer of 1986. *Signs* followed by archiving the court depositions of Rosenberg and Kessler-Harris.[46] But the women's culture debate had moved beyond the boundaries of feminist academic journals. Rosenberg's testimony, and feminist scholars' reaction to it, was covered by the community feminist press, the radical press, the popular press, and traditional academic journals. Those outside the culture of feminist scholarship condemned feminist reaction against Rosenberg.[47] After nearly two decades of insular debate and development, the culture of feminist scholarship, its scholarly and political criteria, and its goals were opened to public scrutiny.

In letters and interviews published in the *New York Times, Ms. Magazine, The Nation, Society,* and *The Chronicle of Higher Education,* Rosenberg has said that she refuses to subordinate scholarship to political goals.[48] Many members of the popular press and traditional scholarly press agreed with her assessment. For example, the *Washington Post's* literary critic, Jonathan Yardley, argued that her treatment reveals that women's studies is merely the classroom advocacy of feminist propaganda. "Sears won the case, but in academic-feminist circles, Rosenberg came off the loser. She has been severely criticized in several academic journals . . . devoted to feminist revisionism. . . . One can only wonder how well these people sleep at night. They are scholars . . . yet what they are saying is that the obligation to feminist orthodoxy is higher than the obligation to scholarly integrity."[49]

The *Washington Post* carried an editorial that accused women's history scholars of "feminist McCarthyism" and "blindly applying a party line."[50] Thomas Haskell, a Rice University historian, called feminist criticism of Rosenberg "a stifling of academic freedom" reminiscent of the "shallow backwaters of Marxism." In the same article, Gwendolyn Wright, a Columbia University architectural historian said, "The stifling of discourse is extremely dangerous. It's terrible to say we can only use knowledge in certain ways—it's very distressing for the Women's Movement."[51] The conservative literary scholar Carol Iannone accused feminist scholars of "intellectual perjury": "The majority view among feminist historians today is apparently that truth should be suppressed or even distorted in the service of feminist politics. . . . Feminism's precise complaint against 'patriarchal history' is that it suppresses or distorts the truth of women's experience. But we now find feminists willing to suppress, change, slant the record that they themselves have documented if it conflicts with their version of women's interests."[52]

Such reactions against Rosenberg's critics do not reflect an understanding of the culture of feminist scholarship, but an understanding produced by adherence to dominant American cultural ideology. To comprehend the ideology and motives of the culture of feminist scholarship accurately, Rosenberg's "violation" must be placed within the context of scholarly and political understanding expressed in the journals' discussion of women's culture.[53]

In the Rosenberg controversy, outsiders "see" feminist McCarthyism—the suppression of truth to serve political ideology, intellectual perjury, a stifling of objective discourse and academic freedom. Insiders "see" an emerging, contested, controversial, as yet unsubstantiated interpretation of history being presented as factual evidence in a politically charged event that substantially damaged the material conditions of working women. Those who had followed the journal's discussion of women's culture knew that the literature on working women in the twentieth century is still relatively thin, and the women's culture debate in particular is an unfolding and contested area of scholarship.[54]

As Ruth Milkman, the editor *Feminist Studies,* points out, Rosenberg and Kessler-Harris "testified under the peculiar constraints of the courtroom—constraints that demanded yes or no answers to complex questions and prohibited any expert witness from acknowledging disagreements or controversy within her field without losing her legitimacy as an expert."[55] Many participants in the culture of feminist scholarship understand that "equality" and "difference" need not be paired dichotomously, and the Sears case structured an impossible choice. In the spring 1988 issue of *Feminist Studies,* the historian Joan W. Scott attempted to resolve the equality-difference split.

> The Sears case offers a sobering lesson in the operation of a discursive, that is a political field. . . . If one opts for equality, one is forced to accept the notion that difference is antithetical to it. If one opts for difference, one admits that equality is unattainable. That, in a sense, is the dilemma. . . . Feminists cannot give up "difference;" it has been our most creative analytic tool. We cannot give up "equality," at least as long as we want to speak to the principles and values of our political system. But it makes no sense for the feminist movement to let its arguments be forced into preexisting categories and its political disputes to be characterized by a dichotomy we did not invent. How then do we recognize and use notions of sexual difference and yet make arguments for equality? The only response is a double one: the unmasking of the power relationship constructed by posing equality as the antithesis of difference and the refusal of its consequent dichotomous construction of political choice.[56]

Scott's solution is incomplete, however, because on a deeper level defenders and critics of Rosenberg are not engaged in a debate about the issue of equality versus difference. Very few members of the popular and traditional scholarly press are familiar with the theoretical nuances of feminist scholarship. The responses to feminist criticism of Rosenberg reveal a more fundamental cultural conflict between epistemological worldviews of the dominant American culture and that of feminist scholarship.

The premise of feminist scholarship fundamentally challenges the dominant American cultural conception of politics and scholarship. Dominant American culture operates on a liberal, Enlightenment model of knowledge that posits that scholars can and should detach the substance of their work from issues of politics and power. Scholars "discover" objective, monolithic "facts" whose meanings exist independently of their contexts and uses. Feminist epistemology, on the other hand, argues that truth is plural and that its foundations lie in the shared historical and cultural meanings of the social world. Knowledge is not a monolithic truth achieved through abstraction, but "is always situated, perspectival, engaged, and involved. It is based on unavoidable prejudgement and is, hence, always 'biased.' " [57]

According to the epistemology of the dominant culture, Rosenberg must eschew political ideology and speak the objective "truth," whether in a book, an academic article, or a courtroom. Feminists argue that her scholarship is neither "truth" nor "apolitical." As the historian Kathryn Kish Sklar explains, "Nobody has a monopoly on truth—history is an art as well as a science—but when you go into a courtroom and claim to know the truth about women, that's a very political act." [58] Carol Sternhell, a scholar and journalist, observes that by bringing scholarship into the courtroom Rosenberg put it in service of political goals, the particular political goals of Sears Roebuck and Company. "Academic research may (occasionally) be 'disinterested'; a trial never is. . . . The debate here isn't really about scholarship at all; it's about the political uses of scholarship." [59]

It was the potential misuse of women's culture theory that originally prompted *Feminist Studies* and *Signs* to critique the work of Smith-Rosenberg and Gilligan. Certainly neither the radical and lesbian feminists who created the community-based women's culture movement in the 1970s, nor the pioneering scholars who introduced it to scholarship, intended to defend the hiring and promotion practices of American corporations.

Through the combined scholarly and political scrutiny of feminist academic journals, the political misuse of women's culture, and all other products of feminist scholarship, was examined. Reasserting the beliefs that first inspired the use of political and scholarly criteria in the culture of feminist scholarship, Milkman explains, "If feminist scholars can learn anything from the Sears case, it is that we ignore the political dimensions of the equality-versus-difference debate at our peril, especially in a period of conservative resurgence like the present. . . . As long as this is the political context in which we find ourselves, feminist scholars must be aware of the real danger that arguments about 'difference' or 'women's culture' will be put to uses other than those for which they were originally developed." [60]

The controversy surrounding the Sears case foreshadowed the current debate over what has been termed "politically correct" scholarship. Without the insights afforded by the negotiation of women's culture in feminist academic journals, that debate will continue to be fundamentally misdirected. In order to determine the appropriate relationship between scholarship and politics, the discussion must take account of the profoundly disparate epistemologies upon which it relies. Charges that feminist scholarship simply adheres to a "party line" obscure the complex social process that produces and legitimates scholarly knowledge.

Rosenberg's use of women's culture scholarship, and critical reaction to it, was the product of competing ideologies, discursive practices, and institutional structures, each operating in wider political contexts that further shaped its meaning. The concept of women's culture as understood within the context of community-based feminism was a differentiated female world, considered a superior and perhaps authentically feminist challenge to dominant culture ideology. When it crossed into the context of the university, feminist editors interpreted women's culture as an intuitive, romantic understanding of gendered relations and attempted to ameliorate its political consequences by subjecting it to the university's rationalist codes and conventions. When women's culture moved into the wider conservative political context of the U.S. Circuit Court of Chicago, it was again reshaped—this time as a gendered sphere in which women choose material deprivation in order to uphold traditional domestic ideology. Given such consequences, denying the political dimensions and uses of scholarship within specific historical contexts does not render scholarship impartial, but rather incomplete.

Amy Farrell, a scholar of feminist publishing, has observed that feminist "gatekeepers" apparently only control the "gate" of academia in one direction.[61] Feminist scholars gained enough authority to negotiate the meaning of women's culture as it entered academic discourse but were unable to retain that power of definition when women's culture expanded. How is it that the content of such scholarship can be so easily appropriated, and its politics so easily evacuated, when used in larger social contexts? Although the possibility for social change can be created through the process of academic legitimation, the features of rational discourse can also be used to absorb and defuse oppositional knowledge.[62]

According to Habermas, discursive practice based on rationality "fulfills an emancipatory function in equalizing all participants in public discourse. Within the boundaries of the public sphere differences in rank and class are in theory subordinate to the demands of critical reasoned debate. 'Access is guaranteed to all citizens.'"[63] Like the principle of academic freedom, feminists can successfully use the theory of equal access to rationalist discourse to "prove" the social reality of exclusion. In fact, they have been able to exercise power within the university through their expert use of rational discourse and academic forms. Their scholarly journals have created a "cultural space," enabling feminists to become active participants within academic discourse rather than remain "outsiders defined, objectified, and reified by that discourse."[64]

The rhetoric of equal access can be used to subdue the politics of feminist inquiry and reinforce dominant ideology, however. The academy's abstract, rationalist forms can mute the narrative voice and the political intent of any piece of scholarship, allowing any voice with any political intent equal access to the language and form of feminist scholarship. Consequently, women's culture scholarship could be stripped of its original lesbian feminist voices and distanced from its radical political intent to serve the dominant social relations as expressed in the Sears decision.

In addition to filtering politics and muting voices, rationalist forms and language effectively exclude oppositional knowledge more adequately expressed in nonacademic forms. As Barbara Christian, an editor, argues, the privileging academic language silences other "native tongues": "Academic language has become the new metaphysic through which we turn leaden idiom into golden discourse. But by writing more important thinking exclusively in this language, we not only speak but to ourselves, we also are in danger of not asking those critical questions which our native *tongues* insist we ask. Whether anyone in the academy knows it or not, the old Afro-American refrain 'God don't like ugly' . . . is very different from its translation into current linguistic practice."[65]

Mindful of the silences within their textual structure, the editors of *Feminist Studies, Frontiers,* and *Signs* developed experimental forms, put traditional forms to new use, and called for submissions in community forms. *Signs,* once the most politically removed of the journals, has created "Forum," which its editors hope will connect the "multivocality" of academy and community concerns: "By establishing 'Forum,' we wish to reconnect with the activist concerns of the women's movement that provided the energy to create the field of feminist studies itself, For us, activism and scholarship are not contradictory or mutually exclusive concepts. To the contrary, we believe that their connection is a source of energy for the engaged debate that has historically enlivened our field."[66]

Although "Forum" has yet to be tested, the history of unanswered calls for manifestos reveals that such silences are not governed by the political value of various literary strategies but reflect the larger stratifications of power both within and without the contemporary women's movement. As Christian observes, "Although everything (in the philosophical discussion about race and gender) has changed, everything (as to whose voices are privileged in institutions, publishing outlets, universities) remains the same."[67]

Notes

1. C. Hugh Holman, ed., *Handbook to Literature* (New York: Macmillan Publishing Co., 1986), 211.

2. A.P.A. Council of Editors, *Publication Manual of the American Psychological Association,* 3d ed. (Washington: American Psychological Association, 1983), 22.

3. Margaret F. Steig, *The Origin and Development of Scholarly Historical Periodicals* (University: University of Alabama Press, 1986), 27.

4. Mary Claire VanLeuner, *A Handbook for Scholars* (New York: Alfred A. Knopf, 1978), 7–8.

5. Feminist discussions of "feminine" form can be found in: Ann Rosalind Jones, "Writing the Body: Toward an Understanding of L'Ecriture Feminine," *Feminist Studies* 7 (Summer 1981): 247–63; Andrea E. Goldsmith, "Notes on the Tyranny of Language Usage," *Women's Studies International Quarterly* 3, nos. 2–3 (1980): 179–91; Josephine Donovan, "Feminism and Aesthetics," *Critical Inquiry* 3, no. 3 (1977): 605–8; Silvia Bovenschen, "Is There Feminine Aesthetic?" *Heresies* 1, no. 4 (1977–78): 10–12; Irene Klepfisz, "Criticism, Form, and Function in Lesbian Literature," *Sinister Wisdom* 9 (1979): 27–30; Annette Kolodny, "Some Notes on Defining a 'Feminist Literary Criticism,'" *Critical*

Inquiry 2, no. 1 (1975): 75–92; Shari Benstock, "Reading the Signs of Women's Writing," *Tulsa Studies in Women's Literature* 4 (Spring 1985): 7–27.

6. Interview with editor Catharine Stimpson, New Brunswick, New Jersey, August 5, 1985.

7. Interviews with Barbara Gelpi, Claire Novak, and Susan Johnson, Palo Alto, California, June 3, 1985; Kathi George, Boulder Colorado, January 15, 1985; Deborah Rosenfelt, San Francisco, California, May 31, 1985.

8. Ann Allen et al., "Commentary: Response to Margarete Sandelowski's 'Fault Lines: Infertility and Imperiled Sisterhood,'" *Feminist Studies* 17 (Spring 1991): 149–51.

9. Nilufer Cagatay, Caren Grown, and Aida Santiago, "The Nairobi Women's Conference: Toward a Global Feminism (Commentary)," *Feminist Studies* 12 (Summer 1986): 401–12; Vasantha Kannabiran, "Report from SSS: A Women's Group in Hyderabad, Andhra Pradesh, India (Commentary)," *Feminist Studies* 12 (Fall 1986): 601–12; Tessie P. Lui, "Race and Gender in the Politics of Group Formation: A Comment on Notions of Multiculturalism," *Frontiers* 12, no. 2 (1991): 155–65.

10. "A Word to Prospective Contributors," *Feminist Studies* 4 (February 1978): 225.

11. Interview with editor Rayna Rapp, New York, October 9, 1986.

12. Mary S. Pollock, "The Politics of Women's Music: A Conversation with Linda Tillery," *Frontiers* 10, no. 1 (1987): 14–19; Mary S. Pollock, "Recovery and Integrity: The Music of Meg Christian," *Fontiers* 9, no. 2 (1986): 29–34.

13. Interview with editor Joan Burstyn, New Brunswick, New Jersey, August 5, 1985.

14. Sections of the journals used for this function include *Signs'* "U.S. Notes," "International Notes," "Reports and Revsions," and "Conference Reports"; *Feminist Studies'* "Notes and Letters"; and *Frontiers'* "Reviews and Responses."

15. Interview with editors Rayna Rapp and Ruth Milkman, New York, October 9, 1985.

16. Carol Nagy Jacklin, "Viewpoint: On *In a Different Voice:* An Interdisciplinary Forum," *Signs* 11 (Winter 1986): 304.

17. Annette Kolodny, "Dancing through the Minefield: Some Observations on the Theory, Practice, and Politics of a Feminist Literary Criticism," *Feminist Studies* 6 (Spring 1980): 9; interview with editor Claire Moses, Reston, Virginia, May 17, 1985.

18. Carroll Smith-Rosenberg, "The Female World of Love and Ritual: Relations between Women in Nineteenth-Century America," *Signs* 1 (Autumn 1975): 1–2.

19. Ellen DuBois et al., "Politics and Culture in Women's History: A Symposium," *Feminist Studies* 6 (Spring 1980): 62.

20. Gayle Kimball, "Women's Culture: Themes and Images," in *Women's Culture: The Women's Renaissance of the Seventies,* ed. Gayle Kimball (Metuchen: Scarecrow Press, 1981), 2.

21. Ruth Iskin, "Institutions of Women's Culture," in *Women's Culture,* ed. Kimball, 288.

22. Interview with editor Estelle Freedman, Palo Alto, California, June 3, 1985.

23. Interview with editor Mary Ryan, Palo Alto, California, June 3, 1985.

24. With its emphasis on materialist-historical analysis, it is not surprising that *Feminist Studies* would initiate this debate on the ahistorical, universalizing aspects of women's culture. As Ryan explains, "Among the editors is a lack of sympathy with cultural feminism. . . . in this fundamental way we look more toward social and materialist things and have a sense of gender as more complex than just female experience." Interview, June 3, 1985.

25. In her critique of Smith-Rosenberg's concept of a "female world," Ellen DuBois traced the term *women's culture* in Nancy Cott, *Roots of Bitterness* (New York: E. P. Dutton, 1972); Christine Stansell and Johnny Faragher, "Women and Their Families on the Overland Trail to California and Oregon, 1842–1867," *Feminist Studies* 2 (1975): 150–66; Kathryn Kish Sklar, *Catherine Bucher: A Study in American Domesticity* (New Haven: Yale University Press, 1973); Ann Douglass Wood, "The 'Scribbling Women' and Fanny Fern: Why Women Wrote," *American Quarterly* 23 (Spring 1971): 3–24; and Mary P. Ryan, "The Power of Women's Networks: A Case of Female Moral Reform in Antebellum America," *Feminist Studies* 5 (Spring 1979): 66–85. Similarly, DuBois parallels women's culture with recent scholarship on slave culture, including: John W. Blassingame, *The Slave Community: Plantation Life in the Antebellum South* (New York: Oxford University Press, 1972); Herbert Gutman, *The Black Family in Slavery and Freedom, 1750–1925* (New York: Pantheon Books, 1974); and Stanley Elkins, *Slavery* (Chicago: University of Chicago Press, 1959). See notes 4 and 5 in DuBois, "Politics and Culture in Women's History," 35.

26. Women's culture approaches profoundly influenced feminist literary and art analyses in the early 1980s. See Sandra Gilbert and Susan Gubar, "Introduction," *Women's Studies* Special Issue 7, no. 1 (1980): 1; and Joan Semmel and April Kingsley, "Sexual Imagery in Women's Art," *Women's Art Journal* 1 (Spring-Summer 1980): 1–6.

27. Carol Gilligan, "In a Different Voice: Women's Conceptions of Self and Morality," *Harvard Educational Review* 47, no. 4 (1977): 481–82.

28. Interview with editor Judith Stacey, Berkeley, California, June 16, 1985.

29. Judy Auerbach et al., "Commentary: On Gilligan's *In a Different Voice*," *Feminist Studies* 11 (Spring 1985): 159.

30. Jessica Benjamin, "Review: *In a Different Voice: Psychological Theory and Women's Development*," *Signs* 9 (Winter 1983): 297.

31. Benjamin, "Review," 307.

32. Carol Nagy Jacklin, "Editor's Note to *In a Different Voice*," 304.

33. Zella Luria, "A Methodological Critique," *Signs* 11 (Winter 1986): 317.

34. Carol B. Stack, "The Culture of Gender: Women and Men of Color," *Signs* 11 (Winter 1986): 321–24.

35. Linda Kerber, "Some Cautionary Words for Historians," *Signs* 11 (Winter 1986): 304–10.

36. Carol Gilligan, "Reply by Carol Gilligan," *Signs* 11 (Winter 1986): 331.

37. Luria, "A Methodological Critique," 320.

38. Information for this description of the trial and testimony is drawn from Ruth Milkman, "Women's History and the Sears Case," *Feminist Studies* 12 (Summer 1986): 375–400; "Archives: Women's History Goes to Trial: *EEOC vs. Sears Roebuck, and Company*," *Signs* 11 (Summer 1986): 751–79; Carol Sternhell, "Life in the Mainstream: What Happens When Feminists End Up on Both Sides of the Court," *Ms.*, July 1986, 48–51, 86–91; David Tell, "Disparity or Discrimination: Women's History vs. Sears. Interview with Rosalyn Rosenberg" and "Differences and Inequality: Interview with Alice Kessler-Harris," *Society* 24 (September–October 1987): 4–16.

39. Rosenberg has acknowledged that the fact her former husband worked for Morgan Associates, the law firm that represented Sears, "played a role" in her decision to become involved in the case. "Women's History Goes to Trial," 385.

40. Ibid., 757.

41. Sternhell, "Life in the Mainstream," 51; Rosenberg, "Women's History Goes to Trial," 779.

42. Cf. Peter Novick, *That Noble Dream* (Cambridge: Cambridge University Press, 1990), 505.

43. For more on the importance of considering social context in assessing the outcome of the Sears case, see Stephanie Riger, "Comment on 'Women's History Goes to Trial': *EEOC v. Sears, Roebuck and Company*," *Signs* 13 (Summer 1988): 897–903.

44. Sternhell, "Life in the Mainstream," 48–49.

45. Ibid., 86.

46. Milkman, "Women's History and the Sears Case," 376; Rosenberg, "Women's History Goes to Trial," 751–67.

47. "The Sears Case: Feminist Bashing in the Popular Press," *New Directions for Women* 15 (October 1986): 1.

48. Milkman, "Women's History and the Sears Case," 392.

49. Jonathan Yardley, "When Scholarship and the Cause Collide," *Washington Post*, June 16, 1986, C-2.

50. "Editorial: Misusing History," *Washington Post*, June 10, 1986.

51. Sternhell, "Life in the Mainstream," 89, 86.

52. Carol Iannone, "The Barbarism of Feminist Scholarship," *Intercollegiate Review* 23 (Fall 1987): 37.

53. In the ethnographic approach, the interpretation of cultural behavior relies on discovering the "emic," or insider's point of view. The "etic," or outsider's perspective, can provide a useful and necessary counterpoint, but the assignment of motives to cultural behavior from an etic perspective often distorts the culture's meaning system to fit the interpretive schema of the observer. The systematic discovery of the knowledge cultural participants use to organize and interpret their own behavior is essential in anthropological terms. Consequently, although Rosenberg herself may grasp and contest the motives of feminist scholarship, few popular press critics are emic enough to that culture to reconstruct its intentions accurately. For a discussion of emic and etic perspectives, see James Spradley and David McCurdy, *The Cultural Experience:*

Ethnography in Complex Society (Chicago: Science Research Associates, 1972), and Clifford Geertz, *The Interpretations of Cultures* (New York: Basic Books, Inc., 1973).

54. Rosenberg, "Women's History Goes to Trial," 752.

55. Milkman, "Women's History and the Sears Case," 394.

56. Joan W. Scott, "Deconstructing Equality-Versus-Difference," *Feminist Studies* 14 (Spring 1988): 43–44.

57. Susan Hekman, "From Monism to Pluralism," *Women and Politics* (Fall 1987): 88.

58. Sternhell, "Life in the Mainstream," 88.

59. Ibid., 90–91.

60. Milkman, "Women's History and the Sears Case," 394.

61. Amy Farrell, "Comments on 'Gatekeepers and Gatecrashers': Feminisms and Institutional Power in American Culture," paper presented at American Studies Association Annual Meeting, Baltimore, Maryland, 1991.

62. For an excellent account of the uses and limits of dominant ideology and institutions, see Kimberlé Williams Crenshaw, "Race, Reform, and Retrenchment: Transformation and Legitimation in Antidiscrimination Law," *Harvard Law Review* 101 (May 1988): 1331–87; and Frances Fox Piven and Richard Cloward, *Poor People's Movements: How They Succeed, How They Fail* (New York: Pantheon Books, 1977).

63. Jurgen Habermas, *Structural Transformations in the Public Sphere,* translated by Thomas Burger (Cambridge: MIT Press, 1989), 52, cf. Rita Felski, *Beyond Feminist Aesthetics: Feminist Literature and Social Change* (Cambridge: Harvard University Press, 1989), 164.

64. Crenshaw, "Race, Reform, and Retrenchment," 1359.

65. Barbara Christian, "Conference Call," *differences* 2, no. 3 (1990): 64.

66. "Editorial," *Signs* 16 (Spring 1991): 435.

67. Christian, "Conference Call," 62.

chapter seven

Feminist Academic Journals and Feminist Knowledge in the 1990s

My final words are to remember that history and our own work ebb and flow, but keeping alive the core of what we are about through those hard times has been done by women in the past and they can serve as guideposts for us in facing the future.[1]

Charlotte Bunch, editor,
Quest

In the summer of 1992, Ruth-Ellen Boetcher Joeres of *Signs* published a remarkable editorial statement:

> If feminism is to be inside the academy, it goes without saying that it will take on characteristics of that institution. It will begin to define itself as a discipline, for example, because it will want to lessen its reputation as being made up of magpies and nomads who, after all, really don't belong. . . . And in the effort to give ourselves the prestige we seek—to mirror those who are successful in the ways in which the academy defines success—we may try to align ourselves with those who represent High Theory, which speaks a language not known for its accessibility. In all of these cases, the institutionalizing process has not always been beneficial or benign for us.

They then offered the most recognized journal of the field as "an alternative space within the academy that might represent a way back to our origins as a nomadic people whose acceptance of/in the institution as home is never entirely unproblematic: a space that can allow for difference in the ways we communicate with each other."[2]

In 1975, Catharine Stimpson had set out to beat the academics at their own game by making *Signs* a scholarly journal beyond reproach.[3] Consequently, the 1992 statement of profound institutional ambivalence seems extraordinary unless viewed in light of current concerns in the continuing production of knowledge within feminist discourse.

In 1975, feminist scholars had a relatively small selection of academic journals to support their work. By the end of the 1980s, the field was populated by scores of publications serving a multiplicity of specialized interests.[4] This proliferation repositioned *Signs, Feminist Studies,* and *Frontiers* as representatives of "traditional," perhaps even what the literary critic Gayatri Spivak calls "hegemonic feminism," within the university.[5] No longer academic renegades, the journals are authoritative publications—the pillars of "established" feminism, cited and contested, internally and externally, in the ongoing struggle in the cultural production of knowledge.

According to Peter Berger, a sociologist, institutions pattern human activity into stable, predictable, and controlled behavior and cognition. Legitimation provides the plausible justification that maintains and reproduces institutions as authoritative structures.[6] The model of scholarly political publication created and developed by the editors of journals like *Feminist Studies, Frontiers,* and *Signs* is now a "stable, predictable, and controlled" pattern of scholarship that can be reproduced and contested, but never ignored, by new journals in the field.

The full measure of these journals as legitimized academic institutions can be seen in the creation of *NWSA Journal,* which was founded in 1988 by MaryJo Wagner and Susan Hartmann at the Ohio State Center for Women's Studies as the official publication of the National Women's Studies Association. Since the mid 1970s, the National Women's Studies Association has been the most visible and important manifestation of feminist ambivalence within the university. Throughout its history, the association has continually struggled between the impetus of activism and the validity of scholarship as useful feminist strategies. Robin Leidner, a sociologist, has extensively analyzed the history of public dramas and internal conflicts surrounding the NWSA's use of hybrid political-scholarly organizational structures.[7]

The publication's more recent creation as an unambivalently scholarly journal is a sign that the NWSA is gradually coming to terms with itself as an academic professional association. The current editor,

Patrocinio Schweickart, explains that "historically, the political/scholarly tension at NWSA has been resolved in favor of political action. The balance in the journal is different, the basic principle guiding the journal is 'scholarship can be social action.' One of the core constituencies for NWSA is an academic constituency. The journal is vital for the production of scholarship, but also for the production of scholars. Both are vital to the cultural project of feminism."[8]

It is important to note that in the process of becoming a more fully legitimized institution for its academic constituency the NWSA created a journal that replicates the model established by *Feminist Studies, Frontiers,* and *Signs.* MaryJo Wagner studied and adopted versions of their editorial structures and publishing formats. The journal shares *Frontiers'* commitment to accessibility by avoiding highly specialized academic language. Like *Feminist Studies* and *Frontiers,* its mission is explicitly political, and it remains attentive to the concerns of the contemporary women's movement. In addition, *NWSA Journal* is not committed to exclusively conventional scholarly forms; its use of "Observations," "Reports," and "Forum" parallels *Feminist Studies'* own "Commentary," "Notes and Letters," and "Forum."[9] Its rotation of institutional sponsorship, editorial structure, and extensive use of review essays most closely resembles that of *Signs.* The overall scholarly political criteria that define the parameters of its scholarship were developed during the earliest years of *Frontiers, Feminist Studies,* and *Signs.*

Yet *NWSA Journal* does more than simply replicate the earlier model. It extends the model into wider institutional settings and more diverse constituencies. The NWSA has always considered itself to be a central resource for women's studies educators, administrators, students, and activists within a number of settings: kindergarten through twelfth grade, community colleges, community educational projects, and universities. As Schwieckart points out, "It is important for the scholarly conversation to reach these other sections of the feminist community. I want *NWSA Journal* to be a useful vehicle for those constituencies. For this reason, the conventional standards of scholarship are not the sole basis for selecting the articles we publish; some articles are selected with an eye to their value to scholars in community colleges, K-12 teachers, students, and activists in women's centers and the community."

In a further attempt to include feminist practicioners in a variety of educational settings, fully 35 percent of each issue is devoted to review essays, including such features on materials for classroom use as "The Evolution of Texts for Women's Studies Students," "The Lesbian Teacher in Front of the Classroom," and "Teaching Materials on Women, Health and Healing in the U.S." In addition, the regular "On Learning and Teaching" section addresses the practical, political, and pedagogical issues confronting teachers in women's studies classrooms. By combining these features with articles that meet the strictest standards of academic convention, *NWSA Journal* extends and transforms the cognitive models of feminist scholarship pioneered by *Frontiers, Feminist Studies,* and *Signs* into recognized institutional practices.

However, as the theorist Barbara Johnson notes, institutions are articulations of power that mobilize some impulses and deactivate others.[10] Thus, if the journals do exercise the power of "hegemonic feminism," to what extent do they contain, appropriate, or replenish the rest of feminist discourse? Unlike *NWSA Journal,* other new feminist academic journals were created to contest the assumptions of "traditional" feminist journals explicitly and seek to "activate" particular tensions in feminist discourse, especially those surrounding the current sites of struggle and negotiation in feminist scholarship—poststructuralist theory and multiculturalism.[11] As poststructuralist critiques grew in influence, feminist scholars continued to attach theory to the academy and its exclusivity. As marginalized scholars challenged the centrality of white, feminist frameworks, multiculturalism remained implicitly attached to the community and its activism. Rather than reifying this academy-community dichotomy, such new journals as *differences: A Journal of Feminist Cultural Studies* (Indiana University Press), *Genders* (University of Texas), and *SAGE: A Scholarly Journal on Black Women* (SAGE Women's Educational Press, Inc.) sought more innovative positions within the tensions surrounding theory and multiculturalism.

Editors at *differences* and *Genders* characterize their journals as "theoretically informed" investigations of difference. Although distinct in important ways, both were created in response to the promise of theories associated with poststructuralism and its attendant fields, cultural studies and critical studies. The continued development and influence of such increasingly complex theories within feminist scholarship has intensified debate concerning the appropriate relationship between academic feminism and feminist activism. Although not specifically directed at the work featured in *differences* or *Genders,* the editors of

Signs have reiterated the fundamental feminist conviction: "We are not writing into the wind, . . . what we investigate and what we write about is meant to have some clear benefit for women."[13]

In the spring of 1992, *differences* deliberately reopened "theorizing politics and theorizing politically" as "significantly contested elements of feminist practice." In a special issue on politics, power, and culture, the editors challenged the fundamental political criteria that had defined feminist scholarship, and feminist academic journals, since the 1970s.

> *Feminist political theory*—a curious phrase, perhaps for some even striking, if only in its apparent redundancy. Is not *feminist theory* sufficient? Is it not necessarily *political* precisely insofar as it is *feminist?* That these questions invite a response in the indicative might occasion an initial pause, a hesitation before multiple closures requisite to their resolution; for the definitional clarity they demand entails a demarcation of the boundaries, a setting of the limits, not only of "feminism" but of "politics" and "theory" as well.
>
> The sensibility informing this special issue of *differences* might be characterized as an attempt to activate that hesitation, to render it productive, by foregrounding the imbrication of feminist theory with the more general unsettling of certainties associated with postmodernity.[13]

Will such deliberate destabilizing of established feminist political assumptions extend the range of possibilities for understanding women's oppression, or will the prevalence of such theories inexorably lead to a further distancing of feminist scholarship from feminist activism?

The editors of *differences* and *Genders* argue that feminist scholarship, of necessity, must account for its relationship to the growing sophistication in scholarly discourse. Founding editor Elizabeth Weed conceptualized *differences* while working at the Pembroke Center for Teaching and Research on Women at Brown University in 1989. The center provided the scholarly climate, institutional support, and much of the editorial board for the journal. According to another editor, Naomi Schor, and Weed, the title is not intended to signal "pluralism," but something closer to the film theorist Teresa de Lauretis's "multiple subjectivities."

differences is not simply concerned with women's issues or gender issues, but with any work that uses the "dilemma of difference" as a form of extensive cultural criticism.[14] Consequently, although the nucleus of each issue rests in feminist theory, *differences* was not modeled on traditional feminist academic journals. According to Schor, the journal's format and theoretical sophistication more closely resemble several poststructuralist journals: *Diacritics, October,* and *Representations.*[15] This turn to cultural theory has produced ground-breaking special issues, including "Reproductive Technologies and AIDS" (Volume 1, number 1), "Notes from the Beehive: Feminism and Institutions" (Volume 2, number 3), "Politics/Power/Culture: Postmodernity and Feminist Political Theory" (Volume 3, number 1), and the best-selling "The Essential Difference: Another Look at Essentialism" (Volume 1, number 2), which included the work of Teresa de Lauretis, Luce Irigaray, and Gayatri Spivak.

The term *poststructuralism* covers a multitude of diverse, often competing, critical inquiries. It is not surprising, then, that *differences* is not the first voice in the field. *Genders* was initiated by culture studies theorist Anne Kibbey in 1988 as a recognition that gender had become a category of extensive cultural analysis. She found that critical studies of gender were too often generated within social science frameworks or relied upon elite canons within the art history. Now housed at the University of Colorado at Boulder, *Genders* became the first academic journal to make mass and elite constructions of gender within the arts and humanities its principal concern. Consequently, the journal easily juxtaposes essays on Madonna, Oprah Winfrey, and Mapplethorpe with analyses of Descartes, Shakespeare, and Matisse.[16]

Journals such as *Genders* and *differences* help institutionalize and legitimate poststructuralist influence in the production of feminist scholarship. Beyond that, they present a more fundamental challenge to established feminist academic journals because they intentionally decenter the category of "woman" as the defining criterion for feminist scholarship. For years, "gender" was used as a synonym for "women" in feminist scholarship.[17] By the late 1980s, however, *Genders* and *differences* had initiated the reconsideration and recognition of "woman." The editors of *Genders* challenged the equation of "gender" with "women" by insisting that gender is not just women's work.[18] In contrast to the exclusive focus on women in earlier feminist journals, "*Genders* sees its task as one that must involve men as well as women at all levels. . . . One of the effects of this integration has been a reframing of major issues in feminist theory to take a stronger account of social context."[19]

Similarly, the editors of *differences* do not want to limit contributions only to those that "thematize women." *differences* editor and Pembroke founder Joan W. Scott argues that doing so opens a range of possibilities of theorizing gender as a "primary way of signifying relationships of power."[20] Work reflecting the potential of such approaches include *differences'* special issues on "Male Subjectivity" (Volume 1, number 3) and "The Phallus Issue" (Volume 4, number 1) and *Genders'* special issue "The Politics of the Sexual Body" (Issue 7, March 1990).

An article in *Genders* by the Iranian writer Abouli Farmanfarmaian particularly exemplifies the possibilities of such an approach. In "Sexuality in the Gulf War: Did You Measure Up?" (Spring 1992), Farmanfarmaian examined the role of race and sexuality as not metaphors but determinants of the Gulf War. He analyzed how fears concerning rape, miscegenation, family, and "manhood" were structurally and discursively intertwined in generating outrage against Iraq. He then placed these determining fears in the larger context of the use of race and sexuality in the history of American imperialism.

Yet the question remains, Can gender studies readily accommodate, or will it inadvertently evacuate, the feminist politics of women's studies? As Rita Felski observes, "Feminist discourse originates from women's experiences of oppression and recognizes their ultimate authority in speaking of its effects, feminism as a critique of values is also engaged in a more general and public process of revising and refuting male-defined cultural and discursive frameworks."[21]

A focus on "gender," rather than "women," does indeed offer a more fully investigated analysis of male subjectivities and the construction of male-defined culture. The editors of *differences* and *Genders* facilitate feminist examinations of how historically conferred, unstable, multiple identifications of masculinity constitute power in society. However the question that the journals pose concerns whether women's subjectivities will remain the preferred authorized position from which feminist scholars critique, revise, and refute such male-defined frameworks.

By 1988, the term *gender* had acquired such rapidly shifting, fluid meanings that the editors of *Signs* devoted an editorial to the subject in their spring issue. They concluded that the prevailing definition of gender "is subtle, contextual—it shifts with the purpose of the author" and warned, "As we develop this conceptual category, how do we avoid occluding the centrality of relations among women?" Similarly, the editors of *Feminist Studies,* in the Preface to the spring 1992 issue, asked of proponents of postmodernism, "Whose experience? Whose desire? Whose authority of interpretation? In other words, again and always, 'What do women want?'" And, after arguing the usefulness of deconstruction, Judith Newton, a former editor of *Feminist Studies,* reiterated the "preconditions" of feminist uses of poststructuralist approaches:

> Feminist appropriations of Foucault, however, have largely deviated from those of nonfeminist men and again the difference has much to do with needs, desires, and politics. Despite the fact that feminists have been influenced by skeptical poststructuralist philosophy, and despite the political setbacks of the last few years, many feminist critics still operate not only out of a belief and investment in change. . . . Belief in the possibility of identifying power, belief in the possibility of progressive agency and change are, of course, preconditions for feminist and all oppositional politics and have been the preconditions for the scholarly projects that grew from them."[22]

In response to such concerns, proponents of feminist poststructuralism resist pressures to classify poststructuralism as feminist "ally, enemy, fellow traveler, [or] fifth column."[23] The editors at *differences* and *Genders* argue that embedded in their challenge is perhaps the most exciting contribution of their journals—the potential of decentering white privilege in the construction of feminist inquiry. By moving away from a thematized focus on women, difference becomes implicated in the conception and construction of power itself—opening investigations of the complex connections between sexual difference, gender difference, racial difference, national difference, and more. The transformative potential of rethinking gender and diversity in poststructuralist feminist inquiry is illustrated by *differences'* special issue "Queer Theory: Lesbian and Gay Sexualities" (Volume 3, number 2), guest-edited by de Lauretis, and *Genders'* special issue "Theorizing Nationality, Sexuality, and Race" (Issue 10, Spring 1991), which includes "U.S. Third World Feminism: The Theory and Method of Oppositional Consciousness in the Postmodern World" by Chela Sandoval.

Even though feminist scholars at *differences* and *Genders* have moved rapidly forward in addressing questions of difference and the social constructions of power, Evelyn Brooks Higginbotham, a black historian, is concerned that "the general trend has been to mention black and Third World feminists who first called attention to the glaring fallacies in essentialist analysis and to claims of a homogeneous 'womanhood,' 'woman's culture,' and 'patriarchal oppression of women.' Beyond this recognition, however, white feminist scholars pay hardly more than lip service to race as they continue to analyze their own experience in ever more sophisticated forms."[24]

The feminist academic journal that most successfully centers race and community interest in its analysis is *SAGE: A Scholarly Journal on Black Women*. In the summer of 1983, founding editors Patricia Bell-Scott, Beverly Guy-Sheftall, and Ruby Sales conducted a candid, all-night discussion about the absence of material on women of color in feminist academic journals and African-American academic journals. At the time, only the *Psychology of Women Quarterly* and the *Black Scholar* produced special issues on African-American women. Academic discourses in black studies and women's studies had moved to the point of serious and intense theoretical debate, but, according to Bell-Scott, published material on black women remained underdeveloped in scholarly debate.[25] By morning, the women decided that rather than focusing their energies on the established journals, a new "pro-woman," "pro-black" publication was needed. The first issue of *SAGE*, designed to provide an interdisciplinary forum for feminist critical discussion of issues related to black women, appeared in the spring of 1984. The journal is based at the Women's Research and Resource Center at Spelman College.

The editors and contributors of *SAGE* have a broader definition of scholarship than the predominantly white academic journals. To convey the meaning of "pro-black" and "pro-woman" scholarship, the editors, at times, rely on Alice Walker's preferred term, *womanist*. Walker has explained that the term is drawn from "the black folk expression of mothers to female children, 'You acting womanish,' i.e., like a woman. Usually referring to outrageous, audacious, courageous, or *willful* behavior. . . . Interchangeable with another black folk expression, 'You trying to be grown.' Responsible. In charge. Serious. . . . Loves struggle. *Loves* the folk. Loves herself." Higginbotham also agrees that "some black women scholars adopt the term *womanist* instead of *feminist* in rejection of gender-based dichotomies that lead to a false homogenizing of women."[26]

Perhaps *SAGE*'s most notable difference from other new feminist academic journals lies in its relentless dedication to including themes of active resistance and community connection. This commitment has informed the journal's content, format, and focus from its inception. Thus, although *differences* and *Genders* pose the problem of how to move from scholarly critiques to women's lived experience, *SAGE* explores how to use women's lived experience to produce accurate, effective critical perspectives. Its editors seek to publish work considered "scholarly" in the broadest sense—accessible analyses of black women's experiences wherever the women reside and whatever their perspectives. Although conventional academics are the journal's core constituency, unlike *Feminist Studies, Frontiers,* and *Signs,* the editors of *SAGE* have a specific image of the nonacademic community it wishes to address—students, teenagers, senior citizens, and readers without college educations who populate their families and community institutions. As Bell-Scott explains,

> Our objective has been to democratize intellectual discourse by including the widest possible range of voices. If you look through back issues, you will see anything from fairly sophisticated literary criticism to interviews to personal narratives. Our authors have been respected scholars, community activists, students—we have published an eleven-year-old and an eighty-seven-year-old. Our desire to reach the next generation has been heightened largely because of the decreasing numbers of young Black Americans who are going to college. Of those who do, some of the best and the brightest have chosen to go to law school and medical school. We think it's important to have scholars, too. We saw a critical need to reach out and focus on young people. In the summer of 1988 we had a whole issue done by students.[27]

Grappling with many of the same concerns as *Frontiers, SAGE* has deliberately assumed a community posture from within an academic setting. Against the strong advice of established journal editors, *SAGE* was designed to appear less academic and formidable. In order to appeal to readers of all educational backgrounds, *SAGE* publishes short articles, uses engaging visuals and photographic essays, and has a 8.5 by 11 inch magazine format. According to Bell-Scott, the editors hope to promote literacy and critical reading among nonacademic readers. "We don't mind if non-academics think *SAGE* is a magazine. If an adolescent saw the journal on a table, they might initially be encouraged to pick it up because the cover was enticing. Then, if they flipped through it, they may see the photographic essays and be encouraged to read further. This is the scenario we hope for."[28]

Reiterating the insights of the black theorist bell hooks, the editors of *SAGE* assert that institutional power is simply one form of power. Indeed, there is, according to hooks, enormous "power in having a public audience for one's work that may not be particularly academic; power that comes from writing in ways that enable people to think critically about everyday life."[29]

To date, this community posture has not diminished *SAGE*'s academic credibility. The journal has published work by many esteemed scholars: hooks; the anthropologist Lynn Bolles; writer Paula Giddings; sociologist Joyce Ladner, a social work scholar; Barbara Smith, a literary critic; Rosalyn Terborg-Penn, a historian; and Michele Wallace, Alice Walker, and Audre Lorde, who are writers. The journal is self-sustained by an academic subscription base and by abundant reprint requests from other scholarly publications and for classroom use. *SAGE*'s academic reputation has been further enhanced by the critical and market success of *Double Stitch: Black Women Write about Mothers and Daughters*, an anthology based on two special issues that is in its second printing and has been released in paperback.[30]

Yet the editors are careful not to reproduce organicist, romantic, or monolithic conceptualizations of black women, "black identity," and "black community." In the special issue "Mothers and Daughters II" (Fall 1987), contributors present analyses of "contradictory, ambivalent, courageous, ambiguous, and sympathetic mothers."[31] The multiple aspects of black motherhood are variously grieved by the authors and daughters as constructions of racist and sexist oppression, celebrated as imperfect sites of humanizing resistance, and analyzed as culturally complex intersections of Afrocentric and Eurocentric ideologies. For example, in "Mothers of Mind," the historian Elsa Barkley Brown illustrates how centralizing community interests and women's lived experiences in the production of knowledge radically reshapes feminist theory. It was only through "placing one's self inside one's community and inside one's scholarship" that she was able to complete her study of washerwomen in the African-American community of Louisville, Kentucky. Brown details the lessons that caused her to retheorize the project:

My academic training has been designed to teach me paradigms for and theories about Africanamerican people and historical development and to teach me to use them as the basis of my analysis of the people whose lives I study. But I, like many Africanamerican scholars before me, have often had to question that training; it has, after all, been designed to teach me how to interpret an Afrocentric community in terms of a Eurocentric world view. And, as I question the applicability of my historical training, I have to look for other ways to analyze my community. It is in this discovery of new directions that my mother has influenced my work, and thus what follows could most appropriately be subtitled, "How My Mother Taught Me To Be A Historian In Spite of My Academic Training."[32]

Brown discovered that her Eurocentric training contradicted the historical record that her mother had passed down at the family's kitchen table. Standard histories had misinterpreted the economic importance of washerwomen. By relying on her mother's historical record of her own washerwoman mother, however, Brown was able to ask "the right questions" that revealed the institutional importance of washerwomen. They did not work in isolation, as had been assumed, but organized themselves as entrepreneurs. They used this entrepreneurial organization to create churches, schools, mutual benefit societies, factories, and banks for African-American communities. Washerwomen were not simply wage-earners, they were "organizers, planners, policymakers, leaders, and developers of the community and its institutions." Brown, like other contributors to *SAGE*, concludes that theory must be embedded in concrete community connections: "Black Studies (and to some degree Women's Studies) began from an understanding of the necessity of connecting the people doing the research and the people who were the subjects of the inquiry—to have the academy informed by those whose very lives spoke to that about which we intellectualize."[33]

So far, the success of *SAGE* has been unique. Two smaller specialized journals, the *Zora Neale Hurston Forum* and the *Journal of the National Black Nurses Association,* have appeared, but the editors of *SAGE* had hoped to see other journals on African-American women's history or black women's literature.[34] *SAGE* never intended to carry the full burden of feminist research on, and perspectives by, women of color, but it remains a vital but token publication in the culture of feminist scholarship.

Feminist academic inquiry remains a dynamic, ever-shifting, terrain. The production of feminist knowledge is a scholarly, political, and institutionally complex negotiation. As always, *Frontiers, Feminist Studies,* and *Signs* continue to respond. In one of the most intimate self-scrutinies, *Signs* published an article that examined its editorial board and that of *Feminist Studies* in 1985 and concluded:

> Despite white, middle-class feminists' frequent expressions of interest and concern over the plight of minority and working-class women, those holding the gatekeeping positions at these journals are as white as those at any mainstream social science or humanities publication.
>
> . . . it is more difficult to delineate the ways that classism excludes both whites and women of color who are working class. The information *Signs* gives about the institutional affiliations of its editors and consultants, however, can be used to illustrate other biases in the gatekeeping positions. None of the fifty women in these positions represents traditionally Black institutions; only six represent schools whose students are primarily constituted of working-class students; and only three are from the South, where the highest concentrations of minorities continue to live.[35]

About a year before the publication of the article, both journals conducted similar reassessments. The changes that ensued give some indication of how the publications intend to address certain omissions on their boards and in their pages. The original white, middle-class, primarily heterosexual editors are now esteemed, established scholars, no longer the activist students and fledgling academics who created a politicized scholarship from the margins of the campus and community. Indeed, the 1988–93 editorial boards of *Frontiers, Feminist Studies,* and *Signs* were primarily comprised of tenured and widely published associate and full professors.

In a partial attempt to replicate their own history, a number of the original editors of *Feminist Studies* stepped down to make room for younger, more diverse scholars. The journal infused its close-knit editorial collective with scholars whose color, sexual preference, or age have marginalized their work in academe.[36] Yet this "marginalized representation" does not mean that the new editors are necessarily peripheral or marginal academics. Editors such as Lynn Bolles, Barbara Christian, Rosalyn Terborg-Penn, and Martha Vicinus of *Feminist Studies* may represent marginalized constituencies, but each woman is a highly successful scholar and much in demand in academia. The editors did not design this policy to simply place scholars with "marginalized identities" on the boards, but, as Claire Moses explains, to access networks of diverse political and scholarly interest in wider feminist communities.

> We've been adding editors—not just those whose personal identity are Third World, but whose contacts, networks, and fields of interest expand our discussions around these issues. And we've also addressed the heterosexual bias of what is published in *Feminist Studies*. . . . not only getting the word out among people producing theory and scholarship in lesbian studies, but also by increasing our contacts by adding editors and consultants whose ties are in those areas. We're not just interested in someone's personal identity as lesbian . . . but in the creation of new scholarship and theory.[37]

The editors do not rely on "essentialized" identities, rather they understand that the social construction of race, class, and gender has effectively made it difficult for marginalized scholars to access the most powerful networks and institutions of academic discourse.

Similarly, *Signs* has used its institutional rotations of editorship to expand and pluralize its board. After the tightly hierarchical editorship of Catharine Stimpson at Barnard College from 1975 to 1980, Barbara Gelpi and her colleagues at Stanford University (1980–85) "stressed the importance of feminist connection among editors, contributors, reviewers, and readers as they put their energies to a common task." In addition, the Stanford group chose to move away from Stimpson's purely academic focus by publishing work explicitly designed to stimulate social change: "We see our responsibility to the feminist community as one which involves intellectual commitment to the best and most interesting ideas in all academic fields as well as participatory commitment in the process whereby ideas become action."[38] This "participatory commitment" generated articles on rape avoidance strategies, sexual harassment, unemployment compensation, the meaning of the vote, and a special issue addressing the feminization of poverty.[39]

Perhaps even more notable was the journal's move to North Carolina (1986–91) under Jean O'Barr and the dual auspices of Duke University and the University of North Carolina at Chapel Hill. Relocating *Signs* at a state university in the South was a conscious effort to "pursue, with renewed emphasis, the intellectual promise of the diversity of women's lives, particularly in those areas that pertain to race, class, and regional studies."[40] The Duke–UNC board widened the journal's scope with frequent analyses of marginalized populations and increasing attention to multiculturalism. Although the North Carolina group sponsored a special issue, "Common Grounds and Crossroads: Race, Ethnicity, and Class in Women's Lives" (Volume 14, number 4), increased attention to diversity was common in many regular issues, for example, Volume 15, number 2.

But the most substantial changes in *Signs'* history have come from another rotation of editorship. In 1992, the journal came to the University of Minnesota Center for Advanced Feminist Studies under the interdisciplinary editorship of Ruth-Ellen Boetcher Joeres, a literary historian, and Barbara Laslett, a sociologist. The Minnesota group has chosen to emphasize the "multivocality" of the field: "The number of voices speaking in the name of feminism has multiplied so enormously that we can no longer speak comfortably of a feminism or, indeed, of a single feminist theory. . . . *Signs* is a journal of many voices, many stories."[41] To encourage and accommodate this multivocality, the Minnesota board finally broke the journal's strict adherence to academic form and language. While stressing the inevitability of increasingly complex language to convey increasingly sophisticated scholarship, the board called upon scholars "mired in . . . the disciplinary, jargonistic, alienating language so prominent in academe" to recall the field's origin in activism.

The editors codified their convictions in a revised editorial policy: fewer scholarly articles, more accessible prose, increased use of authorial voice, reduction of substantive notes, and—after nearly two decades of protecting the genre's borders—"loosening the ban on the personal." Most significantly, the editors singled out the essay, with its subjective voice, lack of documentation, and political immediacy, as the journal's preferred form. They describe the essay as a "borderline genre" that provides "an alternative avenue for feminist critical writing in the academy."[42] Then, the editors showcased personal and political scholarly essays by Marilyn Frye and Alice Kessler-Harris in a forum titled "On Being Labeled Politically (In)Correct."

Signs and *Feminist Studies* have increased the content on women of color, diversified their editorial boards, and amended their academic forms, yet it is not clear whether these actions will substantially reshape the journals. Critics have claimed that "polite pluralism" cannot substitute for fundamental rearrangements of institutional power. In *Signs'* "The Cost of Exclusionary Practices in Women's Studies," Maxine Baca Zinn and others warned that "such work is often tacked on, its significance for feminist knowledge still unrecognized and unregarded." [43]

In this world of multiplicity and diversity, feminist scholarship is losing its visceral connections to the nonacademic women's movement. For *Feminist Studies* editor Barbara Christian, the problem is "not so much the split between the real world outside and the unreal world of the institution inside, but the academy behaves as if it *is* the world, the only world, and that which lies *outside* it is but raw material which it transforms into ideas." [44] In a similar analysis, Barbara Johnson argues that distinctions between the university and the "real world" are nothing other than perceptions of the boundaries of institutions. "Whether one is in the university or in the army, the real world seems to exist outside the institution. It is as though institutions existed precisely to create boundaries between the unreal and the real, to assure docility, paradoxically, through the assumption of unreality. Yet institutions are nothing if not *real* articulations of power." [45] Chela Sandoval also warns that U.S.–third world feminist theories of oppositional consciousness have been sublimated, assimilated, and "made deeply invisible by the manner of its appropriation, in the terms of what has become a hegemonic feminist theory." [46] U.S.–third world feminist theory, she argues, forces fully institutionalized hegemonic feminism to recenter its constructions of oppositional consciousness. Although the academy has been successfully used as a site of power for articulating feminist knowledge, it is now in danger of becoming a site of feminist hegemonic privilege and a vehicle for feminist containment and appropriation.

Frontiers, which has always pursued diversity, has faced different challenges that, ironically, have led to both to a deeper involvement with the structures and standards of academe and a centralizing of traditionally marginalized scholarships. Since its inception, *Frontiers* had struggled to remain financially self-supporting. But by the mid 1980s, the journal was floundering because its subscription base had remained small and because community bookstore sales, advertising, and even sales of single issues as classroom texts had failed to bring in enough revenue to stabilize the journal. The editorial collective opened negotiations with several university presses, seeking a home within a journals division. All negotiations were unsuccessful. *Frontiers* then sought greater funding, on a permanent basis, from the University of Colorado, which had previously funded the journal with modest, single-action grants.[47]

As the editorial board waited to hear whether funds would be available for the 1987–88 fiscal year, Kathi George, its community-minded editor, left the journal to pursue a career in publishing.[48] Michèle Barale, the board member whom George supported as her successor, was rejected by the university and denied a tenure-track position. The decision led to a struggle within the editorial board. The journal floundered, and *Frontiers* opened negotiations with the university presses. Without George's personally financed editorship, the board faced either dismantling the journal or seeking a closer affiliation with the university.

Historian Elizabeth Jameson, a founding member of the original *Frontiers* collective and the head of women's studies at the University of New Mexico, was able to propose an editorial structure and operating budget that interested the University of New Mexico and the University Press of Colorado. To ensure continuity, the new board is made up of three scholars from the host university (the University of New Mexico), a member of the original 1975 *Frontiers* collective, and one member from the later University of Colorado at Boulder collective. The board is assisted by an expanded editorial collective that includes scholars from the University of New Mexico, community artists and activists, and two representatives from the Technical Vocational Institute Community College of Albuquerque. In addition, twenty-nine highly diverse feminist scholars based in the West review and consult for the journal. The well-known anthropologist Louise Lamphere was persuaded to act as editor during the publication's five-year tenure at the University of New Mexico.

The changes signaled a fundamental repositioning of *Frontiers* as a journal claiming academic legitimacy. George observes that "*Frontiers* is now all grown up, it's mature, it's traditional, it's a real academic journal of 6 by 9 size, it's established, it's legitimate, it's respectable and very well thought of, the masthead is dripping in big women's studies names, with all kinds of publishing prestige, affiliations and credentials. It has been a success in its goal of becoming institutionalized. It's a journal you can take to the dean!"[49]

Despite this accumulation of university-sanctioned affiliations, the editors wished to retain control of the journal and independently in-corporated themselves as "Board of *Frontiers, Inc.*" The journal's inde-pendent ownership, institutional arrangements, editorial structure, and review process are now quite similar to those of *Feminist Studies.* Like the early *Feminist Studies,* when the journal was in transition and aca-demically sanctioned work had to be gathered on short notice, *Frontiers* compiled a special issue of papers from the Berkshire Conference on the History of Women to signal its academic seriousness.[50] The inclu-sion of an "Archives" section and the plan to rotate host editorships every five years among competing institutions is quite similar to *Signs'* organization. Furthermore, with changes in journal size, design, type, and format, *Frontiers* now closely resembles its more academic sister journals. Its continuing emphasis on bridging community and academy concerns and on multiculturalism and regionalism are unique, however.

Ironically, it was *Frontiers'* identity as a journal of regional and multi-cultural feminist interest that provided it an attractive "market niche" in contemporary academic publishing.[51] Reflecting the recently enhanced status of studies on the American West and calls for multicultural scholarship, the journal reasserted its commitment to bridging "aca-demic and popular views on issues common to women everywhere— with an emphasis on women in the West. We are also committed to making *Frontiers* a place where work by women of color is not simply welcome but essential."[52] Its new editorial collective decided not to con-tinue *Frontiers'* tradition of special issues on women of color, but rather to centralize such perspectives in each issue.[53]

The first volume under the new collective's direction (12, numbers 2 and 3) featured the work of African-American feminist lesbian poet Audre Lorde; two newly discovered pieces by Zora Neale Hurston; Vicki Ruiz's case study of Mexican-American resistance in the Hou-chon settlement of El Paso; Valerie Matsumoto's analysis of Japanese-American cross-cultural gender construction; Barbara Babcock's re-thinking of Ruth Benedict's study of the Zuni; Louise Lamphere's study of the anthropological treatment of the Navajo; and Cherrie Moraga's familial analysis of the Latino theater movement, as well as Mohawk poetry, pieces on women in the Caribbean and multiculturalism in the American Southwest, and a special section on "Issues of Identity and Identity Politics."

Frontiers' commitment to anchoring the insights of "high" theory in the reality of multicultural experience is clearly evident in the cluster of articles on identity politics. In "The Challenge and Theory of Feminist Identity Politics: Working on Racism" (Volume 12, number 2), Nancie Caraway, a political theorist, combines academically derived poststructuralist arguments concerning subjectivity with the community-based political actions of black feminist organizer Bernice Johnson Reagon and white lesbian poet Minnie Bruce Pratt to suggest strategies for recentering feminist discourse and creating multiracial coalitions. Also in Volume 12, number 2, the anthropologist Patricia Zavella uses the self-described heterogeneous identities of Chicanas to deconstruct the overly inclusive and imposed identity of "Hispanic." In "Reflections on Diversity among Chicanas" she draws upon poststructualist theory to argue the importance of the diverse social locations, cultural backgrounds, and self-constructions of Chicana women to reconstitute the center of feminist scholarship.

The promise of centralizing such work as a means of resisting the academic appropriation of feminist scholarship is reflected in the collective's manifesto-style declaration that "academics, . . . writers and readers of the new women's literature, native and immigrant women, lesbians, mothers, grandmothers, young women just waking to our collective strengths, women who are differently abled, African-Americans, Hispanics, Native Americans, and Asian-Americans, all the diverse members of our different communities: the *Frontiers* Editorial Collective hopes you will continue to claim this journal as your own." [54]

The preponderance of this multicultural work was generated by placing *Frontiers* deeper within the professionalized culture of feminist scholarship. By including a wider variety of established scholars with regional and multicultural interest, the journal gained better access to the academic conferences and professional networks that thrive because of the demands and structures of academic life. By turning to traditional academic structures but insisting on nontraditional content, *Frontiers* has been able to more fully center marginalized scholarship within the university.

But where does this leave the voices of the community? According to Lamphere, community contributions are still expressed primarily in community forms—poetry, photography, personal essays, and fiction. The most community-identified forms—poetry, fiction, and photography—are integrated into *Frontiers'* pages but compartmentalized within the editorial process. Academic editors continue to find "borderline genres," for example, the personal essay or informal talk, troubling and less easily contained. Such genre-blurring forms use rationalist prose and political critique but do not rely on academic conventions of argument and substantiation.[55] Perhaps the threat of encroachment could be reconsidered as a form that might more fully accommodate community and academic voices, but Lamphere hopes to increase community participation by accessing networks of community bookstores and community colleges.

Frontiers is a clear indication that a community posture from the fringe of the academy is no longer a viable position. Within the current political context, feminist academic journals only seem to address feminist concerns from deep within the protection of academic structures and conventions. Like much of publishing in the 1980s, American liberal and leftist political publishing encountered decreased reader responsiveness coupled with exorbitantly increased nonprofit postal rates.[56] For example, *Ms.*'s loss of its Educational Foundation's nonprofit status, combined with the long-term struggle to attract advertisers, so increased its postal costs that founders Gloria Steinem and Pat Carbine were compelled to sell the magazine. After it changed hands several times, its publication was suspended in October 1989. Although the magazine had 550,000 subscribers at the time, it still failed to show a profit.[57] The magazine reappeared in 1990 with a format that combines the look of a glossy monthly with the subscription rates and production schedule of a scholarly journal. The fact that ensuring the publication of political criticism requires stable financial sponsorship in one form or another is an unavoidable reality. For feminist publishing, and for many other political publishing ventures, grass-roots sponsorship proves too fragile in reactionary contexts.

Such developments indicate that feminist academic journals have been drawn completely inside the university and have only tenuous connections to the splintered and withered community movement. The editors of *Feminist Studies, Frontiers,* and *Signs* understand that the university is not an isolated terrain of struggle for feminists, that the dichotomy between scholarly thought and political action is a social construction, and that the wider feminist movement is an integral part of their scholarship. They are self-consciously examining the issues raised by the "duality of their position—its claim to acceptance by the academic establishment, and its participation in feminism's challenge to it."[58] Both *Frontiers* and *Signs* have devoted entire issues to the questions raised by a feminist presence in the academy. And such examinations are becoming acutely reflexive, as in *Signs'* discussion of conflict and competition among feminist academics, *Feminist Studies'* symposium on the meaning and ethics of book reviewing in feminist publications, and *Frontiers'* analysis of why feminists leave academic life voluntarily.[59] Whether the inherent contradictions of using a patriarchal institution as a feminist sanctuary—and the fact that the university is neither a permanent nor a safe solution—will prove ultimately precarious remains to be seen. Certainly, feminist scholars and their journals ignore the university's threat of exclusivity and absorption at the risk of endangering the contemporary women's movement.

Of the various feminist scholarly journals, *Feminist Studies* remains the most explicitly attentive to both political relevance and scholarly rigor. *Signs,* always preeminent and consciously molded in strict compliance with the university's most rigorous criteria, has maintained its academic credibility while developing a more egalitarian and political reputation. Without a journal such as *Signs,* even if it occasionally disavows explicit politics, feminist scholarship would be further marginalized. However, as the discipline risks becoming completely insular and ineffective, *Frontiers,* with its small circulation, tenuous funding, and dedication to "bridging the gap between the academy and the community," seems to be taking a promising turn for the future production of feminist scholarship, as indicated by the success of *SAGE* and the revisions at *Signs.*

The combined strength of the journals is that they provide a model for mitigating the needs of the feminist movement and the demands of the patriarchal university in the production of oppositional cultural knowledge. That the journals even suggest this coalescence is remarkable. *Feminist Studies, Frontiers,* and *Signs* embody an ensemble of contradictions. They are rooted in the anarchist impulse of the underground press and the formalized structures of nineteenth-century German scholarly publications. The unusual historical moment in which they were created left the indelible imprint of both a revolutionary social movement and a conservative patriarchal institution. With the expansion of feminist influence in the university, the journals became the public forum for a new cultural entity—a professionalized "culture of feminist scholarship." The journals attended to, but were not wholly of, either the traditional university or the community feminist movement. Yet the former provided their locus of intellectual value and the latter their source of political authenticity.

But, as Audre Lourde has asked, can the master's tools be used to dismantle the master's house?[60] Can institutions constructed by patriarchal ideology be used to oppose patriarchal ideology? Gayle Greene, a literary critic, observes that we are all ultimately culture bound: "There is no 'Archimedean standpoint outside of social life,' no place beyond ideology, beyond language."[61] If feminists insist on the use of the university as a site of resistance—and if the university continues to view politics and scholarship as essentially distinct—feminists cannot completely abandon rationalist discourse and forms without losing the legitimated power to construct oppositional knowledge disseminated throughout society. As the African-American legal scholar Kimberlé Crenshaw notes, "Oppressed people sometimes advance by creating ideological and political crisis, but the form of the crisis producing challenge must reflect the institutional logic of the system. . . . Challenges and demands made from outside the institutional logic would have accomplished little because Blacks, as subordinate 'other,' were already perceived as being outside the mainstream. The struggle . . . of all subordinate groups is . . . an attempt to manipulate elements of the dominant ideology to transform the experience of domination. It is a struggle to create a new status quo through the ideological and political tools that are available."[62] Similarly, Chela Sandoval argues that "the subject-citizen can learn to identify, develop, and control the means of ideology, that is, marshal the knowledge necessary to 'break the ideology' while also speaking in and from within the ideology."[63] Consequently, during the 1990s, feminist academic journals must produce oppositional knowledge from within the confines of patriarchal culture. Indeed, by locating their journals within the university, feminist scholars have been able to turn patriarchal authority against itself.

The culture of feminist scholarship has successfully laid claim to the authoritative and autonomous study of women in contemporary American society. In doing so, it has helped create "an oppositional public arena" for articulations of women's needs and critical opposition to male-defined society, not from the margins but from the heart of dominant sanctioned discourse.[64] Most important, the journals' position within the "institutional logic" of the university can be used as an effective entry for unheard challenges and demands that subordinated others make outside that institutional logic.

Feminist Studies, Frontiers, and *Signs* are positioned at the entrance to socially sanctioned rationalist discourse on women, where private speculation becomes socially sanctioned and publicly available information. That feminists stand at this entrance is important because the university is "the center to which practitioners trace the theoretical basis of knowledge upon which they establish authority; the source of a usable history, economics, political science, and sociology."[65]

The journals have become a critical vehicle for the production, legitimation, and preservation of new feminist knowledge. Through their application of criteria in manuscript selection and editing, their negotiation of new political and scholarly critiques, and their role as a forum for articulating the intellectual structures and consequences of movement practices, the journals sustain the cultural challenge and contradiction that feminist scholarship poses. The successful institutionalization of feminist academic journals has ensured Sally Gearhart's "bubble of freedom," Rita Felksi's "discursive space," and Kimberlé Crenshaw's "counter hegemony," which balance precariously between total co-option by the institution and the repression that could occur if feminist scholarship became too overtly threatening. Ultimately, *Feminist Studies, Frontiers, Signs*, NWSA *Journal, SAGE, Genders, differences, Women's Studies*, and others guarantee that feminist voices will be heard.

Notes

1. Charlotte Bunch, "Women in Print Conference," *Sinister Wisdom* 13 (1980): 77.

2. "Editorial: On Writing Feminist Academic Prose," *Signs* 17 (Summer 1992): 704.

3. Interview with editor Catharine Stimpson, New Brunswick, New Jersey, August 5, 1985.

4. Feminist journals created during the 1980s to serve various academic constituencies include: *Affilia: Journal of Women and Social Work* (1986), *Berkeley Women's Law Journal* (1986), *differences: A Journal of Feminist Cultural Studies* (1989), *Feminist Issues* (1980), *Feminist Teacher* (1984), *Genders* (1988), *Gender and Society* (1987), *Hypatia* (1986), *Journal of Feminist Family Therapy* (1989), *Journal of Women and Aging* (1989), *Journal of Women's History* (1989), NWSA *Journal* (1988), *SAGE: A Scholarly Journal on Black Women* (1984), *Tulsa Studies in Women's Literature* (1982), *Women: A Cultural Review* (1990), *Women and Criminal Justice* (1989), *Women and Politics* (1980), *Women and Therapy* (1982), and *Yale Journal of Law and Feminism* (1989). In addition, two quarterly guides, *Feminist Collections: A Quarterly of Women's Studies Resources* and *Feminist Periodicals: A Current Listing of*

Contents, are published by Susan Searing, the University of Wisconsin women's studies librarian.

5. *Frontiers, Feminist Studies,* and *Signs* were consistently referred to as "established women's studies journals" or "traditional women's studies journals" during interviews with editors from *differences, Genders,* and *SAGE.* Gayatri Spivak, "The Rani of Sirmur," in *Europe and Its Others: Proceedings of the Essex Conference on the Sociology of Literature,* ed. Francis Barker (Essex: University of Essex, 1985), 147.

6. Peter Berger and Thomas Luckmann, *The Social Construction of Reality* (New York: Doubleday, 1966), 74–76.

7. Robin Leidner, "Stretching the Boundaries of Liberalism: Democratic Innovation in a Feminist Organization," *Signs* 16 (Winter 1991): 263–89; Robin Leidner, "Constituency, Accountability, and Deliberation: Reshaping Democracy in the National Women's Studies Association," *NWSA Journal* 5 (Spring 1993): 4–27.

8. Interview with editor Patrocinio Schweickart, March 4, 1993.

9. The most successful of these has been "Forum," which, under Schweickart's direction, has featured an extensive and illuminating debate on the relationship of feminism and science in the 1900s. "Forum" participants in Volume 4, number 3 and Volume 5, number 1 include Anne Fausto-Sterling, Sandra Harding, Ruth Hubbard, Nancy Tuana, and Susan Rosser.

10. Barbara Johnson, *A World of Difference* (Baltimore: Johns Hopkins University Press, 1987), 3.

11. For an articulation of poststructuralist theory and multiculturalism as the primary sites of feminist inquiry in the 1990s, see Isis Berger, Elsa Barkley Brown, and Nancy A. Hewitt, "Symposium: Intersections and Collision Courses: Women, Blacks, and Workers Confront Gender, Race, and Class," *Feminist Studies* 18 (Summer 1992): 283–328.

12. "On Writing Feminist Academic Prose," 701.

13. Kathy Ferguson and Kirstie McClure, "Politics/Power/Culture: Postmodernity and Feminist Political Theory: preliminary," *differences* 3 (Spring 1991): iii.

14. Interview with editor Naomi Schor, January 3, 1992; Liz McMillen, "For Nearly Every Kind of Feminism, a Scholarly Journal of Its Own, *Chronicle of Higher Education,* March 10, 1993, A13.

15. *Diacritics: A Review of Contemporary Criticism* (Johns Hopkins University Press); *October* (M.I.T. Press); *Representations* (University of California Press).

16. Susan McClary, "Madonna's Resurrection of the Fleshly," *Genders* 7 (March 1990): 1–21; Gloria-Jean Masciarotte, "C'mon Girl: Oprah Winfrey and the Discourse of Feminine Talk," *Genders* 11 (Fall 1991): 81–110; Paul Morrison, "Coffee Table Sex: Robert Mapplethorpe and the Sadomasochism of Everyday Life," *Genders* 11 (Fall 1991): 17–36; Jonathan Dollimore, "The Cultural Politics of Perversion: Augustine, Shakespeare, Freud, Foucault," *Genders* 8 (July 1990): 1–16; Jacquelyn N. Zita, "Transsexualized Origins: Reflections

on Descartes' *Mediations,*" *Genders* 5 (July 1989): 86–105; Marilynn Lincoln Board, "Constructing Myths and Ideologies in Matisse's Odalisques," *Genders* 5 (July 1989): 21–49.

17. Joan W. Scott, *Gender and the Politics of History* (New York: Columbia University Press, 1988), 31.

18. Interview with editor Ann Kibbey, February 14, 1992.

19. *"Genders," Texas Journal* 12 (Spring-Summer 1990): 57.

20. Interview with Naomi Schor; Scott, *Gender and the Politics of History,* 42–45.

21. Rita Felski, *Beyond Feminist Aesthetics: Feminist Literature and Social Change* (Cambridge: Harvard University Press, 1989), 167.

22. Judith Newton, "Historicisms New and Old: 'Charles Dickens' Meets Marxism, Feminism, and West Coast Foucault," *Feminist Studies* 16 (Fall 1990): 464.

23. Karen Offen, "Feminism and Sexual Difference in Historical Perspective," in *Theoretical Perspectives on Sexual Difference,* ed. Deborah Rhode (New Haven: Yale University Press, 1990), 13–20; cf. Ferguson and McClure, "Politics/Power/Culture," v.

24. Evelyn Brooks Higginbotham, "African-American Women's History and the Metalanguage of Race," *Signs* 17 (Winter 1992): 251–52.

25. Interview with editor Patricia Bell-Scott, March 19, 1992.

26. Alice Walker, *In Search of Our Mothers' Gardens* (New York: Harcourt Brace Jovanovich, 1983), xi; Higginbotham, "African-American Women's History," 273. Higginbotham (273) observes that "by doing so they follow in the spirit of black scholar and educator Ann J. Cooper, who in *A Voice from the South* (1892), inextricably linked her racial identity to the 'quiet, undisputed dignity' of her womanhood."

27. In addition, *SAGE* has established a student awards program and co-sponsors a model student writer-scholars internship program at Spelman College. Interview with Patricia Bell-Scott.

28. Ibid.

29. bell hooks, *Yearning: Race, Gender, and Cultural Politics* (Boston: South End Press, 1990), 129–30.

30. Patricia Bell-Scott et al., eds., *Double Stitch: Black Women Write about Mothers and Daughters* (Boston: Beacon Press, 1991; paperback, New York: Harper Collins, 1993).

31. Joyce Pettis, "Difficult Survival: Mothers and Daughters in *The Bluest Eye,*" *SAGE* 4 (Fall 1987): 26.

32. Elsa Barkley Brown, "Mothers of Mind," *SAGE* 6 (Summer 1989): 4.

33. Brown, "Mothers of Mind," 7, 9.

34. Other publications include *Berkeley Women of Color Newsletter* (Institute for Study of Social Change, University of California, Berkeley), *Between Ourselves: A Women of Color Newsletter* (Durham, North Carolina), *Black Women's Health Project News* (Martin Luther King Community Center, Atlanta), and *UPFRONT: A Black Woman's Newspaper* (Washington, D.C.).

35. Maxine Baca Zinn et al., "The Costs of Exclusionary Practices in Women's Studies," *Signs* 11 (Winter 1985): 290–303.

36. By the fall of 1993, the twelve-member editorial board included five women of color and three lesbians. Interview with Claire Moses, August 27, 1993.

37. Interview with Claire Moses, Reston, Virginia, May 17, 1985.

38. "Editorial," *Signs* 6 (Spring 1981): 363–64.

39. Pauline B. Bart and Patricia O'Brien, "Stopping Rape: Effective Avoidance Strategies," *Signs* 10 (Autumn 1984): 4–26; Bernice Lott et al., "Sexual Harassment: A Campus Community Case Study," *Signs* 8 (Winter 1982): 296–319; Judith Berman Brandenberg, "Sexual Harassment in the University: Guidelines for Establishing a Grievance Procedure," *Signs* 8 (Winter 1982): 320–36; Diana M. Pearce, "Toil and Trouble: Women Workers and Unemployment Compensation," *Signs* 10 (Spring 1985): 439–59; Mary Fainsod Katzenstein, "Feminism and the Meaning of the Vote," *Signs* 10 (Autumn 1984): 4–26; "Special Issue: Addressing Women and Poverty," *Signs* 10 (Winter 1984).

40. "Editorial," *Signs* 11 (Spring 1986): 436.

41. "Editorial," *Signs* 16 (Spring 1991): 435.

42. Ibid., 703, 704.

43. Zinn et al., "The Cost of Exclusionary Practices," 296.

44. Barbara Christian, "Conference Call," *differences* 2, no. 3 (Fall 1990): 59.

45. Johnson, *A World of Difference*, 3.

46. Chela Sandoval, "U.S. Third World Feminism: The Theory and Method of Oppositional Consciousness in the Postmodern World," *Genders*, no. 10 (Spring 1991): 1–24.

47. When interviewed in 1985, editors Michèle Barale, Kathi George, and Lee Chambers-Schiller expressed concern about the University of Colorado's continued support of *Frontiers*.

48. Kathi George is now a freelance editor, independent publishing consultant, and copy editing instructor working in San Diego. For a firsthand account of her experiences at *Frontiers*, and an analysis of the important function of independent feminist scholars, see "On the Fringes of Academe: Creating the Pathway Panel Conversation at the Tenth Anniversary Celebration of San Diego Independent Scholars," *Journal of Unconventional History* 4 (Winter 1993): 7–27.

49. George, "On the Fringes of Academe," 7.

50. The first issue of *Frontiers* produced under the University of New Mexico collective (Volume 12, no. 1, 1991) showcased selected papers presented at a symposium at the Eighth Berkshire Conference on the History of Women, held at Douglass College, Rutgers University, June 7–10, 1990.

51. Interview with editor Louise Lamphere, February 14, 1992.

52. "From the Editors," *Frontiers* 12, no. 1 (1991): ix.

53. Interview with Louise Lamphere.

54. "From the Editors," xii.

55. Interview with Louise Lamphere.

56. Dick Bunce, "The Crisis in Political Publishing," *Socialist Review* 15 (July–October 1985): 8.

57. Judy Mann, *"Ms.* Dead: Woman Bashing Isn't," *Washington Post,* November 15, 1989; interview with editor Martha Nelson, Palo Alto, California, June 4, 1985.

58. "Editorial," *Signs* 8 (Autumn 1982): 2.

59. "Special Issue: Reconstructing the Academy," *Signs* 12 (Winter 1987): 203–417; Evelyn Fox Keller and Helen Moglen, "Competition and Feminism: Conflicts for Academic Women," *Signs* 12 (Spring 1987): 493–511; "Special Issue: The Women's Studies Movement: A Decade Inside the Academy," *Frontiers* 8 (Winter 1985): Natalie Zemon Davis et al., "A Symposium: Feminist Book Reviewing," *Feminist Studies* 14 (Fall 1988): 601–22; Esther Rothblum, "Leaving the Ivory Tower: Factors Contributing to Women's Voluntary Resignation from Academia," *Frontiers* 10, no. 2 (1988): 14–17.

60. Audre Lourde, "The Master's Tools Will Never Dismantle the Master's House," in *This Bridge Called My Back: Writings by Radical Women of Color,* ed. Cherrie Moraga and Gloria Anzaldua (Watertown: Persephone Press, 1981).

61. Gayle Greene, "The Uses of Quarreling," in *Feminist Institutions: Dialogues on Feminist Theory,* ed. Linda Kauffman (Cambridge: Basil Blackwell, Ltd., 1989), 64.

62. Kimberlé Williams Crenshaw, "Race, Reform, and Retrenchment: Transformation and Legitimation in Antidiscrimination Law," *Harvard Law Review* 101 (May 1988): 1386.

63. Sandoval, "U.S. Third World Feminism," 2.

64. Felski, *Beyond Feminist Aesthetics,* 166.

65. Ibid., 289.

appendix

Feminist Academic Journals in the United States

Affilia: Journal of Women and Social Work (1986)
Berkeley Women's Law Journal (1986)
Columbia Journal of Gender and Law (1991)
differences: A Journal of Feminist Cultural Studies (1989)
Feminisms (1988)
Feminist Collections: A Quarterly of Women's Studies Resources (1980)
Feminist Issues (1980)
Feminist Periodicals: A Current Listing of Contents
Feminist Studies (1972)
Feminist Teacher (1984)
Frontiers: A Journal of Women's Studies (1975)
Gender and Society (1987)
Genders (1988)
Harvard Women's Law Journal (1978)
Hypatia (1986)
Journal of Feminist Family Therapy (1989)
Journal of Women and Aging (1989)
Journal of Women's History (1989)
Legacy: A Journal of American Women Writers (1984)
NWSA Journal (1988)
Psychology of Women Quarterly (1976)
SAGE: A Scholarly Journal on Black Women (1984)
Sex Roles: A Journal of Research (1975)
Signs: A Journal of Women in Culture and Society (1975)
Tulsa Studies in Women's Literature (1982)
Wisconsin Women's Law Journal (1985)
Women and Criminal Justice (1989)
Women and Politics (1980)
Women's Studies (1972)
Women's Studies Quarterly (1972)
Women and Therapy (1982)
Yale Journal of Law and Feminism (1989)

Index

Trivia: A Journal of Ideas, 2
Tulsa Studies in Women's Literature, 184

Una, 18
underground press, 18–19; defined, 20;
    feminist critique of, 23–27; history of,
    20–25; sex advertisments and, 23
Underground Press Syndicate (UPS), 22,
    25
University of Chicago Press, 53, 96, 98,
    102–3, 106n34
University of Colorado at Boulder, 85
university: defined, 3–4; radical move-
    ments and, 44–50, 59n5, 59n12,
    60n26; as site of feminist resistance, 7,
    182–84; women's studies and, 43–52
University of Maryland, 78–79, 83n42,
    103
University of Michigan Papers in
    Women's Studies, 17, 52, 75
University of Minnesota Center for
    Advanced Feminist Studies, 176
University of New Mexico, 178
University of North Carolina, 176
University Press of Colorado, 178
university presses, 76–77, 82n37
UPFRONT: A Black Woman's News-
    paper, 186

Vance, Carole, 116–17, 119
Vicinus, Martha, 55, 114, 119, 175
Victorian Studies, 55
Village Voice, 20
Voices of Women's Liberation, 30

Wagner, MaryJo, 163–64
Walker, Alice, 170, 172
Walkowitz, Judith, 68, 116
Wallace, Michele, 172
Walstedt, Joyce Jennings, 91
Washington Post, 31, 152
Weathermen, 23
Weatherwomen, 25
Weed, Elizabeth, 166
Weedon, Chris, 120
Wellesley College Conference on Women
    and Development, 103
Whisler, Sandra, 102
Williams, Raymond, 57

Willis, Ellen, 31–32
Wilson, Catherine, 104
Wise, Gene, 44–45
Wittig, Monique, 120
Wolf, Dan, 20
Woman's Journal, 18
Womanspirit, 77
Women: A Cultural Review, 184
Women Against Pornography (WAP),
    114–15
Women Against Violence Against Women
    (WAVA), 114–15
Women: A Journal of Women's Libera-
    tion, 66
Women and Criminal Justice, 184
Women and Politics, 184
Women and Therapy, 184
Women in Distribution (WIND), 35
women's culture: community-based, 143–
    44; community publications and,
    144–45; feminist scholarship and,
    142–57
Women's Liberation, 25
women's movement, 65, 98, 102, 108,
    126, 132, 138–40, 182; civil rights
    movement and, 58; New Left and, 58,
    23–30; politicos vs. radical feminists,
    31–34; radical and reform, 28–31,
    45–46
Women's Press, 66
Women's Rights Law Reporter, 73, 75
Women's School of Planning and Archi-
    tecture, 6
Women's Studies, 3, 17, 52, 75, 96
Women's Studies Abstracts, 52
Women's Studies International, 17
Women's Studies International Forum, 17
Women's Studies Newsletter, 75
Woodson, Carter G., 55
Wright, Gwendolyn, 152

Yale Journal of Law and Feminism, 184
Yardley, Jonathan, 152
Yippies, 22–23

Zavella, Patricia, 180
Zimmerman, Bonnie, 125, 128–29, 131
Zinn, Howard, 56
Zora Heale Hurston Forum, 173

PATRICE McDERMOTT is an assistant professor of American studies and women's studies at the University of Maryland, Baltimore County Campus.